1980 EDITION

ARMS CONTROL AND DISARMAMENT AGREEMENTS

TEXTS AND HISTORIES OF NEGOTIATIONS

UNITED STATES
ARMS CONTROL
AND
DISARMAMENT
AGENCY

WASHINGTON, D.C., 20451

United States Arms Control and Disarmament Agency
August 1980

Contents

Foreword

This edition has been revised to include the progress made in arms control since 1977. This publication contains the texts of the Geneva Protocol of 1925 and, in chronological order, all major arms control agreements in which the United States has been a participant since World War II, as well as lists of Signatories and Parties to those agreements. Each agreement is preceded by a brief background discussion prepared by the United States Arms Control and Disarmament Agency.

Introduction

Efforts to prevent or limit war have a long history and have taken many forms. Men have tried to erect religious and ethical barriers against war, to outlaw it, to create codes and tribunals for peaceful arbitration and settlement of disputes. Nations have tried to avert war by withdrawing into isolation or neutrality, or by joining with others in leagues and alliances for the collective defense of peace and security.

In past eras efforts to control weapons of war were seldom successful or lasting. The coming of the nuclear era, however, brought such vast new dimensions of potential destructiveness that concepts of waging war and keeping the peace were transformed.

Until comparatively recent times, disarmament and arms control were chiefly measures imposed by the victors on the vanquished. Only rarely was arms limitation the result of freely negotiated agreement.

A notable example of freely negotiated and successful arms control in "modern" times was the Rush-Bagot agreement of 1817 between the United States and Great Britain, limiting naval forces on the Great Lakes and Lake Champlain to a few vessels on each side.

In the late 19th century the control of armaments took on new importance. The techniques of industrialization applied to the manufacture of weapons, mounting imperialist rivalries, nationalism, competing alliance systems—all contributed to an increasingly dangerous and costly arms race.

At the invitation of Tsar Nicholas II, International Peace Conferences met at The Hague in 1899 and 1907. The Hague Conferences brought advances in codifying the rules of war and in establishing institutions and procedures for settling international disputes—notably the Permanent Court of Arbitration at The Hague, antecedent of the Permanent Court of International Justice and of the present International Court of Justice.

Declarations signed at the 1899 conference prohibited the use of dum-dum bullets, asphyxiating gases, and the launching of projectiles and explosives from balloons or by other new methods of similar nature. The use of poison or poisoned weapons was forbidden by regulations annexed to both the 1899 and 1907 conventions; and a convention prohibiting or restricting the use of specific automatic contact mines and torpedoes was adopted in 1907.

The Hague Conferences were the first attempts at a worldwide approach to the problems of war and peace. They were the outgrowth of recognition that the control of modern weapons and the effects of modern warfare concerned the interests of all nations and required their collective action. Plans for a third conference, however, fell victim to the antagonisms and military competition that preceded World War I, as did many of the arms control declarations.

World War I was fought on a scale previously unknown and new weapons—tanks, submarines, aircraft, poison gas—increased its deadliness. The war gave fresh momentum to the creation of international peacekeeping institutions and to negotiations for disarmament. Following the cessation of hostilities, the Covenant of the League of Nations declared that "the maintenance of peace requires the reduction of national armaments to the lowest point consistent with national safety and the enforcement by common action of international obligations." The Treaty of Versailles imposed drastic limitations on Germany's armament and demilitarized the Rhineland. And in a series of postwar negotiations the Allied powers sought to impose agreed restrictions on certain weapons.

In 1921, on American initiative, a conference was convened at Washington to discuss arms limitations, one of its purposes being to curb an emerging naval race among the victorious allies. The resulting agreement established fixed ratios and tonnage limits for the capital ships of the leading naval powers, and a freeze on naval fortifications and bases in the western Pacific. In 1930 a subsequent treaty signed in London limited other classes of warships and provided for a third naval conference in 1935. That conference was unable to reach any effective agreement, and the naval treaties expired in 1936, following Japanese refusal to continue the arrangements.

The use of poison gas in the battles of World War I had evoked especially strong condemnation. In 1925, as the result of a U.S. initiative, a protocol was signed at Geneva prohibiting the use in war of poison gas and bacteriological weapons. By World War II most countries had ratified it, including all the great powers except the United States and Japan. The protocol was generally observed during that war, although Italy used poison gas in the Ethiopian war. Japan ratified the protocol in 1970; U.S. ratification took place in 1975. When the protocol was originally submitted to the U.S. Senate in 1926, there was strong lobbying against it, and Senate action was not completed. It was resubmitted by President Nixon in 1970, but disagreement about the protocol's application to riot-control agents and herbicides delayed Senate consent to ratification. (The administration took the position that the protocol did not apply to these.)

In 1928 the Kellogg-Briand Pact, initiated by the United States and France and signed by 63 nations, renounced war as an instrument of national policy. The pact included no provisions for insuring compliance with its obligations, and many signatories attached sweeping qualifications or unilateral interpretations, which made the agreement meaningless.

In 1932, after 7 years of preparation, a general disarmament conference was held under the auspices of the League of Nations. A wide variety of measures to limit armed forces, weapons, and expenditures was proposed, including a French proposal for an international police force under the League, a Soviet proposal for general and complete disarmament, and a U.S. plan to reduce forces and to abolish chemical warfare, tanks, bombers, and heavy artillery. No agreement was achieved. Germany demanded the right to rearm unless other nations disarmed to her level, and after Hitler came to power, Germany left the conference and the League. Sporadic sessions of the conference continued until 1937, when it dissolved in deadlock.

New levels of violence and devastation were reached in World War II. Even before its close, the nations fighting the Axis powers began a new effort to prevent war through a system of collective security. The U.N. Charter envisaged international forces under the Security Council to keep the peace. "Armed forces, assistance, and facilities" were to be contributed by all U.N. members. Unlike the Covenant of the League, the Charter gave disarmament no immediate priority; the five great powers would maintain their armaments, policing the disarmament of Germany and Japan and maintaining the peace until the United Nations had developed its own effective military forces. Under Article 11 the General Assembly was "to consider the general principles of cooperation in the maintenance of international peace and security, including the principles governing disarmament and the regulation of armaments," and make recommendations to the Security Council. Article 47 provided that the Military Staff Committee would advise the Security Council on "the regulation of armaments and possible disarmament." Only in these two articles does the word "disarmament" occur.

The Charter of the United Nations was signed at San Francisco on June 26, 1945; on August 6, a new weapon exploded over Hiroshima. Its stupendous power, shattering old concepts of war and weaponry, imposed new urgencies and demanded new perspectives on international efforts to control armaments.

The first American proposal for the control of nuclear weapons recognized that this new force involved the interests of the entire world community. In 1946 the U.S. Representative to the U.N. Atomic Energy Commission, Bernard Baruch, presented a U.S. plan that called for placing all the atomic resources of the world under the ownership or control of an independent international authority. It would have exclusive authority over all the stages of nuclear production, from mining to manufacture, and over the eventual destruction of all nuclear weapons. If the plan were adopted, the United States, the only nuclear power, would give up its atomic arsenal. All nations would submit to inspection by the international authority. If violations called for action by the Security Council, the veto could not be exercised. The plan was to be carried out in stages; the control system was to be in effective operation before the nuclear weapons were removed from the U.S. arsenal.

Although the plan was endorsed by a large majority of U.N. members, the Soviet Union objected to the ownership, staging, and enforcement provisions. Soviet counterproposals left nuclear activities under the control of national governments. The international authority would be empowered only to conduct periodic inspection of declared nuclear facilities. The United States and most other nations considered the Soviet plan's verification provisions altogether inadequate, and negotiations became deadlocked.

Meanwhile, the development of technology brought new dangers and complexities. In September 1949 President Truman announced that the Soviet Union had detonated a nuclear device. In 1952 the United States exploded the first hydrogen device. The first atomic bomb had had the power of 15,000 tons of TNT—15 kilotons. The destructive power of the new weapons was measured in megatons, the equivalent of millions of tons of TNT. In 1953 the Soviet Union announced that they too had exploded a hydrogen bomb. Rivalry in nuclear weapons was paralleled by rivalry in the development of delivery systems.

Among earlier efforts of the nuclear era to control armaments were broad, inclusive proposals, including (by 1959) proposals for "General and Complete Disarmament," with carefully interlocked stages for reducing or eliminating weapons and armed forces, and with precisely stipulated timing to assure that the process of disarming would not leave any nation's security weakened. This exacting requirement for establishing the pace and order of reductions and assuring their equitable impact put great difficulties in the way of agreements. Each nation defined its security needs differently; each possessed differing arrays of weapons and armed forces designed to defend its particular interests. Disparities and differences were accompanied by strong ideological conflicts that intensified wariness and suspicion. And the obstacle of verification stubbornly persisted.

The General Assembly's sessions devoted increasing attention to disarmament issues, and the nonnuclear powers demonstrated heightened concern as the spread of nuclear technology and the continued testing of weapons sharpened world awareness of the implications of nuclear warfare. Successive subsidiary bodies were created as forums for arms control negotiations. The U.N. Disarmament Commission, created in 1952, operated at first chiefly through a Subcommittee of Five—the United States, Great Britain, France, Canada, and the Soviet Union. As debates continued without agreement, membership in disarmament bodies was broadened and efforts were made to blunt the sharpness of East-West division by the participation of nonaligned, nonnuclear nations. The Eighteen Nation Disarmament Committee (ENDC), which began meeting in 1962, became the Conference of the Committee on Disarmament (CCD) in 1969, when its membership was enlarged. The ENDC and the CCD played important roles in achieving the multinational agreements that finally emerged. The Committee on Disarmament (CD), a still larger forum comprising 40 member states, was established in 1978 and began negotiations in 1979. France was a member of both the ENDC and the CCD but had never taken its seat in either. It is an active participant in CD meetings. China has also been an active participant since January 1980.

The creation of such active organizations for multilateral negotiations marked a step forward; so did the convening of special meetings with the participation of experts to deal with particular issues, such as the Geneva Conference on the Discontinuance of Nuclear Tests. The broad continuing effort was supported by active diplomatic exchanges and high-level meetings among the nuclear powers. The special responsibility of the major nuclear powers was subsequently manifested in the bilateral Strategic Arms Limitation Talks (SALT) between the United States and the Soviet Union that began in 1969.

By the middle of the 1950s, past production of nuclear materials could no longer be reliably accounted for, and control systems could not assure that none had been diverted to clandestine weapons manufacture or illegal stockpiles. A point of no return seemed to have been passed. As negotiations and debate continued, emphasis thus shifted gradually from programs of comprehensive disarmament to more limited measures. This brought a new flexibility and pragmatism into negotiations and, while general and complete disarmament remained a goal, willingness to consider partial solutions of limited scope helped to make solid step-by-step progress possible.

Moreover, advanced technology brought qualitative and quantitative changes in weaponry that radically altered concepts of national security and supplied a compelling incentive for pursuing arms control agreements. In the past it was the generally accepted assumption that more armed strength equaled more security. But this equation is no longer valid for the United States and the Soviet Union, which possess arsenals able to destroy the other many times over. More armaments do not guarantee more security. They may in fact have an opposite effect, creating new dangers by causing a potential adversary to overreact in his own weapons program—in response to what he perceives as a threat to his own security. The continuing arms race also increases the possibility of an accident.

Arms control is no longer an intermittent enterprise. It has become a central and continuing concern of governments and an integral aspect of foreign policy and national security. Thus the United States—the first government to do so—established a separate agency in 1961 to deal with disarmament issues. The U.S. Arms Control and Disarmament Agency (ACDA) is charged with formulating, coordinating, and carrying out arms control policies; for conducting and coordinating research; for preparation and management of U.S. participation in negotiations; and for public dissemination of information about arms control.

Some of the agreements printed here have been signed by almost all the world's nations. Others have been negotiated among the chief nuclear powers, who bear the greatest responsibility for averting conflict that would tragically affect nations and peoples everywhere. Some of the treaties are essentially "nonarmament" agreements, designed to keep free of conflict and nuclear weaponry the environments that science has made newly accessible and significant, and whose resources must be preserved for all—for example, outer space or the seabed—or geographic regions where nuclear weapons have not been introduced—Antarctica and Latin America. Some agreements reflect a growing concern with the need to prevent a war that might occur through accident, unauthorized or lawless action, human error, or mechanical failure. And some reflect a conscious decision by the major nuclear powers to limit their own strategic offensive and defensive weapons.

Protocol for the Prohibition of the Use in War of Asphyxiating, Poisonous or Other Gases, and of Bacteriological Methods of Warfare

At the end of World War I, the victorious Allies decided to reaffirm in the Versailles treaty (1919) the prewar prohibition of the use of poisonous gases (see Introduction) and to forbid Germany to manufacture or import them. Similar provisions were included in the peace treaties with Austria, Bulgaria, and Hungary.

Drawing upon the language of these peace treaties, the United States—at the Washington Disarmament Conference of 1922—took the initiative of introducing a similar provision into a treaty on submarines and noxious gases. The U.S. Senate gave its advice and consent to ratification of this treaty without a dissenting vote. It never entered into force, however, since French ratification was necessary, and France objected to the submarine provisions.

At the 1925 Geneva Conference for the Supervision of the International Traffic in Arms, the United States similarly took the initiative of seeking to prohibit the export of gases for use in war. At French suggestion, it was decided to draw up a protocol on non-use of poisonous gas; and at the suggestion of Poland, the prohibition was extended to bacteriological weapons. Signed on June 17, 1925, the Geneva Protocol thus restated the prohibition previously laid down by the Versailles and Washington treaties and added a ban on bacteriological warfare.

Before World War II the protocol was ratified by many countries, including all the great powers except the United States and Japan. When they ratified or acceded to the protocol, some nations—including the United Kingdom, France, and the U.S.S.R.—declared that it would cease to be binding on them if their enemies, or the allies of their enemies, failed to respect the prohibitions of the protocol. Although Italy was a party to the protocol, it used poison gas in the Ethiopian war. On the other hand, the protocol was generally observed in World War II. Referring to reports that the Axis powers were considering the use of gas, President Roosevelt said on June 8, 1943:

Use of such weapons has been outlawed by the general opinion of civilized mankind. This country has not used them, and I hope that we never will be compelled to use them. I state categorically that we shall under no circumstances resort to the use of such weapons unless they are first used by our enemies.

Although the Senate Foreign Relations Committee had favorably reported the protocol in 1926, there was strong lobbying against it, and the Senate had never voted on it. After the war, President Truman withdrew it from the Senate, together with other inactive older treaties. Little attention was paid to the protocol for several years thereafter. During the Korean war, however, the Communist side falsely accused the United States of using bacteriological weapons in Korea; however, they rejected American proposals for international investigation of their charges. In the Security Council, the Soviet Union introduced a draft resolution calling on all U.N. members to ratify the protocol. At that time, the United States was not willing to agree to prohibit the use of any weapons of mass destruction unless they could be eliminated through a disarmament agreement with effective safeguards. On June 26, 1952, the Soviet resolution was rejected by a vote of 1 to 0, with 10 abstentions (including the United States, the United Kingdom, and France).

In 1966 the Communist countries strongly criticized the United States for using tear gas and chemical herbicides in Vietnam. In the General Assembly, Hungary charged that the use in war of these agents was prohibited by the protocol and other provisions of international law. The United States denied that the protocol applied to nontoxic gases or chemical herbicides. Joined by Canada, Italy, and the United Kingdom, the United States introduced amendments to a Hungarian resolution that would have made the use of any chemical and bacteriological weapons an international crime. In its final form, the resolution called for "strict observance by all states of the principles and objectives" of the protocol, condemned "all actions contrary to those objectives," and invited all states to accede to the protocol. During the debate, the U.S. Representative stated that it would be up to each country to decide whether or how to adhere to the protocol, "in the light of constitutional and other considerations."

Interpretation of the protocol remained a thorny problem. In his foreword to a U.N. report on chemical and biological weapons (July 1, 1969), Secretary General Thant recommended a renewed appeal for accession to the protocol and a "clear affirmation" that it covered the use in war of all chemical and biological weapons, including tear gas and other harassing agents. Discussion in the Conference of the Committee on Disarmament (CCD) showed that most members agreed with the Thant recommendations. Swedish Ambassador Myrdal, a strong advocate of the broad interpretation, stressed the danger of escalation if nonlethal chemical agents were permitted. She also pointed out that the military use of tear gases should be distinguished from their use for riot control and that there was a similar difference between using herbicides in war and employing them for peaceful purposes. On the other hand, U.K. Disarmament

Minister Mulley held that only the parties to the protocol were entitled to say what it meant.

In the General Assembly, the 12 nonaligned members of the CCD, joined by 9 other nations, introduced a resolution condemning as contrary to international law the use in international armed conflict of all chemical and biological agents. Opposing the resolution, the U.S. Representative reaffirmed the American interpretation of the protocol and took the position that it was inappropriate for the General Assembly to interpret treaties by means of a resolution. The 21-nation resolution was adopted on December 16, 1969, by a vote of 80 to 3 (Australia, Portugal, the United States), and 36 abstentions (including France and the United Kingdom). France and many other abstainers accepted the broad interpretation of the protocol but considered the resolution undesirable on other grounds.

While the General Assembly debate was still underway, President Nixon announced on November 25, 1969, that he would resubmit the protocol to the Senate. He reaffirmed U.S. renunciation of the first use of lethal chemical weapons and extended this renunciation to incapacitating chemicals. It was on this occasion that he also announced the unilateral U.S. renunciation of bacteriological (biological) methods of warfare.

Some support for the American interpretation of the protocol now came from the United Kingdom and Japan. During the 1930 discussion at Geneva in the Preparatory Commission for the Disarmament Conference, the United Kingdom had taken the position that the protocol covered tear gas. In February 1970 the British Foreign Secretary told Parliament that this was still the British position, but that the riot-control agent CS, unlike older tear gases, was not harmful to man and was therefore not covered by the protocol. During the Diet debate on Japanese ratification of the protocol, Foreign Minister Aichi took the position that it did not prohibit riot-control agents and herbicides. Japan ratified the protocol in May 1970.

In a report of August 11, 1970, to the President, Secretary of State Rogers recommended that the protocol be ratified with a reservation of the right to retaliate with gas if an enemy state or its allies violated the protocol. He also reaffirmed the position that the protocol did not apply to the use in war of riot-control agents and herbicides. President Nixon resubmitted the protocol to the Senate on August 19.

The Foreign Relations Committee did not accept the Administration's interpretation regarding riot-control agents and herbicides. In a letter of April 15, 1971, to the President, Senator Fulbright (Dem., Ark.), the Chairman, said many members thought that it would be in the interest of the United States either to ratify the protocol without "restrictive understandings" or to postpone action until this became possible. The Committee thus deferred action. It also held in abeyance the Biological Weapons Convention, which was submitted to it on August 10, 1972, pending resolution of this issue.

In the latter part of 1974, the Ford Administration launched a new initiative to obtain Senate consent to ratification of the protocol (and, simultaneously, of the Biological Weapons Convention). The new approach was set forth to the Committee by ACDA Director Fred Ikle on December 10, when he announced that the President, while reaffirming the Administration's view as to the scope of the protocol, was prepared "to renounce as a matter of national policy: (1) first use of herbicides in war except use, under regulations applicable to their domestic use, for control of vegetation within U.S. bases and installations or around their immediate defensive perimeters; (2) first use of riot-control agents in war except in defensive military modes to save lives such as:

(a) Use of riot-control agents in riot-control circumstances to include controlling rioting prisoners of war. This exception would permit use of riot-control agents in riot situations in areas under direct and distinct U.S. military control;

(b) Use of riot-control agents in situations where civilian casualties can be reduced or avoided. This use would be restricted to situations in which civilians are used to mask or screen attacks;

(c) Use of riot-control agents in rescue missions. The use of riot-control agents would be permissible in the recovery of remotely isolated personnel such as downed aircrews (and passengers);

(d) Use of riot-control agents in rear echelon areas outside the combat zone to protect convoys from civil disturbances, terrorists and paramilitary organizations."

In addition, Dr. Ikle testified that "the President, under an earlier directive still in force, must approve in advance any use of riot-control agents and chemical herbicides in war."

Two days later, on December 12, the Committee voted unanimously to send the protocol and the convention to the Senate floor, and on December 16 the Senate voted its approval, also unanimously. The Committee, in recommending advice and consent to ratification of the protocol indicated that it attached particular importance to Dr. Ikle's response to the following question posed in connection with his December 10 testimony:

Question: "Assuming the Senate were to give its advice and consent to ratification on the grounds proposed by the Administration, what legal impediment would there be to subsequent Presidential decisions broadening the permissible uses of herbicides and riot-control agents?

Answer: "There would be no formal legal impediment to such a decision. However, the policy which was presented to the Committee will be inextricably linked with the history of Senate consent to ratification of the Protocol with its consent dependent upon its observance. If a future administration should change this policy without Senate consent whether in practice or by a formal policy change, it would be inconsistent with the history of the ratification, and could have extremely grave political repercussions and as a result is extremely unlikely to happen."

The protocol and the convention were ratified by President Ford on January 22, 1975. The U.S. instrument of ratification of the convention was deposited on March 26, 1975, and of the protocol on April 10, 1975.

Protocol for the Prohibition of the Use in War of Asphyxiating, Poisonous or Other Gases, and of Bacteriological Methods of Warfare

Signed at Geneva June 17, 1925
Entered into force February 8, 1928
Ratification advised by the U.S. Senate December 16, 1974
Ratified by U.S. President January 22, 1975
U.S. ratification deposited with the Government of France April 10, 1975
Proclaimed by U.S. President April 29, 1975

The Undersigned Plenipotentiaries, in the name of their respective Governments:

Whereas the use in war of asphyxiating, poisonous or other gases, and of all analogous liquids, materials or devices, has been justly condemned by the general opinion of the civilized world; and

Whereas the prohibition of such use has been declared in Treaties to which the majority of Powers of the World are Parties; and

To the end that this prohibition shall be universally accepted as a part of International Law, binding alike the conscience and the practice of nations;

Declare:

That the High Contracting Parties, so far as they are not already Parties to Treaties prohibiting such use, accept this prohibition, agree to extend this prohibition to the use of bacteriological methods of warfare and agree to be bound as between themselves according to the terms of this declaration.

The High Contracting Parties will exert every effort to induce other States to accede to the present Protocol. Such accession will be notified to the Government of the French Republic, and by the latter to all signatory and acceding Powers, and will take effect on the date of the notification by the Government of the French Republic.

The present Protocol, of which the French and English texts are both authentic, shall be ratified as soon as possible. It shall bear today's date.

The ratifications of the present Protocol shall be addressed to the Government of the French Republic, which will at once notify the deposit of such ratification to each of the signatory and acceding Powers.

The instruments of ratification of and accession to the present Protocol will remain deposited in the archives of the Government of the French Republic.

The present Protocol will come into force for each signatory Power as from the date of deposit of its ratification, and, from that moment, each Power will be bound as regards other powers which have already deposited their ratifications.

IN WITNESS WHEREOF the Plenipotentiaries have signed the present Protocol.

DONE at Geneva in a single copy, this seventeenth day of June, One Thousand Nine Hundred and Twenty-Five.

States Parties to the Protocol for the Prohibition of the Use in War of Asphyxiating, Poisonous or Other Gases, and of Bacteriological Methods of Warfare, Done at Geneva June 17, 1925

States which have deposited instruments of ratification or accession, or continue to be bound as the result of succession agreements concluded by them or by reason of notification given by them to the Secretary-General of the United Nations:

	Argentina—May 12, 1969
1 a b	Australia—Jan. 22, 1930
	Austria—May 9, 1928
1 a b 2	Bahamas, The
2	Barbados—June 22, 1976
1 a b	Belgium—Dec. 4, 1928
6	Bhutan—June 12, 1978[6]
1 a b 2	Botswana
	Brazil—Aug. 28, 1970
1 a b	Bulgaria—Mar. 7, 1934
1 a b 2	Burma
1 a b	Canada—May 6, 1930
	Central African Republic—July 31, 1970
1 a b	Chile—July 2, 1935
1 a b	China, People's Republic of—Aug. 9, 1952
	China (Taiwan)—Aug. 7, 1929
7	Comoros
	Cuba—June 24, 1966
	Cyprus—Dec. 12, 1966
1 b	Czechoslovakia—Aug. 16, 1938
	Denmark—May 5, 1930
7	Djibouti
	Dominican Republic—Dec. 8, 1970
	Ecuador—Sept. 16, 1970
	Egypt—Dec. 6, 1928
1 a b	Estonia—Aug. 28, 1931
	Ethiopia—Sept. 18, 1935
1 a b	Fiji—Mar. 21, 1973
	Finland—June 26, 1929
1 a b 3	France—May 9, 1926
	Gambia, The—Nov. 16, 1966
	German Democratic Republic
	Germany, Federal Republic of—Apr. 25, 1929
	Ghana—May 3, 1967
	Greece—May 30, 1931

See footnotes pages 17 and 18.

1 a b	Grenada
1 a b 2	Guyana
	Holy See—Oct. 18, 1966
	Hungary—Oct. 11, 1952
	Iceland—Nov. 2, 1967
1 a b	India—Apr. 9, 1930
	Indonesia—Jan. 26, 1971
	Iran—July 4, 1929
1 a b	Iraq—Sept. 8, 1931
	Ireland—Aug. 18, 1930
1 a b	Israel—Feb. 20, 1969
	Italy—Apr. 3, 1928
	Ivory Coast—July 27, 1970
	Jamaica—July 31, 1970
	Japan—May 21, 1970
1 a b d	Jordan—Jan. 20, 1977
	Kenya—July 6, 1970
1 a b d	Kuwait—Dec. 15, 1971
	Latvia—June 3, 1931
	Lebanon—Apr. 17, 1969
	Lesotho—Mar. 15, 1972
	Liberia—Apr. 2, 1927
1 b d	Libya—Dec. 29, 1971
	Lithuania—June 15, 1933
	Luxembourg—Sept. 1, 1936
	Madagascar—Aug. 12, 1967
	Malawi—Sept. 14, 1970
	Malaysia—Dec. 10, 1970
	Maldive Islands—Jan. 6, 1967
	Mali—Nov. 19, 1966
	Malta—Oct. 15, 1970
	Mauritius—Jan. 8, 1971
	Mexico—Mar. 15, 1932
	Monaco—Jan. 6, 1967
1 b	Mongolia—Dec. 6, 1968
	Morocco—Oct. 13, 1970
	Nepal—May 9, 1969
1 c 4	Netherlands—Oct. 31, 1930
1 a b	New Zealand—Jan. 22, 1930
	Niger—Apr. 19, 1967
1 a b	Nigeria—Oct. 15, 1968
	Norway—July 27, 1932
	Pakistan—June 9, 1960

See footnotes pages 17 and 18.

	Panama—Dec. 4, 1970
	Paraguay—Jan. 14, 1969
	Philippines—May 29, 1973
	Poland—Feb. 4, 1929
1 a b	Portugal—July 1, 1930
	Qatar—Sept. 16, 1976
1 a b	Romania—Aug. 23, 1929
	Rwanda—June 25, 1964
	Saudi Arabia—Jan. 27, 1971
1 a b 2	Seychelles
	Sierra Leone—Mar. 20, 1967
1 a b 2	Singapore
1 a b	South Africa—Jan. 22, 1930
1 a b	Spain—Aug. 22, 1929
	Sri Lanka—Jan. 20, 1954
1 c 4	Suriname
1 a b 2	Swaziland
	Sweden—Apr. 25, 1930
	Switzerland—July 12, 1932
1 d	Syrian Arab Republic—Dec. 17, 1968
	Tanzania—Apr. 22, 1963
	Thailand—June 6, 1931
	Togo—Apr. 5, 1971
	Tonga—July 28, 1971
	Trinidad and Tobago—Nov. 30, 1970
	Tunisia—July 12, 1967
	Turkey—Oct. 5, 1929
	Uganda—May 24, 1965
1 a b	Union of Soviet Socialist Republics—Apr. 5, 1928
1 a b 5	United Kingdom—Apr. 9, 1930
1 c	United States—Apr. 10, 1975
	Upper Volta—Mar. 3, 1971
	Uruguay—Apr. 12, 1977
	Venezuela—Feb. 8, 1928
	Yemen Arab Republic (Sana)—Mar. 17, 1971
1 b	Yugoslavia—Apr. 12, 1929
1 a b 2	Zambia

---

1 a, b, c, d With reservations to Protocol as follows:

a—binding only as regards relations with other parties.
b—to cease to be binding in regard to any enemy States whose armed forces or allies do not observe provisions.
c—to cease to be binding as regards use of chemical agents with respect to any enemy State whose armed forces or allies do not observe provisions.
d—does not constitute recognition of or involve treaty relations with Israel.

[2]By virtue of agreement with former parent State or notification to the Secretary General of the United Nations of succession to treaty rights and obligations upon independence.

[3]Applicable to all French territories.

[4]Applicable to Suriname and Curacao.

[5]It does not bind India or any British Dominion which is a separate member of the League of Nations and does not separately sign or adhere to the Protocol. It is applicable to all colonies.

[6]Deposited accession on June 12, 1978, but the French Government asked that accession take effect on date of notification by them—Feb. 19, 1979.

[7]Included in declaration by France. Continued application has apparently not been determined.

The Antarctic Treaty

The Antarctic Treaty, the earliest of the post-World War II arms limitation agreements, has significance both in itself and as a precedent. It internationalized and demilitarized the Antarctic Continent and provided for its cooperative exploration and future use. It has been cited as an example of nations exercising foresight and working in concert to prevent conflict before it develops. Based on the premise that to exclude armaments is easier than to eliminate or control them once they have been introduced, the treaty served as a model, in its approach and even provisions, for later "nonarmament" treaties—the treaties that excluded nuclear weapons from outer space, from Latin America, and from the seabed.

By the 1950s seven nations—Argentina, Australia, Chile, France, New Zealand, Norway, and the United Kingdom—claimed sovereignty over areas of Antarctica, on the basis of discovery, exploration, or geographic propinquity. Claims of Argentina, Chile, and the United Kingdom overlapped. Eight other nations—the United States, the Soviet Union, Belgium, Germany, Poland, Sweden, Japan, and South Africa—had engaged in exploration but had put forward no specific claims. The United States did not recognize the claims of other governments and reserved the right to assert claims based on exploration by its citizens. The Soviet Union took a similar position.

Activities in the Antarctic had generally been conducted peacefully and cooperatively. Yet the possibility that exploitable economic resources might be found meant the possibility of future rivalry for their control. Moreover, isolated and uninhabited, the continent might at some time become a potential site for emplacing nuclear weapons.

Fortunately, scientific interests rather than political, economic, or military concerns dominated the expeditions sent to Antarctica after World War II. Fortunately, too, international scientific associations were able to work out arrangements for effective cooperation. In 1956 and 1957, for example, American meteorologists "wintered over" at the Soviet post, Mirnyy, while Soviet meteorologists "wintered over" at Little America. These cooperative activities culminated in the International Geophysical Year of 1957–1958 (IGY), a joint scientific effort by 12 nations—Argentina, Australia, Belgium, Chile, France, Japan, New Zealand, Norway, South Africa, the Soviet Union, the United Kingdom, and the United States—to conduct studies of the Earth and its cosmic environment.

In these years the desire to keep the continent demilitarized was general and some diplomatic discussion of the possibility had taken place. On May 3, 1958, the United States proposed to the other 11 nations participating in the IGY that a conference be held, based on the points of agreement that had been reached in informal discussions:

(1) that the legal *status quo* of the Antarctic Continent remain unchanged;
(2) that scientific cooperation continue;
(3) that the continent be used for peaceful purposes only.

All accepted the U.S. invitation. The Washington Conference on Antarctica met from October 15 to December 1, 1959. No insurmountable conflicts or issues divided the conference, and negotiations culminated in a treaty signed by all 12 nations on December 1, 1959. Approved by the U.S. Senate, U.S. ratification was deposited August 18, 1960, and the treaty entered into force on June 23, 1961, when the formal ratifications of all the participating nations had been received.

The treaty provides that Antarctica shall be used for peaceful purposes only. It specifically prohibits "any measures of a military nature, such as the establishment of military bases and fortifications, the carrying out of military maneuvers, as well as the testing of any type of weapons." Military personnel or equipment, however, may be used for scientific research or for any other peaceful purpose. Nuclear explosions and the disposal of radioactive waste material in Antarctica are prohibited, subject to certain future international agreements of these subjects. All Contracting Parties entitled to participate in the meetings referred to in Article IX of the treaty have the right to designate observers to carry out inspections in all areas of Antarctica, including all stations, installations and equipment, and ships and aircraft at discharge or embarkation points. Each observer has complete freedom of access at any time to any or all areas of Antarctica. Contracting Parties may also carry out aerial inspections. There are provisions for amending the treaty; for referring disputes that cannot be handled by direct talks, mediation, arbitration, or other peaceful means to the International Court of Justice; and for calling a conference in 30 years to review the operation of the treaty if any parties request it.

Argentina, Australia, New Zealand, the United Kingdom, and the United States have all exercised the right of inspection. The United States in 1964 inspected stations operated by six nations—Argentina, Chile, France, New Zealand, the United Kingdom, and the Soviet Union; in 1967, eight stations operated by seven nations were visited during a 5-week, 8,500-mile voyage; inspections have taken place in 1971, 1975, 1977, and 1980. All American inspections included Soviet facilities. They reported essentially the same findings. No military activities, armaments, or prohibited nuclear activities were observed, and all scientific programs were in accord with previously published plans. The observed activities at each station were in compliance with the provisions and spirit of the Antarctic Treaty.

Ten consultative meetings have been held in accordance with Article IX of the treaty. Numerous recommendations on measures in furtherance of the principles and objectives of the treaty have been adopted, many of which have now entered into force. The eleventh consultative meeting will be held in Argentina during 1981. The Contracting Parties entitled to participate in these meetings are the 12 original signatory states and Poland, whose entitlement to consultative status, pursuant to paragraph 2 of Article IX, was recognized at a special consultative meeting in London in July 1977.

The Antarctic Treaty

Signed at Washington December 1, 1959
Ratification advised by U.S. Senate August 10, 1960
Ratified by U.S. President August 18, 1960
U.S. ratification deposited at Washington August 18, 1960
Proclaimed by U.S. President June 23, 1961
Entered into force June 23, 1961

The Governments of Argentina, Australia, Belgium, Chile, the French Republic, Japan, New Zealand, Norway, the Union of South Africa, the Union of Soviet Socialist Republics, the United Kingdom of Great Britain and Northern Ireland, and the United States of America,

Recognizing that it is in the interest of all mankind that Antarctica shall continue forever to be used exclusively for peaceful purposes and shall not become the scene or object of international discord;

Acknowledging the substantial contributions to scientific knowledge resulting from international cooperation in scientific investigation in Antarctica;

Convinced that the establishment of a firm foundation for the continuation and development of such cooperation on the basis of freedom of scientific investigation in Antarctica as applied during the International Geophysical Year accords with the interests of science and the progress of all mankind;

Convinced also that a treaty ensuring the use of Antarctica for peaceful purposes only and the continuance of international harmony in Antarctica will further the purposes and principles embodied in the Charter of the United Nations;

Have agreed as follows:

Article I

1. Antarctica shall be used for peaceful purposes only. There shall be prohibited, *inter alia,* any measures of a military nature, such as the establishment of military bases and fortifications, the carrying out of military maneuvers, as well as the testing of any type of weapons.

2. The present Treaty shall not prevent the use of military personnel or equipment for scientific research or for any other peaceful purposes.

Article II

Freedom of scientific investigation in Antarctica and cooperation toward that end, as applied during the International Geophysical Year, shall continue, subject to the provisions of the present Treaty.

Article III

1. In order to promote international cooperation in scientific investigation in Antarctica, as provided for in Article II of the present Treaty, the Contracting Parties agree that, to the greatest extent feasible and practicable:

(a) information regarding plans for scientific programs in Antarctica shall be exchanged to permit maximum economy and efficiency of operations;

(b) scientific personnel shall be exchanged in Antarctica between expeditions and stations;

(c) scientific observations and results from Antarctica shall be exchanged and made freely available.

2. In implementing this Article, every encouragement shall be given to the establishment of cooperative working relations with those Specialized Agencies of the United Nations and other international organizations having a scientific or technical interest in Antarctica.

Article IV

1. Nothing contained in the present Treaty shall be interpreted as:

(a) a renunciation by any Contracting Party of previously asserted rights of or claims to territorial sovereignty in Antarctica;

(b) a renunciation or diminution by any Contracting Party of any basis of claim to territorial sovereignty in Antarctica which it may have whether as a result of its activities or those of its nationals in Antarctica, or otherwise;

(c) prejudicing the position of any Contracting Party as regards its recognition or non-recognition of any other State's right of or claim or basis of claim to territorial sovereignty in Antarctica.

2. No acts or activities taking place while the present Treaty is in force shall constitute a basis for asserting, supporting or denying a claim to territorial sovereignty in Antarctica or create any rights of sovereignty in Antarctica. No new claim, or enlargement of an existing claim, to territorial sovereignty in Antarctica shall be asserted while the present Treaty is in force.

Article V

1. Any nuclear explosions in Antarctica and the disposal there of radioactive waste material shall be prohibited.

2. In the event of the conclusion of international agreements concerning the use of nuclear energy, including nuclear explosions and the disposal of radioactive waste material, to which all of the Contracting Parties whose representatives are entitled to participate in the meetings provided for under Article IX are parties, the rules established under such agreements shall apply in Antarctica.

Article VI

The provisions of the present Treaty shall apply to the area south of 60° South Latitude, including all ice shelves, but nothing in the present Treaty shall prejudice or in any way affect the rights, or the exercise of the rights, of any State under international law with regard to the high seas within that area.

Article VII

1. In order to promote the objectives and ensure the observance of the provisions of the present Treaty, each Contracting Party whose representatives are entitled to participate in the meetings referred to in Article IX of the Treaty shall have the right to designate observers to carry out any inspection provided for by the present Article. Observers shall be nationals of the Contracting Parties which designate them. The names of observers shall be communicated to every other Contracting Party having the right to designate observers, and like notice shall be given of the termination of their appointment.

2. Each observer designated in accordance with the provisions of paragraph 1 of this Article shall have complete freedom of access at any time to any or all areas of Antarctica.

3. All areas of Antarctica, including all stations, installations and equipment within those areas, and all ships and aircraft at points of discharging or embarking cargoes or personnel in Antarctica, shall be open at all times to inspection by any observers designated in accordance with paragraph 1 of this Article.

4. Aerial observation may be carried out at any time over any or all areas of Antarctica by any of the Contracting Parties having the right to designate observers.

5. Each Contracting Party shall, at the time when the present Treaty enters into force for it, inform the other Contracting Parties, and thereafter shall give them notice in advance, of

(a) all expeditions to and within Antarctica, on the part of its ships or nationals, and all expeditions to Antarctica organized in or proceeding from its territory;

(b) all stations in Antarctica occupied by its nationals; and

(c) any military personnel or equipment intended to be introduced by it into Antarctica subject to the conditions prescribed in paragraph 2 of Article I of the present Treaty.

Article VIII

1. In order to facilitate the exercise of their functions under the present Treaty, and without prejudice to the respective positions of the Contracting Parties relating to jurisdiction over all other persons in Antarctica, observers designated under paragraph 1 of Article VII and scientific personnel exchanged under subparagraph 1(b) of Article III of the Treaty, and members of the staffs accompanying any such persons, shall be subject only to the jurisdiction of the Contracting Party of which they are nationals in respect of all acts or omissions occurring while they are in Antarctica for the purpose of exercising their functions.

2. Without prejudice to the provisions of paragraph 1 of this Article, and pending the adoption of measures in pursuance of subparagraph 1(e) of Article IX, the Contracting Parties concerned in any case of dispute with regard to the exercise of jurisdiction in Antarctica shall immediately consult together with a view to reaching a mutually acceptable solution.

Article IX

1. Representatives of the Contracting Parties named in the preamble to the present Treaty shall meet at the City of Canberra within two months after the date of entry into force of the Treaty, and thereafter at suitable intervals and places, for the purpose of exchanging information, consulting together on matters of common interest pertaining to Antarctica, and formulating and considering, and recommending to their Governments, measures in furtherance of the principles and objectives of the Treaty, including measures regarding:

(a) use of Antarctica for peaceful purposes only;

(b) facilitation of scientific research in Antarctica;

(c) facilitation of international scientific cooperation in Antarctica;

(d) facilitation of the exercise of the rights of inspection provided for in Article VII of the Treaty;

(e) questions relating to the exercise of jurisdiction in Antarctica;

(f) preservation and conservation of living resources in Antarctica.

2. Each Contracting Party which has become a party to the present Treaty by accession under Article XIII shall be entitled to appoint representatives to participate in the meetings referred to in paragraph 1 of the present Article, during such time as that Contracting Party demonstrates its interest in Antarctica by conducting substantial scientific research activity there, such as the establishment of a scientific station or the despatch of a scientific expedition.

3. Reports from the observers referred to in Article VII of the present Treaty shall be transmitted to the representatives of the Contracting Parties participating in the meetings referred to in paragraph 1 of the present Article.

4. The measures referred to in paragraph 1 of this Article shall become effective when approved by all the Contracting Parties whose representatives were entitled to participate in the meetings held to consider those measures.

5. Any or all of the rights established in the present Treaty may be exercised as from the date of entry into force of the Treaty whether or not any measures facilitating the exercise of such rights have been proposed, considered or approved as provided in this Article.

Article X

Each of the Contracting Parties undertakes to exert appropriate efforts, consistent with the Charter of the United Nations, to the end that no one engages in any activity in Antarctica contrary to the principles or purposes of the present Treaty.

Article XI

1. If any dispute arises between two or more of the Contracting Parties concerning the interpretation or application of the present Treaty, those Contracting Parties shall consult among themselves with a view to having the dispute resolved by negotiation, inquiry, mediation, conciliation, arbitration, judicial settlement or other peaceful means of their own choice.

2. Any dispute of this character not so resolved shall, with the consent, in each case, of all parties to the dispute, be referred to the International Court of Justice for settlement; but failure to reach agreement on reference to the International Court shall not absolve parties to the dispute from the responsibility of continuing to seek to resolve it by any of the various peaceful means referred to in paragraph 1 of this Article.

Article XII

1. (a) The present Treaty may be modified or amended at any time by unanimous agreement of the Contracting Parties whose representatives are entitled to participate in the meetings provided for under Article IX. Any such modification or amendment shall enter into force when the depositary Government has received notice from all such Contracting Parties that they have ratified it.

(b) Such modification or amendment shall thereafter enter into force as to any other Contracting Party when notice of ratification by it has been received by the depositary Government. Any such Contracting Party from which no notice of ratification is received within a period of two years from the date of entry into force of the modification or amendment in accordance with the provisions of subparagraph 1(a) of this Article shall be deemed to have withdrawn from the present Treaty on the date of the expiration of such period.

2. (a) If after the expiration of thirty years from the date of entry into force of the present Treaty, any of the Contracting Parties whose representatives are entitled to participate in the meetings provided for under Article IX so requests by a communication addressed to the depositary Government, a Conference of all the

Contracting Parties shall be held as soon as practicable to review the operation of the Treaty.

(b) Any modification or amendment to the present Treaty which is approved at such a Conference by a majority of the Contracting Parties there represented, including a majority of those whose representatives are entitled to participate in the meetings provided for under Article IX, shall be communicated by the depositary Government to all the Contracting Parties immediately after the termination of the Conference and shall enter into force in accordance with the provisions of paragraph 1 of the present Article.

(c) If any such modification or amendment has not entered into force in accordance with the provisions of subparagraph 1(a) of this Article within a period of two years after the date of its communication to all the Contracting Parties, any Contracting Party may at any time after the expiration of that period give notice to the depositary Government of its withdrawal from the present Treaty; and such withdrawal shall take effect two years after the receipt of the notice of the depositary Government.

Article XIII

1. The present Treaty shall be subject to ratification by the signatory States. It shall be open for accession by any State which is a Member of the United Nations, or by any other State which may be invited to accede to the Treaty with the consent of all the Contracting Parties whose representatives are entitled to participate in the meetings provided for under Article IX of the Treaty.

2. Ratification of or accession to the present Treaty shall be effected by each State in accordance with its constitutional processes.

3. Instruments of ratification and instruments of accession shall be deposited with the Government of the United States of America, hereby designated as the depositary Government.

4. The depositary Government shall inform all signatory and acceding States of the date of each deposit of an instrument of ratification or accession, and the date of entry into force of the Treaty and of any modification or amendment thereto.

5. Upon the deposit of instruments of ratification by all the signatory States, the present Treaty shall enter into force for those States and for States which have deposited instruments of accession. Thereafter the Treaty shall enter into force for any acceding State upon the deposit of its instrument of accession.

6. The present Treaty shall be registered by the depositary Government pursuant to Article 102 of the Charter of the United Nations.

Article XIV

The present Treaty, done in the English, French, Russian and Spanish languages, each version being equally authentic, shall be deposited in the archives of the Government of the United States of America, which shall transmit duly certified copies thereof to the Governments of the signatory and acceding States.

IN WITNESS WHEREOF the undersigned Plenipotentiaries, duly authorized, have signed the present Treaty.

DONE at Washington this first day of December, one thousand nine hundred and fifty-nine.

Antarctic Treaty

Country	Date of Signature	Date of Deposit of Ratification	Date of Deposit of Accession
Argentina	12/1/59	6/23/61	
Australia	12/1/59	6/23/61	
Belgium	12/1/59	7/26/60	
Brazil			5/16/75
Bulgaria			9/11/78
Chile	12/1/59	6/23/61	
Czechoslovakia			6/14/62
Denmark			5/20/65
France	12/1/59	9/16/60	
German Democratic Republic			11/19/74
Germany, Federal Republic of			2/5/79
Japan	12/1/59	8/4/60	
Netherlands			3/30/67
New Zealand	12/1/59	11/1/60	
Norway	12/1/59	8/24/60	
Poland			6/8/61
Romania			9/15/71
South Africa	12/1/59	6/21/60	
Union of Soviet Socialist Republics	12/1/59	11/2/60	
United Kingdom	12/1/59	5/31/60	
United States	12/1/59	8/18/60	
Uruguay			1/11/80
Total	12	12	10

Memorandum of Understanding Between the United States of America and the Union of Soviet Socialist Republics Regarding the Establishment of a Direct Communications Link (With Annex)

The need for assuring quick and reliable communication directly between the heads of government of nuclear-weapons states first emerged in the context of efforts to reduce the danger that accident, miscalculation, or surprise attack might trigger a nuclear war. These risks, arising out of conditions which are novel in history and peculiar to the nuclear-armed missile age, can of course threaten all countries, directly or indirectly.

The Soviet Union had been the first nation to propose, in 1954, specific safeguards against surprise attack; it also expressed concern about the danger of accidental war. At Western initiative, a Conference of Experts on Surprise Attack was held in Geneva in 1958, but recessed without achieving conclusive results, although it stimulated technical research on the issues involved.

In its "Program for General and Complete Disarmament in a Peaceful World," presented to the General Assembly by President Kennedy on September 25, 1961, the United States proposed a group of measures to reduce the risks of war. These included advance notification of military movements and maneuvers, observation posts at major transportation centers and air bases, and additional inspection arrangements. An international commission would be established to study possible further measures to reduce risks, including "failure of communication."

The United States draft treaty outline submitted to the ENDC[1] on April 18, 1962, added a proposal for the exchange of military missions to improve communications and understanding. It also proposed "establishment of rapid and reliable communications" among the heads of governments and with the Secretary General of the United Nations.

The Soviet draft treaty on general and complete disarmament (March 15, 1962) offered no provisions covering the risk of war by

---

[1]Eighteen-Nation Disarmament Committee, which met at Geneva from 1962 on. In 1969, with the addition of new members, the name was changed to Conference of the Committee on Disarmament (CCD). A yet larger group, the Committee on Disarmament, was established in 1978–79.

surprise attack, miscalculation, or accident; on July 16, however, it introduced amendments to its draft that called for (1) a ban on joint maneuvers involving the forces of two or more states and advance notification of substantial military movements, (2) exchange of military missions, and (3) improved communications between heads of governments and with the U.N. Secretary General. These measures were not separable, however, from the rest of the Soviet program.

The Cuban missile crisis of October 1962 compellingly underscored the importance of prompt, direct communication between heads of states. On December 12 of that year, a United States working paper submitted to the ENDC urged consideration of a number of measures to reduce the risk of war; these measures, the United States argued, offered opportunities for early agreement and could be undertaken either as a group or separately. Included was establishment of communication links between major capitals to insure rapid and reliable communication in times of crisis. The working paper suggested that it did not appear either necessary or desirable to specify in advance all the situations in which a special communications link might be used:

> . . . In the view of the United States, such a link should, as a general matter, be reserved for emergency use; that is to say, for example, that it might be reserved for communications concerning a military crisis which might appear directly to threaten the security of either of the states involved and where such developments were taking place at a rate which appeared to preclude the use of normal consultative procedures. Effectiveness of the link would not be degraded through use for other matters.

On June 20, 1963, at Geneva the American and Soviet representatives to the ENDC completed negotiations and signed the "Memorandum of Understanding Between the United States of America and the Union of Soviet Socialist Republics Regarding the Establishment of a Direct Communications Link." The memorandum provided that each government should be responsible for arrangements for the link on its own territory, including continuous functioning of the link and prompt delivery of communications to its head of government. An annex set forth the routing and components of the link and provided for allocation of costs, exchange of equipment, and other technical matters. The direct communications link would comprise:

(1) two terminal points with teletype equipment,
(2) a full-time duplex wire telegraph circuit (Washington-London-Copenhagen-Stockholm-Helsinki-Moscow),
(3) a full-time duplex radiotelegraph circuit (Washington-Tangier-Moscow).

If the wire circuit should be interrupted, messages would be transmitted by the radio circuit. If experience showed the need for an additional wire circuit, it might be established by mutual agreement.

The "Hot Line" agreement, the first bilateral agreement between the United States and the Soviet Union that gave concrete recognition to the perils implicit in modern nuclear-weapons systems, was a limited but practical step to bring those perils under rational control.

The communications link has proved its worth since its installation. During the Arab-Israeli war in 1967, for example, the United States used it to prevent possible misunderstanding of U.S. fleet movements in the Mediterranean. It was used again during the 1973 Arab-Israeli war. The significance of the hot line is further attested by the 1971 agreement to modernize it.

Memorandum of Understanding Between the United States of America and the Union of Soviet Socialist Republics Regarding the Establishment of a Direct Communications Link

Signed at Geneva June 20, 1963
Entered into force June 20, 1963

For use in time of emergency the Government of the United States of America and the Government of the Union of Soviet Socialist Republics have agreed to establish as soon as technically feasible a direct communications link between the two Governments.

Each Government shall be responsible for the arrangements for the link on its own territory. Each Government shall take the necessary steps to ensure continuous functioning of the link and prompt delivery to its head of government of any communications received by means of the link from the head of government of the other party.

Arrangements for establishing and operating the link are set forth in the Annex which is attached hereto and forms an integral part hereof.

DONE in duplicate in the English and Russian languages at Geneva, Switzerland, this 20th day of June, 1963.

FOR THE GOVERNMENT OF THE
UNITED STATES OF AMERICA:

FOR THE GOVERNMENT OF THE
UNION OF SOVIET SOCIALIST
REPUBLICS:

Acting Representative of the United States of America to the Eighteen-Nation Committee on Disarmament

Acting Representative of the Union of Soviet Socialist Republics to the Eighteen-Nation Committee on Disarmament

(SEAL)

31

Annex

To the Memorandum of Understanding Between the United States of America and the Union of Soviet Socialist Republics Regarding the Establishment of a Direct Communications Link

The direct communications link between Washington and Moscow established in accordance with the Memorandum, and the operation of such link, shall be governed by the following provisions:

1. The direct communications link shall consist of:

   a. Two terminal points with telegraph-teleprinter equipment between which communications shall be directly exchanged;

   b. One full-time duplex wire telegraph circuit, routed Washington-London-Copenhagen-Stockholm-Helsinki-Moscow, which shall be used for the transmission of messages;

   c. One full-time duplex radiotelegraph circuit, routed Washington-Tangier-Moscow, which shall be used for service communications and for coordination of operations between the two terminal points.

If experience in operating the direct communications link should demonstrate that the establishment of an additional wire telegraph circuit is advisable, such circuit may be established by mutual agreement between authorized representatives of both Governments.

2. In case of interruption of the wire circuit, transmission of messages shall be effected via the radio circuit, and for this purpose provision shall be made at the terminal points for the capability of prompt switching of all necessary equipment from one circuit to another.

3. The terminal points of the link shall be so equipped as to provide for the transmission and reception of messages from Moscow to Washington in the Russian language and from Washington to Moscow in the English language. In this connection, the USSR shall furnish the United States four sets of telegraph terminal equipment, including page printers, transmitters, and reperforators, with one year's supply of spare parts and all necessary special tools, test equipment, operating instructions, and other technical literature, to provide for transmission and reception of messages in the Russian language.

The United States shall furnish the Soviet Union four sets of telegraph terminal equipment, including page printers, transmitters, and reperforators, with one year's supply of spare parts and all necessary special tools, test equipment, operating instructions and other technical literature, to provide for transmission and reception of messages in the English language.

The equipment described in this paragraph shall be exchanged directly between the parties without any payment being required therefor.

4. The terminal points of the direct communications link shall be provided with encoding equipment. For the terminal point in the USSR, four sets of such equipment (each capable of simplex operation), with one year's supply of spare parts, with all

necessary special tools, test equipment, operating instructions and other technical literature, and with all necessary blank tape, shall be furnished by the United States to the USSR against payment of the cost thereof by the USSR.

The USSR shall provide for preparation and delivery of keying tapes to the terminal point of the link in the United States for reception of messages from the USSR. The United States shall provide for the preparation and delivery of keying tapes to the terminal point of the link in the USSR for reception of messages from the United States. Delivery of prepared keying tapes to the terminal points of the link shall be effected through the Embassy of the USSR in Washington (for the terminal of the link in the USSR) and through the Embassy of the United States in Moscow (for the terminal of the link in the United States).

5. The United States and the USSR shall designate the agencies responsible for the arrangements regarding the direct communications link, for its technical maintenance, continuity and reliability, and for the timely transmission of messages.

Such agencies may, by mutual agreement, decide matters and develop instructions relating to the technical maintenance and operation of the direct communications link and effect arrangements to improve the operation of the link.

6. The technical parameters of the telegraph circuits of the link and of the terminal equipment, as well as the maintenance of such circuits and equipment, shall be in accordance with CCITT and CCIR recommendations.

Transmission and reception of messages over the direct communications link shall be effected in accordance with applicable recommendations of international telegraph and radio communications regulations, as well as with mutually agreed instructions.

7. The costs of the direct communications link shall be borne as follows:

a. The USSR shall pay the full cost of leasing the portion of the telegraph circuit from Moscow to Helsinki and 50% of the cost of leasing the portion of the telegraph circuit from Helsinki to London. The United States shall pay the full cost of leasing the portion of the telegraph circuit from Washington to London and 50% of the cost of leasing the portion of the telegraph circuit from London to Helsinki.

b. Payment of the cost of leasing the radio telegraph circuit between Washington and Moscow shall be effected without any transfer of payments between the parties. The USSR shall bear the expenses relating to the transmission of messages from Moscow to Washington. The United States shall bear the expenses relating to the transmission of messages from Washington to Moscow.

Treaty Banning Nuclear Weapon Tests in the Atmosphere, in Outer Space and Under Water

The test ban treaty of 1963 prohibits nuclear weapons tests "or any other nuclear explosion" in the atmosphere, in outer space, and under water. While not banning tests underground, the treaty does prohibit nuclear explosions in this environment if they cause "radioactive debris to be present outside the territorial limits of the State under whose jurisdiction or control" the explosions were conducted. In accepting limitations on testing, the nuclear powers accepted as a common goal "an end to the contamination of man's environment by radioactive substances."

Efforts to achieve a test ban agreement had extended over 8 years. They involved complex technical problems of verification and the difficulties of reconciling deep-seated differences in approach to arms control and security. The uneven progress of the negotiations reflected, moreover, contemporaneous fluctuations in East-West political relationships.

Prior to SALT, no arms control measure since World War II had enlisted so intensely the sustained interest of the international community. The United States in November 1952, and the Soviet Union in August of the following year, exploded their first hydrogen devices, and rising concern about radioactive fallout and the prospect of even more powerful explosions spurred efforts to halt testing. Succeeding events gave the dangers of fallout concrete and human meaning. In March 1954 the United States exploded an experimental thermonuclear device at Bikini atoll, expected to have the power of 8 million tons of TNT. The actual yield was almost double that predicted—about 15 megatons, and the area of dangerous fallout greatly exceeded original estimates. A Japanese fishing vessel, the *Lucky Dragon,* was accidentally contaminated, and its crew suffered from radiation sickness, as did the inhabitants of an atoll in the area. In another such accident, radioactive rain containing debris from a Soviet hydrogen bomb test fell on Japan.

As knowledge of the nature and effects of fallout increased, and as it became apparent that no region was untouched by radioactive debris, the issue of continued nuclear tests drew widened and intensified public attention. Apprehension was expressed about the possibility of a cumulative contamination of the environment and of resultant genetic damage.

Efforts to negotiate an international agreement to end nuclear tests began in the Subcommittee of Five (the United States, the United Kingdom, Canada, France, and the U.S.S.R.) of the U.N. Disarmament Commission in May 1955, when the Soviet Union included discontinuance of weapons tests in its proposals.

Public interest in the course of the negotiations was active and sustained. In individual statements and proposals, and in international meetings, governments pressed for discontinuance of nuclear tests. A dozen resolutions of the General Assembly addressed the issue, repeatedly urging conclusion of an agreement to ban tests under a system of international controls.

Test Ban and General Disarmament

The relation of a test ban to other aspects of disarmament was for a time a troubling issue. The initial Soviet proposal of a test ban on May 10, 1955, was part of a comprehensive plan to reduce conventional forces and armaments and to eliminate nuclear weapons. Later that year in the General Assembly, the U.S.S.R. advocated a separate test ban. The three Western powers, over the next 3 years, made discontinuance of tests contingent on progress in other measures of arms control, particularly a cut-off in the production of fissionable materials for weapons and safeguards against surprise attack, and insisted that a test ban could not be enforced "in the absence of more general control agreements."

In January 1959 the United States and the United Kingdom dropped the linkage between a test ban and other arms control agreements; France, however, did not. The French continued to maintain that until there was agreement on nuclear disarmament—including an end to weapons production, reconversion of stocks, and a ban on possession and use—French plans to conduct tests would go forward. The Soviet Union abruptly reversed its position in June 1961, when Premier Khrushchev declared during his meeting with President Kennedy in Vienna that the test-ban question must be linked with general and complete disarmament. The Soviet Union refused to modify this position until November, when it proposed a separate test ban with no controls whatever, pending agreement on general and complete disarmament.

Verification

The central and most persistent barrier to a treaty on cessation of tests, however, was the issue of verifying compliance, of agreeing to establish a system of controls and inspection—particularly with regard to underground explosions—that could guarantee against testing in secret. The Western powers were determined to assure that no agreement would be liable to clandestine violation. In test-ban negotiations, as well as in other arms control efforts, they considered that it would be dangerous to their security to accept simple pledges without the means of knowing that they would be observed.

It was further believed that such pledges would mislead concerned world opinion with illusions of secure progress toward disarmament.

Writing to President Eisenhower on October 17, 1956, Premier Bulganin had stated the fundamental Soviet position. "Since any explosion of an atomic or hydrogen bomb cannot, in the present state of scientific knowledge, be produced without being recorded in other countries," he said, there could be an immediate agreement to prohibit tests without any provision for international control:

> Would not the best guarantee against the violation of such an agreement be the mere fact that secret testing of nuclear weapons is impossible and that consequently a government undertaking the solemn obligation to stop making tests could not violate it without exposing itself to the entire world as the violator of an international agreement?

The western countries were not convinced that existing technology for detecting nuclear explosions was adequate to monitor compliance, or that the mere force of world opinion would provide assurance against violations. In his response, President Eisenhower stated that "to be effective, and not simply a mirage," disarmament plans required systems of inspection and control. And in a public statement a few days later, he said

> A simple agreement to stop H-bomb tests cannot be regarded as automatically self-enforcing on the unverified assumption that such tests can instantly and surely be detected. It is true that tests of very large weapons would probably be detected when they occur . . . It is, however, impossible—in my view of the vast Soviet land-mass that can screen future tests—to have positive assurance of such detection, except in the case of the largest weapons.

On June 14, 1957, the Soviet Union for the first time offered test ban proposals that included international control. The proposals were very general: establishment of an international supervisory commission and control posts, on the basis of reciprocity, on the territories of the three nuclear powers and in the Pacific Ocean area. The Western powers suggested that a group of experts work out the details of a control system, while the delegates considered a temporary test ban in relation to other disarmament measures.

The Soviet Union continued to press for an immediate suspension of tests, and the United States for agreement on a control system as a necessary accompanying measure. In March 1958 the Soviet Union announced that it was discontinuing all tests and appealed to the parliaments of other nuclear powers to take similar action. It added, however, that the Soviet Union would "naturally be free" to resume testing if other nuclear powers did not stop their tests. Succeeding Bulganin as Premier, Nikita Khrushchev called on President Eisenhower to end tests. President Eisenhower rejected the proposal, stating that some tests could be conducted "under conditions of secrecy," and renewed the proposal for an experts' group to study control problems. After further summit correspondence and diplomatic exchange, Khrushchev agreed to a conference of experts. Meanwhile U.S. and British tests continued.

The Geneva Conference of Experts met in July and August 1958, attended by representatives from the United States, the United Kingdom, Canada, France, the U.S.S.R., Poland, Czechoslovakia, and Romania. They agreed on the technical characteristics of a control system to monitor a ban on tests in the atmosphere, under water, and underground. Their report proposed an elaborate network of 170–180 land control posts and 10 shipborne posts, as well as regular and special aircraft flights. It recognized that on-site inspections would be needed to determine whether some seismic events were caused by earthquakes or explosions.

The United States and Britain welcomed the experts' report and declared their willingness to negotiate an agreement for suspension of tests and the establishment of an international control system on the basis of the report. They were prepared to suspend tests for a year from the beginning of negotiations unless the U.S.S.R. resumed testing. The suspension could continue on a year-to-year basis, provided that the inspection system was installed and functioning, and "satisfactory progress" was being made on major arms-control measures. Premier Khrushchev's response was to attack the Americans and British for continuing their tests, and for linking the test ban to other matters; he announced that the Soviet Union was released from its self-imposed pledge. The U.S.S.R. resumed tests, and the series continued until November 3.

The negotiating powers refrained from testing for the next 3 years. The "moratorium" was marked by several public statements of intent, by the United States, the United Kingdom, and the Soviet Union, in varying degrees of specificity and with various caveats. At the end of December 1959, President Eisenhower announced that the United States would no longer consider itself bound by the "voluntary moratorium" but would give advance notice if it decided to resume testing. The Soviet Union, with dramatic effect, resumed testing in August of 1961. The United States resumed testing 2 weeks later.

Throughout the various conferences and exchanges on a test ban, the complexity of the central problem brought successive deadlocks, break-offs, and renewals of discussion, shifts in position, searches for compromise and new approaches, and for new techniques of verifications, and successive suspensions and resumptions of tests. The United States continued to be unwilling to accept the Soviet basic proposition that a test ban could be agreed to and controls instituted subsequently, or to accept indefinite test suspensions that were tantamount to endorsing an uncontrolled prohibition. New data from American underground tests, moreover, had shown that techniques recommended earlier for distinguishing between explosions and earthquakes were less effective than had been believed and that a reliable control system to monitor seismic events that registered under 4.75 on the Richter scale required further research and confirmed the need for on-site inspections.

Among the salient points of disagreement on a control system were:

The Veto. The U.S.S.R. initially sought to have all substantive operations of the system subject to veto; the United States insisted that the fact-finding process of inspection, to be effective, must be as automatic as possible.

On-Site Inspections. The Soviet Union placed a limit on permitted inspections in its territory, refusing to allow more than three per year. The United States and the United Kingdom held that the number must be determined by scientific fact and detection capability. As new information became available, the United States eventually indicated that it could accept a minimum of seven, but the U.S.S.R. rejected this quota. There was disagreement, as well, over the size of the area to be inspected, the nationality and composition of inspection teams, and the criteria for identifying events that required inspection.

Control Posts. Although the United States and the United Kingdom had originally proposed that the control posts should be internationally owned and operated, they later agreed to national ownership and operation of the posts, as the U.S.S.R. insisted, with international monitoring and supervision.

There were unresolved differences about the number and location of posts and about the number and location of the automatic seismic observation stations ("black boxes") with which it was proposed to supplement them. The U.S.S.R. also claimed that national control posts and automatic observation devices made any international inspection unnecessary, a position that the United States and the United Kingdom were not willing to accept.

The Organization of the Control Commission. In March 1961 the Soviet Union recommended replacing the single administrator of the proposed Control Commission with a "troika," a tripartite administrative council, consisting of one neutral, one Western, and one Communist member (a proposal paralleling the Soviet effort the previous year to replace the U.N. Secretary General with a tripartite commission). This three-headed administration would be able to function even in routine matters only by unanimous agreement, an arrangement that the Western powers argued was unworkable and would make the Control Commission helpless. The Soviet Union eventually abandoned this demand.

The effort to achieve a test ban, and to resolve the stubborn issues involved, had been pursued in a wide variety of channels. Successive General Assembly sessions had debated the issue. It had been a major item on the agenda of the U.N. Disarmament Commission and its Subcommittee of Five (later ten). The United States, the United Kingdom, and the Soviet Union had engaged in a long tripartite effort—The Conference on the Discontinuance of Nuclear Weapons Tests—in almost continuous session in Geneva from October 31, 1958, to January 29, 1962. Under its auspices three technical working groups of experts had investigated and reported on various aspects of control: one on high altitude tests, another on underground tests, the third on seismic research programs to improve detection capabilities.

After the three-power conference adjourned in January 1962, unable to complete the drafting of a treaty because of the Soviet Union's claim that national means of detection were adequate for all environments, the principal forum for negotiations became the newly formed Eighteen-Nation Disarmament Committee (ENDC), which began its meetings at Geneva under the aegis of the General Assembly in March 1962. On the U.S. side, overall direction of the negotiations was assumed by William C. Foster, first Director of the newly created U.S. Arms Control and Disarmament Agency. Soviet insistence that the West accept Premier Khrushchev's quota of three annual inspections, however, brought these talks to an impasse. The United States and the United Kingdom, in high-level correspondence with the Soviet Union, then sought to arrange three-power talks. Finally, on June 10, 1963, President Kennedy announced that agreement had been reached to hold three-power meetings on the test ban in Moscow. He also pledged that the United States would not be the first to resume tests in the atmosphere.

At this time a shift of Soviet interest to a ban that did not deal with underground tests emerged, although the Soviet Union had rejected an Anglo-American proposal for an agreement of this kind the year before. Premier Khrushchev disclosed this in a speech on July 2, 1963, when he called for an agreement outlawing tests in the atmosphere, in outer space, and under water—environments where both sides agreed their existing verification systems could adequately police a ban.

The three-power meetings began on July 15. The long years of discussion had clarified views and greatly reduced areas of disagreement, and a treaty was negotiated within 10 days. It was initialed on July 25 and formally signed at Moscow on August 5, 1963, by U.S. Secretary of State Dean Rusk; the Foreign Minister of the U.S.S.R., Andrei Gromyko; and the Foreign Minister of the U.K., Lord Home. On September 24, after extensive hearings and almost 3 weeks of floor debate, the Senate consented to ratification of the treaty by a vote of 80 to 19. It was ratified by President Kennedy on October 7, 1963, and entered into force on October 10 when the three original signatories deposited their instruments of ratification.

The parties to the treaty undertake "not to carry out any nuclear weapon test explosion, or any other nuclear explosion," in the atmosphere, under water, or in outer space, or in any other environment if the explosion would cause radioactive debris to be present outside the borders of the state conducting the explosion. As explained by Acting Secretary of State Ball in a subsequent report to President Kennedy, "The phrase 'any other nuclear explosion' includes explosions for peaceful purposes. Such explosions are prohibited by the treaty because of the difficulty of differentiating between weapon test explosions and peaceful explosions without additional controls."

The treaty is of unlimited duration, with provisions for amendment or withdrawal. Article III opens the treaty to all states, and most of the countries of the world have now signed it (108 nations are parties, 15 nations have signed but not ratified it). The treaty has not been signed by France or by the People's Republic of China.

Treaty Banning Nuclear Weapon Tests in the Atmosphere, in Outer Space and Under Water

Signed at Moscow August 5, 1963
Ratification advised by U.S. Senate September 24, 1963
Ratified by U.S. President October 7, 1963
U.S. ratification deposited at Washington, London, and Moscow October 10, 1963
Proclaimed by U.S. President October 10, 1963
Entered into force October 10, 1963

The Governments of the United States of America, the United Kingdom of Great Britain and Northern Ireland, and the Union of Soviet Socialist Republics, hereinafter referred to as the "Original Parties,"

Proclaiming as their principal aim the speediest possible achievement of an agreement on general and complete disarmament under strict international control in accordance with the objectives of the United Nations which would put an end to the armaments race and eliminate the incentive to the production and testing of all kinds of weapons, including nuclear weapons.

Seeking to achieve the discontinuance of all test explosions of nuclear weapons for all time, determined to continue negotiations to this end, and desiring to put an end to the contamination of man's environment by radioactive substances,

Have agreed as follows:

Article I

1. Each of the Parties to this Treaty undertakes to prohibit, to prevent, and not to carry out any nuclear weapon test explosion, or any other nuclear explosion, at any place under its jurisdiction or control:

(a) in the atmosphere; beyond its limits, including outer space; or under water, including territorial waters or high seas; or

(b) in any other environment if such explosion causes radioactive debris to be present outside the territorial limits of the State under whose jurisdiction or control such explosion is conducted. It is understood in this connection that the provisions of this subparagraph are without prejudice to the conclusion of a treaty resulting in the permanent banning of all nuclear test explosions, including all such explosions underground, the conclusion of which, as the Parties have stated in the Preamble to this Treaty, they seek to achieve.

2. Each of the Parties to this Treaty undertakes furthermore to refrain from causing, encouraging, or in any way participating in, the carrying out of any nuclear weapon test explosion, or any other nuclear explosion, anywhere which would take place in any of the environments described, or have the effect referred to, in paragraph 1 of this Article.

Article II

1. Any Party may propose amendments to this Treaty. The text of any proposed amendment shall be submitted to the Depositary Governments which shall circulate it to all Parties to this Treaty. Thereafter, if requested to do so by one-third or more of the

Parties, the Depositary Governments shall convene a conference, to which they shall invite all the Parties, to consider such amendment.

2. Any amendment to this Treaty must be approved by a majority of the votes of all the Parties to this Treaty, including the votes of all of the Original Parties. The amendment shall enter into force for all Parties upon the deposit of instruments of ratification by a majority of all the Parties, including the instruments of ratification of all of the Original Parties.

Article III

1. This Treaty shall be open to all States for signature. Any State which does not sign this Treaty before its entry into force in accordance with paragraph 3 of this Article may accede to it at any time.

2. This Treaty shall be subject to ratification by signatory States. Instruments of ratification and instruments of accession shall be deposited with the Governments of the Original Parties—the United States of America, the United Kingdom of Great Britain and Northern Ireland, and the Union of Soviet Socialist Republics—which are hereby designated the Depositary Governments.

3. This Treaty shall enter into force after its ratification by all the Original Parties and the deposit of their instruments of ratification.

4. For States whose instruments of ratification or accession are deposited subsequent to the entry into force of this Treaty, it shall enter into force on the date of the deposit of their instruments of ratification or accession.

5. The Depositary Governments shall promptly inform all signatory and acceding States of the date of each signature, the date of deposit of each instrument of ratification of and accession to this Treaty, the date of its entry into force, and the date of receipt of any requests for conferences or other notices.

6. This Treaty shall be registered by the Depositary Governments pursuant to Article 102 of the Charter of the United Nations.

Article IV

This Treaty shall be of unlimited duration.

Each Party shall in exercising its national sovereignty have the right to withdraw from the Treaty if it decides that extraordinary events, related to the subject matter of this Treaty, have jeopardized the supreme interests of its country. It shall give notice of such withdrawal to all other Parties to the Treaty three months in advance.

Article V

This Treaty, of which the English and Russian texts are equally authentic, shall be deposited in the archives of the Depositary Governments. Duly certified copies of this Treaty shall be transmitted by the Depositary Governments to the Governments of the signatory and acceding States.

IN WITNESS WHEREOF the undersigned, duly authorized, have signed this Treaty.

DONE in triplicate at the city of Moscow the fifth day of August, one thousand nine hundred and sixty-three.

For the Government of
the United States of
America

For the Government of
the United Kingdom
of Great Britain and
Northern Ireland

For the Government of
the Union of Soviet
Socialist Republics

Limited Test Ban Treaty

Country	Date of[1] Signature	Date of Deposit[1] of Ratification	Date of Deposit[1] of Accession
Afghanistan	8/8/63	3/12/64	
Algeria	8/14/63		
Argentina	8/8/63		
Australia	8/8/63	11/12/63	
Austria	9/11/63	7/17/64	
Bahamas, The			8/13/76
Belgium	8/8/63	3/1/66	
Benin	8/27/63	12/15/64	
Bhutan			6/8/78
Bolivia	8/8/63	8/4/65	
Botswana			1/5/68
Brazil	8/8/63	12/15/64	
Bulgaria	8/8/63	11/13/63	
Burma	8/14/63	11/15/63	
Burundi	10/4/63		
Byelorussian S.S.R.[2]	10/8/63	12/16/63	
Cameroon	8/27/63		
Canada	8/8/63	1/28/64	
Cape Verde			10/24/79
Central African Republic			12/22/64
Chad	8/26/63	3/1/65	
Chile	8/8/63	10/6/65	
China (Taiwan)	8/23/63	5/18/64	
Colombia	8/16/63		
Costa Rica	8/9/63	7/10/67	
Cyprus	8/8/63	4/15/65	
Czechoslovakia	8/8/63	10/14/63	
Denmark	8/9/63	1/15/64	
Dominican Republic	9/16/63	6/3/64	
Ecuador	9/27/63	5/6/64	
Egypt	8/8/63	1/10/64	
El Salvador	8/21/63	12/3/64	
Ethiopia	8/9/63		
Fiji			7/18/72
Finland	8/8/63	1/9/64	
Gabon	9/10/63	2/20/64	
Gambia, The			4/27/65
German Democratic Republic	8/8/63	12/30/63	

See footnotes on page 239.

Country	Date of[1] Signature	Date of Deposit[1] of Ratification	Date of Deposit[1] of Accession
Germany, Federal Republic of	8/19/63	12.1/64	
Ghana	8/8/63	11/27/63	
Greece	8/8/63	12/18/63	
Guatemala	9/23/63	1/6/64	
Haiti	10/9/63		
Honduras	8/8/63	10/2/64	
Hungary	8/8/63	10/21/63	
Iceland	8/12/63	4/29/64	
India	8/8/63	10/10/63	
Indonesia	8/23/63	1/20/64	
Iran	8/8/63	5/5/64	
Iraq	8/13/63	11/30/64	
Ireland	8/8/63	12/18/63	
Israel	8/8/63	1/15/64	
Italy	8/8/63	12/10/64	
Ivory Coast	9/5/63	2/5/65	
Jamaica	8/13/63		
Japan	8/14/63	6/15/64	
Jordan	8/12/63	5/29/64	
Kenya			6/10/65
Korea, Republic of	8/30/63	7/24/64	
Kuwait	8/20/63	5/20/65	
Laos	8/12/63	2/10/65	
Lebanon	8/12/63	5/14/65	
Liberia	8/8/63	5/19/64	
Libya	8/9/63	7/15/68	
Luxembourg	8/13/63	2/10/66	
Madagascar	9/23/63	3/15/65	
Malawi			11/26/64
Malaysia	8/8/63	7/15/64	
Mali	8/23/63		
Malta			11/25/64
Mauritania	9/13/63	4/6/64	
Mauritius			4/30/69
Mexico	8/8/63	12/27/63	
Mongolia	8/8/63	11/1/63	
Morocco	8/27/63	2/1/66	
Nepal	8/26/63	10/7/64	
Netherlands	8/9/63	9/14/64	
New Zealand	8/8/63	10/10/63	

See footnotes on page 239.

Country	Date of[1] Signature	Date of Deposit[1] of Ratification	Date of Deposit[1] of Accession
Nicaragua	8/13/63	1/26/65	
Niger	9/24/63	7/3/64	
Nigeria	8/30/63	2/17/67	
Norway	8/9/63	11/21/63	
Pakistan	8/14/63		
Panama	9/20/63	2/24/66	
Paraguay	8/15/63		
Peru	8/23/63	7/20/64	
Philippines	8/8/63	11/10/65	
Poland	8/8/63	10/14/63	
Portugal	10/9/63		
Romania	8/8/63	12/12/63	
Rwanda	9/19/63	12/27/63	
San Marino	9/17/63	7/3/64	
Senegal	9/20/63	5/6/64	
Sierra Leone	9/4/63	2/21/64	
Singapore			7/12/68
Somalia	8/19/63		
South Africa			10/10/63
Spain	8/13/63	12/17/64	
Sri Lanka	8/22/63	2/5/64	
Sudan	8/9/63	3/4/66	
Swaziland			5/29/69
Sweden	8/12/63	12/9/63	
Switzerland	8/26/63	1/16/64	
Syrian Arab Republic	8/13/63	6/1/64	
Tanzania	9/16/63	2/6/64	
Thailand	8/8/63	11/15/63	
Togo	9/18/63	12/7/64	
Tonga			7/7/71
Trinidad & Tobago	8/12/63	7/14/64	
Tunisia	8/8/63	5/26/65	
Turkey	8/9/63	7/8/65	
Uganda	8/29/63	3/24/64	
Ukrainian S.S.R.[2]	10/8/63	12/30/63	
Union of Soviet Socialist Republics	8/5/63	10/10/63	
United Kingdom	8/5/63	10/10/63	
United States	8/5/63	10/10/63	
Upper Volta	8/30/63		
Uruguay	8/12/63	2/25/63	

See footnotes on page 239.

Country	Date of[1] Signature	Date of Deposit[1] of Ratification	Date of Deposit[1] of Accession
Venezuela	8/16/63	2/22/65	
Western Samoa	9/5/63	1/15/65	
Yemen Arab Republic (Sana)	8/13/63		
Yemen, People's Democratic Republic of (Aden)			6/1/79
Yugoslavia	8/8/63	1/15/64	
Zaire	8/8/63	10/28/63	
Zambia			1/11/65
Total	106	91	17

See footnotes on page 239.

Treaty on Principles Governing the Activities of States in the Exploration and Use of Outer Space, Including the Moon and Other Celestial Bodies

The treaty on outer space and celestial bodies was the second of the so-called "nonarmament" treaties; its concepts and some of its provisions were modeled on its predecessor, the Antarctic Treaty. Like that treaty it sought to prevent "a new form of colonial competition" and the possible damage that self-seeking exploitation might cause.

In early 1957, even before the launching of Sputnik in October, developments in rocketry had led the United States to propose international verification of the testing of space objects. And the development of an inspection system for outer space was part of a Western proposal for partial disarmament put forward in August 1957. The U.S.S.R., however, in the midst of testing its first ICBM and about to orbit its first Earth satellite, did not accept these proposals.

Between 1959 and 1962 the Western powers made a series of proposals that would bar the use of outer space for military purposes. Their successive plans for general and complete disarmament included provisions to ban the orbiting and stationing in outer space of weapons of mass destruction. Addressing the General Assembly on September 22, 1960, President Eisenhower proposed that the principles of the Antarctic Treaty be applied to outer space and celestial bodies.

Soviet plans for general and complete disarmament between 1960 and 1962 included provisions for insuring the peaceful use of outer space. The Soviet Union, however, would not separate outer space from other disarmament issues. It declined to agree to restrict outer space to peaceful uses unless American foreign bases, where short-range and medium-range missiles were stationed, were eliminated also.

The Western powers declined to accept the Soviet approach; the linkage, they held, would upset the military balance and weaken the security of the West.

After the signing of the limited test ban treaty, the Soviet Union's position changed. It ceased to link an agreement on outer space with the question of foreign bases. On September 19, 1963, Foreign

Minister Gromyko told the General Assembly that the Soviet Union wished to conclude an agreement banning the orbiting of objects carrying nuclear weapons. Ambassador Stevenson stated that the United States had no intention of orbiting weapons of mass destruction, installing them on celestial bodies or stationing them in outer space. The General Assembly unanimously adopted a resolution on October 17, 1963, welcoming the Soviet and American statements and calling upon all states to refrain from introducing weapons of mass destruction into outer space.

The United States supported the resolution, despite the absence of any provisions for verification; the capabilities of its space-tracking systems, it was estimated, were adequate for detecting launchings and devices in orbit.

Seeking to sustain the momentum for arms control agreements, the United States in 1965 and 1966 pressed for a treaty that would give further substance to the U.N. resolution.

On June 16, 1966, both the United States and the Soviet Union submitted draft treaties. The American draft dealt only with celestial bodies; the Soviet draft covered the whole outer space environment. The United States accepted the Soviet position on the scope of the treaty, and by September agreement had been reached in discussions at Geneva on most treaty provisions. Differences on the few remaining issues—chiefly involving access to facilities on celestial bodies, reporting on space activities, and the use of military equipment and personnel in space exploration—were satisfactorily resolved in private consultations during the General Assembly session by December.

On the 19th of that month the General Assembly approved by acclamation a resolution commending the treaty. It was opened for signature at Washington, London, and Moscow on January 27, 1967. On April 25 the Senate gave unanimous consent to its ratification, and the treaty entered into force on October 10, 1967.

The substance of the arms control provisions is in Article IV. This article restricts military activities in two ways:

First, it contains an undertaking not to place in orbit around the Earth, install on the moon or any other celestial body, or otherwise station in outer space nuclear or any other weapons of mass destruction.

Second, it limits the use of the moon and other celestial bodies exclusively to peaceful purposes and expressly prohibits their use for establishing military bases, installations, or fortifications; testing weapons of any kind; or conducting military maneuvers.

In the years since the treaty came into force, space exploration has been conducted in an increasingly cooperative spirit, as manifested in United States and Soviet collaboration in jointly planned and manned space enterprises.

Treaty on Principles Governing the Activities of States in the Exploration and Use of Outer Space, Including the Moon and Other Celestial Bodies

Signed at Washington, London, Moscow, January 27, 1967
Ratification advised by U.S. Senate April 25, 1967
Ratified by U.S. President May 24, 1967
U.S. ratification deposited at Washington, London, and Moscow October 10, 1967
Proclaimed by U.S. President October 10, 1967
Entered into force October 10, 1967

The States Parties to this Treaty,

Inspired by the great prospects opening up before mankind as a result of man's entry into outer space,

Recognizing the common interest of all mankind in the progress of the exploration and use of outer space for peaceful purposes.

Believing that the exploration and use of outer space should be carried on for the benefit of all peoples irrespective of the degree of their economic or scientific development,

Desiring to contribute to broad international co-operation in the scientific as well as the legal aspects of the exploration and use of outer space for peaceful purposes,

Believing that such co-operation will contribute to the development of mutual understanding and to the strengthening of friendly relations between States and peoples,

Recalling resolution 1962 (XVIII), entitled "Declaration of Legal Principles Governing the Activities of States in the Exploration and Use of Outer Space," which was adopted unanimously by the United Nations General Assembly on 13 December 1963,

Recalling resolution 1884 (XVIII), calling upon States to refrain from placing in orbit around the Earth any objects carrying nuclear weapons or any other kinds of weapons of mass destruction or from installing such weapons on celestial bodies, which was adopted unanimously by the United Nations General Assembly on 17 October 1963,

Taking account of United Nations General Assembly resolution 110 (II) of 3 November 1947, which condemned propaganda designed or likely to provoke or encourage any threat to the peace, breach of the peace or act of aggression, and considering that the aforementioned resolution is applicable to outer space,

Convinced that a Treaty on Principles Governing the Activities of States in the Exploration and Use of Outer Space, including the Moon and Other Celestial Bodies, will further the Purposes and Principles of the Charter of the United Nations,

Have agreed on the following:

Article I

The exploration and use of outer space, including the moon and other celestial bodies, shall be carried out for the benefit and in the interests of all countries, irrespective of their degree of economic or scientific development, and shall be the province of all mankind.

Outer space, including the moon and other celestial bodies, shall be free for exploration and use by all States without discrimination of any kind, on a basis of equality and in accordance with international law, and there shall be free access to all areas of celestial bodies.

There shall be freedom of scientific investigation in outer space, including the moon and other celestial bodies, and States shall facilitate and encourage international co-operation in such investigation.

Article II

Outer space, including the moon and other celestial bodies, is not subject to national appropriation by claim of sovereignty, by means of use or occupation, or by any other means.

Article III

States Parties to the Treaty shall carry on activities in the exploration and use of outer space, including the moon and other celestial bodies, in accordance with international law, including the Charter of the United Nations, in the interest of maintaining international peace and security and promoting international co-operation and understanding.

Article IV

States Parties to the Treaty undertake not to place in orbit around the Earth any objects carrying nuclear weapons or any other kinds of weapons of mass destruction, install such weapons on celestial bodies, or station such weapons in outer space in any other manner.

The moon and other celestial bodies shall be used by all States Parties to the Treaty exclusively for peaceful purposes. The establishment of military bases, installations and fortifications, the testing of any type of weapons and the conduct of military maneuvers on celestial bodies shall be forbidden. The use of military personnel for scientific research or for any other peaceful purposes shall not be prohibited. The use of any equipment or facility necessary for peaceful exploration of the moon and other celestial bodies shall also not be prohibited.

Article V

States Parties to the Treaty shall regard astronauts as envoys of mankind in outer space and shall render to them all possible assistance in the event of accident, distress, or emergency landing on the territory of another State Party or on the high seas. When astronauts make such a landing, they shall be safely and promptly returned to the State of registry of their space vehicle.

In carrying on activities in outer space and on celestial bodies, the astronauts of one State Party shall render all possible assistance to the astronauts of other States Parties.

States Parties to the Treaty shall immediately inform the other States Parties to the Treaty or the Secretary-General of the United Nations of any phenomena they discover in outer space, including the moon and other celestial bodies, which could constitute a danger to the life or health of astronauts.

Article VI

States Parties to the Treaty shall bear international responsibility for national activities in outer space, including the moon and other celestial bodies, whether such activities are carried on by governmental agencies or by non-governmental entities, and for assuring that national activities are carried out in conformity with the provisions set forth in the present Treaty. The activities of non-governmental entities in outer space, including the moon and other celestial bodies, shall require authorization and continuing supervision by the appropriate State Party to the Treaty. When activities are carried on in outer space, including the moon and other celestial bodies, by an international organization, responsibility for compliance with this Treaty shall be borne both by the international organization and by the States Parties to the Treaty participating in such organization.

Article VII

Each State Party to the Treaty that launches or procures the launching of an object into outer space, including the moon and other celestial bodies, and each State Party from whose territory or facility an object is launched, is internationally liable for damage to another State Party to the Treaty or to its natural or juridical persons by such object or its component parts on the Earth, in air space or in outer space, including the moon and other celestial bodies.

Article VIII

A State Party to the Treaty on whose registry an object launched into outer space is carried shall retain jurisdiction and control over such object, and over any personnel thereof, while in outer space or on a celestial body. Ownership of objects launched into outer space, including objects landed or constructed on a celestial body, and of their component parts, is not affected by their presence in outer space or on a celestial body or by their return to the Earth. Such objects or component parts found beyond the limits of the State Party to the Treaty on whose registry they are carried shall be returned to that State Party, which shall, upon request, furnish identifying data prior to their return.

Article IX

In the exploration and use of outer space, including the moon and other celestial bodies, States Parties to the Treaty shall be guided by the principle of co-operation and mutual assistance and shall conduct all their activities in outer space, including the moon and other celestial bodies, with due regard to the corresponding interests of all other States Parties to the Treaty. States Parties to the Treaty shall pursue studies of outer space, including the moon and other celestial bodies, and conduct exploration of them so as to avoid their harmful contamination and also adverse changes in the environment of the Earth resulting from the introduction of extraterrestrial matter and, where necessary, shall adopt appropriate measures for this purpose. If a State Party to the Treaty has reason to believe that an activity or experiment planned by it or its nationals in outer space, including the moon and other celestial bodies, would cause potentially harmful interference with activities of other States Parties in the peaceful exploration and use of outer space, including the moon and other celestial bodies, it shall undertake appropriate international consultations before proceeding with any such activity or experiment. A State Party to the Treaty which has reason to believe that an activity or experiment planned by another State Party in outer space, including the moon and other celestial bodies, would cause potentially harmful interference with activities in the peaceful exploration and use of outer space, including the moon and other celestial bodies, may request consultation concerning the activity or experiment.

Article X

In order to promote international co-operation in the exploration and use of outer space, including the moon and other celestial bodies, in conformity with the purposes of this Treaty, the States Parties to the Treaty shall consider on a basis of equality any requests by other States Parties to the Treaty to be afforded an opportunity to observe the flight of space objects launched by those States.

The nature of such an opportunity for observation and the conditions under which it could be afforded shall be determined by agreement between the States concerned.

Article XI

In order to promote international co-operation in the peaceful exploration and use of outer space, States Parties to the Treaty conducting activities in outer space, including the moon and other celestial bodies, agree to inform the Secretary-General of the United Nations as well as the public and the international scientific community, to the greatest extent feasible and practicable, of the nature, conduct, locations and results of such activities. On receiving the said information, the Secretary-General of the United Nations should be prepared to disseminate it immediately and effectively.

Article XII

All stations, installations, equipment and space vehicles on the moon and other celestial bodies shall be open to representatives of other States Parties to the Treaty on a basis of reciprocity. Such representatives shall give reasonable advance notice of a projected visit, in order that appropriate consultations may be held and that maximum precautions may be taken to assure safety and to avoid interference with normal operations in the facility to be visited.

Article XIII

The provisions of this Treaty shall apply to the activities of States Parties to the Treaty in the exploration and use of outer space, including the moon and other celestial bodies, whether such activities are carried on by a single State Party to the Treaty or jointly with other States, including cases where they are carried on within the framework of international inter-governmental organizations.

Any practical questions arising in connection with activities carried on by international inter-governmental organizations in the exploration and use of outer space, including the moon and other celestial bodies, shall be resolved by the States Parties to the Treaty either with the appropriate international organization or with one or more States members of that international organization, which are Parties to this Treaty.

Article XIV

1. This Treaty shall be open to all States for signature. Any State which does not sign this Treaty before its entry into force in accordance with paragraph 3 of this article may accede to it at any time.

2. This Treaty shall be subject to ratification by signatory States. Instruments of ratification and instruments of accession shall be deposited with the Governments of the United States of America, the United Kingdom of Great Britain and Northern Ireland and the Union of Soviet Socialist Republics, which are hereby designated the Depositary Governments.

3. This Treaty shall enter into force upon the deposit of instruments of ratification by five Governments including the Governments designated as Depositary Governments under this Treaty.

4. For States whose instruments of ratification or accession are deposited subsequent to the entry into force of this Treaty, it shall enter into force on the date of the deposit of their instruments of ratification or accession.

5. The Depositary Governments shall promptly inform all signatory and acceding States of the date of each signature, the date of deposit of each instrument of ratification of and accession to this Treaty, the date of its entry into force and other notices.

6. This Treaty shall be registered by the Depositary Governments pursuant to Article 102 of the Charter of the United Nations.

Article XV

Any State Party to the Treaty may propose amendments to this Treaty. Amendments shall enter into force for each State Party to the Treaty accepting the amendments upon their acceptance by a majority of the States Parties to the Treaty and thereafter for each remaining State Party to the Treaty on the date of acceptance by it.

Article XVI

Any State Party to the Treaty may give notice of its withdrawal from the Treaty one year after its entry into force by written notification to the Depositary Governments. Such withdrawal shall take effect one year from the date of receipt of this notification.

Article XVII

This Treaty, of which the English, Russian, French, Spanish and Chinese texts are equally authentic, shall be deposited in the archives of the Depositary Governments. Duly certified copies of this Treaty shall be transmitted by the Depositary Governments to the Governments of the signatory and acceding States.

Outer Space Treaty

Country	Date of[1] Signature	Date of Deposit[1] of Ratification	Date of Deposit[1] of Accession
Afghanistan	1/27/67		
Argentina	1/27/67	3/26/69	
Australia	1/27/67	10/10/67	
Austria	2/20/67	2/26/68	
Bahamas, The			8/11/76
Barbados			9/12/68
Belgium	1/27/67	3/30/73	
Bolivia	1/27/67		
Botswana	1/27/67		
Brazil	1/30/67	3/5/69	
Bulgaria	1/27/67	3/28/67	
Burma	5/22/67	3/18/70	
Burundi	1/27/67		
Byelorussian S.S.R.[2]	2/10/67	10/31/67	
Cameroon	1/27/67		
Canada	1/27/67	10/10/67	
Central African Republic	1/27/67		
Chile	1/27/67		
China (Taiwan)	1/27/67	7/24/70	
Colombia	1/27/67		
Cyprus	1/27/67	7/5/72	
Czechoslovakia	1/27/67	5/11/67	
Denmark	1/27/67	10/10/67	
Dominican Republic	1/27/67	11/21/68	
Ecuador	1/27/67	3/7/69	
Egypt	1/27/67	10/10/67	
El Salvador	1/27/67	1/15/69	
Ethiopia	1/27/67		
Fiji			7/14/72
Finland	1/27/67	7/12/67	
France	9/25/67	8/5/70	
Gambia, The	6/2/67		
German Democratic Republic	1/27/67	2/2/67	
Germany, Federal Republic of	1/27/67	2/10/71	
Ghana	1/27/67		
Greece	1/27/67	1/19/71	
Guyana	2/3/67		

See footnotes on page 239.

Country	Date of[1] Signature	Date of Deposit[1] of Ratification	Date of Deposit[1] of Accession
Haiti	1/27/67		
Holy See	4/5/67		
Honduras	1/27/67		
Hungary	1/27/67	6/26/67	
Iceland	1/27/67	2/5/68	
India	3/3/67		
Indonesia	1/27/67		
Iran	1/27/67		
Iraq	2/27/67	12/4/68	
Ireland	1/27/67	7/17/68	
Israel	1/27/67	2/18/77	
Italy	1/27/67	5/4/72	
Jamaica	6/29/67	8/6/70	
Japan	1/27/67	10/10/67	
Jordan	2/2/67		
Korea, Republic of	1/27/67	10/13/67	
Kuwait			6/7/72
Laos	1/27/67	11/27/72	
Lebanon	2/23/67	3/31/69	
Lesotho	1/27/67		
Libya			7/3/68
Luxembourg	1/27/67		
Madagascar			8/22/68
Malaysia	2/20/67		
Mali			6/11/68
Mauritius			4/7/69
Mexico	1/27/67	1/31/68	
Mongolia	1/27/67	10/10/67	
Morocco			12/21/67
Nepal	2/3/67	10/10/67	
Netherlands	2/10/67	10/10/69	
New Zealand	1/27/67	5/31/68	
Nicaragua	1/27/67		
Niger	2/1/67	4/17/67	
Nigeria			11/14/67
Norway	2/3/67	7/1/69	
Pakistan	9/12/67	4/8/68	
Panama	1/27/67		
Peru	6/30/67	2/28/79	

See footnotes on page 239.

Country	Date of[1] Signature	Date of Deposit[1] of Ratification	Date of Deposit[1] of Accession
Philippines	1/27/67		
Poland	1/27/67	1/30/68	
Romania	1/27/67	4/9/68	
Rwanda	1/27/67		
San Marino	4/21/67	10/29/68	
Saudi Arabia			12/17/76
Seychelles			1/5/78
Sierra Leone	1/27/67	7/13/67	
Singapore			9/10/76
Somalia	2/2/67		
South Africa	3/1/67	9/30/68	
Spain			11/27/68
Sri Lanka	3/10/69		
Sweden	1/27/67	10/11/67	
Switzerland	1/27/67	12/18/69	
Syrian Arab Republic			11/19/68
Thailand	1/27/67	9/5/68	
Togo	1/27/67		
Tonga			6/22/71
Trinidad & Tobago	7/24/67		
Tunisia	1/27/67	3/28/68	
Turkey	1/27/67	3/27/68	
Uganda			4/24/68
Ukrainian S.S.R.[2]	2/10/67	10/31/67	
Union of Soviet Socialist Republics	1/27/67	10/10/67	
United Kingdom	1/27/67	10/10/67	
United States	1/27/67	10/10/67	
Upper Volta	3/3/67	6/18/68	
Uruguay	1/27/67	8/31/70	
Venezuela	1/27/67	3/3/70	
Yemen, People's Democratic Republic of (Aden)			6/1/79
Yugoslavia	1/27/67		
Zaire	1/27/67		
Zambia			8/20/73
Total[3]	89	57	19

See footnotes on page 239.

Treaty for the Prohibition of Nuclear Weapons in Latin America

The Treaty for the Prohibition of Nuclear Weapons in Latin America, like the Antarctic Treaty and the Outer Space Treaty, seeks to limit the spread of nuclear weapons by preventing their introduction into areas hitherto free of them. Unlike the other treaties, the Latin American Treaty concerns itself with a populated area— over 7½ million square miles, inhabited by nearly 200 million people. Besides the agreement among the Latin American countries themselves, there are two Additional Protocols dealing with matters that concern non-Latin American countries. Protocol I involves an undertaking by non-Latin American countries that have possessions in the nuclear-free zone. Protocol II involves an undertaking by those powers which possess nuclear weapons. The United States is a party to Protocol II. President Carter signed Protocol I on May 26, 1977, and submitted it to the Senate on May 24, 1978.

The United States has favored the establishment of nuclear-free zones where they would not disturb existing security arrangements and where provisions for investigating alleged violations would give reasonable assurance of compliance. It has also considered it important that the initiative for such zones originate in the geographical area concerned and that all states important to the denuclearization of the area participate. Considering that Soviet proposals for the denuclearization of Central Europe and other areas did not meet these criteria, the United States opposed them. From the start, however, the United States gave support and encouragement to Latin American countries in this undertaking.

Even before the Cuban missile crisis, the Brazilian representative to the U.N. General Assembly had suggested making Latin America a nuclear-weapon-free zone. During the crisis, he submitted a draft resolution calling for such a zone. While asserting support for the principle, Cuba stipulated certain conditions, including the requirement that Puerto Rico and the Panama Canal Zone be included in the zone, and that foreign military bases, especially Guantanamo Naval Base, be eliminated. The draft resolution was not put to a vote at the General Assembly that year.

The Cuban missile crisis of October 1962 brought home to Latin American countries the dangers of nuclear war, and in April 1963 the Presidents of five Latin American countries—Bolivia, Brazil, Chile, Ecuador, and Mexico—announced that they were prepared to sign a multilateral agreement that would make Latin America a nuclear-weapon-free zone. On November 27, 1963, this declaration received the support of the U.N. General Assembly, with the United States voting in the affirmative.

The Latin American nations followed this initiative by extensive and detailed negotiations among themselves. At the Mexico City Conference (November 23–27, 1965) a Preparatory Commission for the Denuclearization of Latin America was created, with instructions to prepare a draft treaty. Important differences among the Latin American countries emerged over questions of defining the boundaries of the nuclear-weapon-free zone, transit, guarantees, and safeguards on peaceful nuclear activities. Most of these differences were eventually resolved.

On February 14, 1967, the treaty was signed at the regional meeting of Latin American countries at Tlatelolco, a section of Mexico City. On December 5, 1967, the U.N. General Assembly endorsed the Treaty of Tlatelolco by a vote of 82–0 with 28 abstentions, the United States voting in support of the treaty. Thus far Cuba has refused to sign. (A question has been raised as to whether Guyana is eligible to sign.) Argentina has signed the treaty and publicly announced its intention to ratify. Although Brazil and Chile have ratified, the treaty is not yet in force for them because they did not waive the entry-into-force provision which, *inter alia*, requires ratification by all eligible countries.

The basic obligations of the treaty are contained in Article I:

1. The Contracting Parties hereby undertake to use exclusively for peaceful purposes the nuclear material and facilities which are under their jurisdiction, and to prohibit and prevent in their respective territories:

   (a) The testing, use, manufacture, production or acquisition by any means whatsoever of any nuclear weapons, by the Parties themselves, directly or indirectly, on behalf of anyone else or in any other way, and

   (b) The receipt, storage, installation, deployment and any form of possession of any nuclear weapons, directly or indirectly, by the Parties themselves, by anyone on their behalf or in any other way.

2. The Contracting Parties also undertake to refrain from engaging in, encouraging or authorizing directly or indirectly, or in any way participating in the testing, use, manufacture, production, possession or control of any nuclear weapon.

Important provisions of the treaty deal with verification. Treaty parties undertake to negotiate agreements with the International

Atomic Energy Agency for application of its safeguards to their peaceful nuclear activities. In addition, the treaty establishes an organization to ensure compliance with treaty provisions—the Agency for the Prohibition of Nuclear Weapons in Latin America. The Council, one of the principal organs of the Agency, is empowered to perform "special inspections."

Of the accompanying protocols, Protocol I calls on nations outside the treaty zone to apply the denuclearization provisions of the treaty to their territories in the zone. All four powers having such territories have signed—the United Kingdom, the Netherlands, France, and the United States. The United Kingdom and the Netherlands have ratified.

Within the Latin American nuclear-weapon-free zone lie the Canal Zone, the Guantanamo Naval Base in Cuba, the Virgin Islands, and Puerto Rico—four areas with differing relationships to the United States. Previous administrations have indicated that they would be prepared to have the Canal Zone included in the treaty, subject to a clear understanding that the well-established rights of transit through the zone would not be affected, and to have Guantanamo included if Cuba joined the treaty. They were not prepared to include Puerto Rico and the Virgin Islands. The Carter Administration assessed the entire question and concluded that it was in the net interest of the United States to sign Protocol I. It is supportive both to U.S.-Latin American relations and to our non-proliferation objective.

In Protocol II, nuclear-weapons states undertake (1) to respect the denuclearized status of the zone, (2) not to contribute to acts involving violation of obligations of the parties, and (3) not to use or threaten to use nuclear weapons against the contracting parties. France, the United Kingdom, the United States, the People's Republic of China, and the Soviet Union have adhered to Protocol II.

In transmitting Protocol II, the President recommended that the Senate give its advice and consent to ratification subject to a statement containing the following understandings and declarations:

— The Treaty and its Protocols have no effect upon the international status of territorial claims.
— The Treaty does not affect the rights of the Contracting Parties to grant or deny transport and transit privileges to non-Contracting Parties.
— With respect to the undertaking in Article 3 of Protocol II not to use or threaten to use nuclear weapons against the Treaty parties, the United States would "have to consider that an armed attack by a Contracting Party, in which it was assisted by a nuclear-weapon state, would be incompatible with the

Contracting Party's corresponding obligations under Article I of the Treaty."

— Considering the technology for producing explosive devices for peaceful purposes to be indistinguishable from that for making nuclear weapons, the United States regards the Treaty's prohibitions as applying to all nuclear explosive devices. However, the Treaty would not prevent the United States, as a nuclear-weapon state, from making nuclear explosion services for peaceful purposes available "in a manner consistent with our policy of not contributing to the proliferation of nuclear weapons capabilities."

— Although not required to do so, the United States will act, with respect to the territories of Protocol I adherents that are within the treaty zone, in the same way as Protocol II requires it to act toward the territories of the Latin American treaty parties.

The Senate Foreign Relations Committee endorsed the Protocol and the statement, which was slightly revised during the course of the hearings. On April 19, 1971, the Senate gave its advice and consent to ratification subject to the statement which was included in the U.S. instrument of ratification. The President ratified the Protocol on May 8, and it entered into force on May 12, 1971, when the U.S. instrument of ratification was deposited in Mexico City.

This was the first time the United States had ever entered into an obligation that restricted the use of nuclear weapons. The Treaty, however, significantly enhances U.S. national security. It includes an undertaking by the Latin American countries party to the treaty to prevent the type of deployment of nuclear weapons in their territory that occurred in the Cuban missile crisis. It provides for verification of compliance with this undertaking not only by the parties themselves, but by the regional organization they have established and given the right to make special inspections. It requires IAEA safeguards on all nuclear materials and facilities under the jurisdiction of the parties. And this regional initiative to curb the spread of nuclear weapons gave important support to efforts to obtain a universal non-proliferation treaty.

Treaty for the Prohibition of Nuclear Weapons in Latin America

Signed at Mexico City February 14, 1967
Entered into force April 22, 1968

Preamble

In the name of their peoples and faithfully interpreting their desires and aspirations, the Governments of the States which sign the Treaty for the Prohibition of Nuclear Weapons in Latin America,

Desiring to contribute, so far as lies in their power, towards ending the armaments race, especially in the field of nuclear weapons, and towards strengthening a world at peace, based on the sovereign equality of States, mutual respect and good neighbourliness,

Recalling that the United Nations General Assembly, in its Resolution 808 (IX), adopted unanimously as one of the three points of a coordinated programme of disarmament "the total prohibition of the use and manufacture of nuclear weapons and weapons of mass destruction of every type,"

Recalling that militarily denuclearized zones are not an end in themselves but rather a means for achieving general and complete disarmament at a later stage,

Recalling United Nations General Assembly Resolution 1911 (XVIII), which established that the measures that should be agreed upon for the denuclearization of Latin America should be taken "in the light of the principles of the Charter of the United Nations and of regional agreements,"

Recalling United Nations General Assembly Resolution 2028 (XX), which established the principle of an acceptable balance of mutual responsibilities and duties for the nuclear and non-nuclear powers, and

Recalling that the Charter of the Organization of American States proclaims that it is an essential purpose of the Organization to strengthen the peace and security of the hemisphere,

Convinced:

That the incalculable destructive power of nuclear weapons has made it imperative that the legal prohibition of war should be strictly observed in practice if the survival of civilization and of mankind itself is to be assured,

That nuclear weapons, whose terrible effects are suffered, indiscriminately and inexorably, by military forces and civilian population alike, constitute, through the persistence of the radioactivity they release, an attack on the integrity of the human species and ultimately may even render the whole earth uninhabitable,

That general and complete disarmament under effective international control is a vital matter which all the peoples of the world equally demand,

That the proliferation of nuclear weapons, which seems inevitable unless States, in the exercise of their sovereign rights, impose restrictions on themselves in order to prevent it, would make any agreement on disarmament enormously difficult and would increase the danger of the outbreak of a nuclear conflagration,

That the establishment of militarily denuclearized zones is closely linked with the maintenance of peace and security in the respective regions,

That the military denuclearization of vast geographical zones, adopted by the sovereign decision of the States comprised therein, will exercise a beneficial influence on other regions where similar conditions exist.

That the privileged situation of the signatory States, whose territories are wholly free from nuclear weapons, imposes upon them the inescapable duty of preserving that situation both in their own interests and for the good of mankind,

That the existence of nuclear weapons in any country of Latin America would make it a target for possible nuclear attacks and would inevitably set off, throughout the region, a ruinous race in nuclear weapons which would involve the unjustifiable diversion, for warlike purposes, of the limited resources required for economic and social development,

That the foregoing reasons, together with the traditional peace-loving outlook of Latin America, give rise to an inescapable necessity that nuclear energy should be used in that region exclusively for peaceful purposes, and that the Latin American countries should use their right to the greatest and most equitable possible access to this new source of energy in order to expedite the economic and social development of their peoples,

Convinced finally:

That the military denuclearization of Latin America—being understood to mean the undertaking entered into internationally in this Treaty to keep their territories forever free from nuclear weapons—will constitute a measure which will spare their peoples from the squandering of their limited resources on nuclear armaments and will protect them against possible nuclear attacks on their territories, and will also constitute a significant contribution towards preventing the proliferation of nuclear weapons and a powerful factor for general and complete disarmament, and

That Latin America, faithful to its tradition of universality, must not only endeavour to banish from its homelands the scourge of a nuclear war, but must also strive to promote the well-being and advancement of its peoples, at the same time co-operating in the fulfilment of the ideals of mankind, that is to say, in the consolidation of a permanent peace based on equal rights, economic fairness and social justice for all, in accordance with the principles and purposes set forth in the Charter of the United Nations and in the Charter of the Organization of American States,

Have agreed as follows:

Obligations

Article I

1. The Contracting Parties hereby undertake to use exclusively for peaceful purposes the nuclear material and facilities which are under their jurisdiction, and to prohibit and prevent in their respective territories:

(a) The testing, use, manufacture, production or acquisition by any means whatsoever of any nuclear weapons, by the Parties themselves, directly or indirectly, on behalf of anyone else or in any other way, and

(b) The receipt, storage, installation, deployment and any form of possession of any nuclear weapons, directly or indirectly, by the Parties themselves, by anyone on their behalf or in any other way.

2. The Contracting Parties also undertake to refrain from engaging in, encouraging or authorizing, directly or indirectly, or in any way participating in the testing, use, manufacture, production, possession or control of any nuclear weapon.

Definition of the Contracting Parties

Article 2

For the purposes of this Treaty, the Contracting Parties are those for whom the Treaty is in force.

Definition of territory

Article 3

For the purposes of this Treaty, the term "territory" shall include the territorial sea, air space and any other space over which the State exercises sovereignty in accordance with its own legislation.

Zone of application

Article 4

1. The zone of application of this Treaty is the whole of the territories for which the Treaty is in force.
2. Upon fulfilment of the requirements of article 28, paragraph 1, the zone of application of this Treaty shall also be that which is situated in the western hemisphere within the following limits (except the continental part of the territory of the United States of America and its territorial waters): starting at a point located at 35° north latitude, 75° west longitude; from this point directly southward to a point at 30° north latitude, 75° west longitude; from there, directly eastward to a point at 30° north latitude, 50° west longitude; from there, along a loxodromic line to a point at 5° north latitude, 20° west longitude; from there, directly southward to a point at 60° south latitude, 20° west longitude; from there, directly westward to a point at 60° south latitude, 115° west longitude; from there, directly northward to a point at 0 latitude, 115° west longitude; from there, along a loxodromic line to a point at 35° north latitude, 150° west longitude; from there, directly eastward to a point at 35° north latitude, 75° west longitude.

Definition of nuclear weapons

Article 5

For the purposes of this Treaty, a nuclear weapon is any device which is capable of releasing nuclear energy in an uncontrolled manner and which has a group of characteristics that are appropriate for use for warlike purposes. An instrument that may be used for the transport or propulsion of the device is not included in this definition if it is separable from the device and not an indivisible part thereof.

Meeting of signatories

Article 6

At the request of any of the signatory States or if the Agency established by article 7 should so decide, a meeting of all the signatories may be convoked to consider in common questions which may affect the very essence of this instrument, including possible amendments to it. In either case, the meeting will be convoked by the General Secretary.

Organization

Article 7

1. In order to ensure compliance with the obligations of this Treaty, the Contracting Parties hereby establish an international organization to be known as the "Agency for the Prohibition of Nuclear Weapons in Latin America," hereinafter referred to as "the Agency." Only the Contracting Parties shall be affected by its decisions.

2. The Agency shall be responsible for the holding of periodic or extraordinary consultations among Member States on matters relating to the purposes, measures and procedures set forth in this Treaty and to the supervision of compliance with the obligations arising therefrom.

3. The Contracting Parties agree to extend to the Agency full and prompt co-operation in accordance with the provisions of this Treaty, of any agreements they may conclude with the Agency and of any agreements the Agency may conclude with any other international organization or body.

4. The headquarters of the Agency shall be in Mexico City.

Organs

Article 8

1. There are hereby established as principal organs of the Agency a General Conference, a Council and a Secretariat.

2. Such subsidiary organs as are considered necessary by the General Conference may be established within the purview of this Treaty.

The General Conference

Article 9

1. The General Conference,the supreme organ of the Agency, shall be composed of all the Contracting Parties; it shall hold regular sessions every two years, and may also hold special sessions whenever this Treaty so provides or, in the opinion of the Council, the circumstances so require.

2. The General Conference:

    (a) May consider and decide on any matters or questions covered by this Treaty, within the limits thereof, including those referring to powers and functions of any organ provided for in this Treaty.

    (b) Shall establish procedures for the control system to ensure observance of this Treaty in accordance with its provisions.

    (c) Shall elect the Members of the Council and the General Secretary.

    (d) May remove the General Secretary from office if the proper functioning of the Agency so requires.

    (e) Shall receive and consider the biennial and special reports submitted by the Council and the General Secretary.

    (f) Shall initiate and consider studies designed to facilitate the optimum fulfilment of the aims of this Treaty, without prejudice to the power of the General Secretary independently to carry out similar studies for submission to and consideration by the Conference.

    (g) Shall be the organ competent to authorize the conclusion of agreements with Governments and other international organizations and bodies.

3. The General Conference shall adopt the Agency's budget and fix the scale of financial contributions to be paid by Member States, taking into account the systems and criteria used for the same purpose by the United Nations.

4. The General Conference shall elect its officers for each session and may establish such subsidiary organs as it deems necessary for the performance of its functions.

5. Each Member of the Agency shall have one vote. The decisions of the General Conference shall be taken by a two-thirds majority of the Members present and voting in the case of matters relating to the control system and measures referred to in article 20, the admission of new Members, the election or removal of the General Secretary, adoption of the budget and matters related thereto. Decisions on other matters, as well as procedural questions and also determination of which questions must be decided by a two-thirds majority, shall be taken by a simple majority of the Members present and voting.

6. The General Conference shall adopt its own rules of procedure.

The Council

Article 10

1. The Council shall be composed of five Members of the Agency elected by the General Conference from among the Contracting Parties, due account being taken of equitable geographic distribution.

2. The Members of the Council shall be elected for a term of four years. However, in the first election three will be elected for two years. Outgoing Members may not be re elected for the following period unless the limited number of States for which the Treaty is in force so requires.

3. Each Member of the Council shall have one representative.

4. The Council shall be so organized as to be able to function continuously.

5. In addition to the functions conferred upon it by this Treaty and to those which may be assigned to it by the General Conference, the Council shall, through the General Secretary, ensure the proper operation of the control system in accordance with the provisions of this Treaty and with the decisions adopted by the General Conference.

6. The Council shall submit an annual report on its work to the General Conference as well as such special reports as it deems necessary or which the General Conference requests of it.

7. The Council shall elect its officers for each session.

8. The decisions of the Council shall be taken by a simple majority of its Members present and voting.

9. The Council shall adopt its own rules of procedure.

The Secretariat

Article 11

1. The Secretariat shall consist of a General Secretary, who shall be the chief administrative officer of the Agency, and of such staff as the Agency may require. The term of office of the General Secretary shall be four years and he may be re-elected for a single additional term. The General Secretary may not be a national of the country in which the Agency has its headquarters. In case the office of General Secretary becomes vacant, a new election shall be held to fill the office for the remainder of the term.

2. The staff of the Secretariat shall be appointed by the General Secretary, in accordance with rules laid down by the General Conference.

3. In addition to the functions conferred upon him by this Treaty and to those which may be assigned to him by the General Conference, the General Secretary shall ensure, as provided by article 10, paragraph 5, the proper operation of the control system established by this Treaty, in accordance with the provisions of the Treaty and the decisions taken by the General Conference.

4. The General Secretary shall act in that capacity in all meetings of the General Conference and of the Council and shall make an annual report to both bodies on the work of the Agency and any special reports requested by the General Conference or the Council or which the General Secretary may deem desirable.

5. The General Secretary shall establish the procedures for distributing to all Contracting Parties information received by the Agency from governmental sources and such information from non-governmental sources as may be of interest to the Agency.

6. In the performance of their duties the General Secretary and the staff shall not seek or receive instructions from any Government or from any other authority external to the Agency and shall refrain from any action which might reflect on their position as international officials responsible only to the Agency; subject to their responsibility to the Agency, they shall not disclose any industrial secrets or other confidential information coming to their knowledge by reason of their official duties in the Agency.

7. Each of the Contracting Parties undertakes to respect the exclusively international character of the responsibilities of the General Secretary and the staff and not to seek to influence them in the discharge of their responsibilities.

Control system

Article 12

1. For the purpose of verifying compliance with the obligations entered into by the Contracting Parties in accordance with article 1, a control system shall be established which shall be put into effect in accordance with the provisions of articles 13–18 of this Treaty.

2. The control system shall be used in particular for the purpose of verifying:

(a) That devices, services and facilities intended for peaceful uses of nuclear energy are not used in the testing or manufacture of nuclear weapons,

(b) That none of the activities prohibited in article 1 of this Treaty are carried out in the territory of the Contracting Parties with nuclear materials or weapons introduced from abroad, and

(c) That explosions for peaceful purposes are compatible with article 18 of this Treaty.

IAEA safeguards

Article 13

Each Contracting Party shall negotiate multilateral or bilateral agreements with the International Atomic Energy Agency for the application of its safeguards to its nuclear activities. Each Contracting Party shall initiate negotiations within a period of 180 days after the date of the deposit of its instrument of ratification of this Treaty. These agreements shall enter into force, for each Party, not later than eighteen months after the date of the initiation of such negotiations except in case of unforeseen circumstances or *force majeure*.

Reports of the Parties

Article 14

1. The Contracting Parties shall submit to the Agency and to the International Atomic Energy Agency, for their information, semi-annual reports stating that no activity prohibited under this Treaty has occurred in their respective territories.

2. The Contracting Parties shall simultaneously transmit to the Agency a copy of any report they may submit to the International Atomic Energy Agency which relates to matters that are the subject of this Treaty and to the application of safeguards.

3. The Contracting Parties shall also transmit to the Organization of American States, for its information, any reports that may be of interest to it, in accordance with the obligations established by the Inter-American System.

Special reports requested by the General Secretary

Article 15

1. With the authorization of the Council, the General Secretary may request any of the Contracting Parties to provide the Agency with complementary or supplementary information regarding any event or circumstance connected with compliance with this Treaty, explaining his reasons. The Contracting Parties undertake to co-operate promptly and fully with the General Secretary.

2. The General Secretary shall inform the Council and the Contracting Parties forthwith of such requests and of the respective replies.

Special inspections

Article 16

1. The International Atomic Energy Agency and the Council established by this Treaty have the power of carrying out special inspections in the following cases:

(a) In the case of the International Atomic Energy Agency, in accordance with the agreements referred to in article 13 of this Treaty;

(b) In the case of the Council:

(i) When so requested, the reasons for the request being stated, by any Party which suspects that some activity prohibited by this Treaty has been carried out or is about to be carried out, either in the territory of any other Party or in any other place on such latter Party's behalf, the Council shall immediately arrange for such an inspection in accordance with article 10, paragraph 5.

(ii) When requested by any Party which has been suspected of or charged with having violated this Treaty, the Council shall immediately arrange for the special inspection requested in accordance with article 10, paragraph 5.

The above requests will be made to the Council through the General Secretary.

2. The costs and expenses of any special inspection carried out under paragraph 1, sub-paragraph (b), sections (i) and (ii) of this article shall be borne by the requesting Party or Parties, except where the Council concludes on the basis of the report on the special inspection that, in view of the circumstances existing in the case, such costs and expenses should be borne by the agency.

3. The General Conference shall formulate the procedures for the organization and execution of the special inspections carried out in accordance with paragraph 1, sub-paragraph (b), sections (i) and (ii) of this article.

4. The Contracting Parties undertake to grant the inspectors carrying out such special inspections full and free access to all places and all information which may be necessary for the performance of their duties and which are directly and intimately connected with the suspicion of violation of this Treaty. If so requested by the authorities of the Contracting Party in whose territory the inspection is carried out, the inspectors designated by the General Conference shall be accompanied by representatives of said authorities, provided that this does not in any way delay or hinder the work of the inspectors.

5. The Council shall immediately transmit to all the Parties, through the General Secretary, a copy of any report resulting from special inspections.

6. Similarly, the Council shall send through the General Secretary to the Secretary-General of the United Nations, for transmission to the United Nations Security Council and General Assembly, and to the Council of the Organization of American States, for its information, a copy of any report resulting from any special inspection carried out in accordance with paragraph 1, sub-paragraph (b), sections (i) and (ii) of this article.

7. The Council may decide, or any Contracting Party may request, the convening of a special session of the General Conference for the purpose of considering the reports resulting from any special inspection. In such a case, the General Secretary shall take immediate steps to convene the special session requested.

8. The General Conference, convened in special session under this article, may make recommendations to the Contracting Parties and submit reports to the Secretary-General of the United Nations to be transmitted to the United Nations Security Council and the General Assembly.

Use of nuclear energy for peaceful purposes

Article 17

Nothing in the provisions of this Treaty shall prejudice the rights of the Contracting Parties, in conformity with this Treaty, to use nuclear energy for peaceful purposes, in particular for their economic development and social progress.

Explosions for peaceful purposes

Article 18

1. The Contracting Parties may carry out explosions of nuclear devices for peaceful purposes—including explosions which involve devices similar to those used in nuclear weapons—or collaborate with third parties for the same purpose, provided that they do so in accordance with the provisions of this article and the other articles of the Treaty, particularly articles 1 and 5.

2. Contracting Parties intending to carry out, or to cooperate in carrying out, such an explosion shall notify the Agency and the International Atomic Energy Agency, as far in advance as the circumstances require, of the date of the explosion and shall at the same time provide the following information:

(a) The nature of the nuclear device and the source from which it was obtained,

(b) The place and purpose of the planned explosion,

(c) The procedures which will be followed in order to comply with paragraph 3 of this article.

(d) The expected force of the device, and

(e) The fullest possible information on any possible radioactive fall-out that may result from the explosion or explosions, and measures which will be taken to avoid danger to the population, flora, fauna and territories of any other Party or Parties.

3. The General Secretary and the technical personnel designated by the Council and the International Atomic Energy Agency may observe all the preparations, including the explosion of the device, and shall have unrestricted access to any area in the vicinity of the site of the explosion in order to ascertain whether the device and the procedures followed during the explosion are in conformity with the information supplied under paragraph 2 of this article and the other provisions of this Treaty.

4. The Contracting Parties may accept the collaboration of third parties for the purpose set forth in paragraph 1 of the present article, in accordance with paragraphs 2 and 3 thereof.

Relations with other international organizations

Article 19

1. The Agency may conclude such agreements with the International Atomic Energy Agency as are authorized by the General Conference and as it considers likely to facilitate the efficient operation of the control system established by this Treaty.

2. The Agency may also enter into relations with any international organization or body, especially any which may be established in the future to supervise disarmament or measures for the control of armaments in any part of the world.

3. The Contracting Parties may, if they see fit, request the advice of the Inter-American Nuclear Energy Commission on all technical matters connected with the application of this Treaty with which the Commission is competent to deal under its Statute.

Measures in the event of violation of the Treaty

Article 20

1. The General Conference shall take note of all cases in which, in its opinion, any Contracting Party is not complying fully with its obligations under this Treaty and shall draw the matter to the attention of the Party concerned, making such recommendations as it deems appropriate.

2. If, in its opinion, such non-compliance constitutes a violation of this Treaty which might endanger peace and security, the General Conference shall report thereon simultaneously to the United Nations Security Council and the General Assembly through the Secretary-General of the United Nations, and to the Council of the Organization of American States. The General Conference shall likewise report to the International Atomic Energy Agency for such purposes as are relevant in accordance with its Statute.

United Nations and Organization of American States

Article 21

None of the provisions of this Treaty shall be construed as impairing the rights and obligations of the Parties under the Charter of the United Nations or, in the case of States Members of the Organization of American States, under existing regional treaties.

Privileges and immunities

Article 22

1. The Agency shall enjoy in the territory of each of the Contracting Parties such

legal capacity and such privileges and immunities as may be necessary for the exercise of its functions and the fulfilment of its purposes.

2. Representatives of the Contracting Parties accredited to the Agency and officials of the Agency shall similarly enjoy such privileges and immunities as are necessary for the performance of their functions.

3. The Agency may conclude agreements with the Contracting Parties with a view to determining the details of the application of paragraphs 1 and 2 of this article.

Notification of other agreements

Article 23

Once this Treaty has entered into force, the Secretariat shall be notified immediately of any international agreement concluded by any of the Contracting Parties on matters with which this Treaty is concerned; the Secretariat shall register it and notify the other Contracting Parties.

Settlement of disputes

Article 24

Unless the Parties concerned agree on another mode of peaceful settlement, any question or dispute concerning the interpretation or application of this Treaty which is not settled shall be referred to the International Court of Justice with the prior consent of the Parties to the controversy.

Signature

Article 25

1. This Treaty shall be open indefinitely for signature by:

(a) All the Latin American Republics, and

(b) All other sovereign States situated in their entirety south of latitude 35° north in the western hemisphere; and, except as provided in paragraph 2 of this article, all such States which become sovereign, when they have been admitted by the General Conference.

2. The General Conference shall not take any decision regarding the admission of a political entity part or all of whose territory is the subject, prior to the date when this Treaty is opened for signature, of a dispute or claim between an extra-continental country and one or more Latin American States, so long as the dispute has not been settled by peaceful means.

Ratification and deposit

Article 26

1. This Treaty shall be subject to ratification by signatory States in accordance with their respective constitutional procedures.

2. This Treaty and the instruments of ratification shall be deposited with the Government of the Mexican United States, which is hereby designated the Depositary Government.

3. The Depositary Government shall send certified copies of this Treaty to the Governments of signatory States and shall notify them of the deposit of each instrument of ratification.

Reservations

Article 27

This Treaty shall not be subject to reservations.

Entry into force

Article 28

1. Subject to the provisions of paragraph 2 of this article, this Treaty shall enter into force among the States that have ratified it as soon as the following requirements have been met:

(a) Deposit of the instruments of ratification of this Treaty with the Depositary Government by the Governments of the States mentioned in article 25 which are in existence on the date when this Treaty is opened for signature and which are not affected by the provisions of article 25, paragraph 2;

(b) Signature and ratification of Additional Protocol I annexed to this Treaty by all extra-continental or continental States having *de jure* or *de facto* international responsibility for territories situated in the zone of application of the Treaty;

(c) Signature and ratification of the Additional Protocol II annexed to this Treaty by all powers possessing nuclear weapons;

(d) Conclusion of bilateral or multilateral agreements on the application of the Safeguards System of the International Atomic Energy Agency in accordance with article 13 of this Treaty.

2. All signatory States shall have the imprescriptible right to waive, wholly or in part, the requirements laid down in the preceding paragraph. They may do so by means of a declaration which shall be annexed to their respective instrument of ratification and which may be formulated at the time of deposit of the instrument or subsequently. For those States which exercise this right, this Treaty shall enter into force upon deposit of the declaration, or as soon as those requirements have been met which have not been expressly waived.

3. As soon as this Treaty has entered into force in accordance with the provisions of paragraph 2 for eleven States, the Depositary Government shall convene a preliminary meeting of those States in order that the Agency may be set up and commence its work.

4. After the entry into force of this Treaty for all the countries of the zone, the rise of a new power possessing nuclear weapons shall have the effect of suspending the execution of this Treaty for those countries which have ratified it without waiving requirements of paragraph 1, sub-paragraph (c) of this article, and which request such suspension; the Treaty shall remain suspended until the new power, on its own initiative or upon request by the General Conference, ratifies the annexed Additional Protocol II.

Amendments

Article 29

1. Any Contracting Party may propose amendments to this Treaty and shall submit its proposals to the Council through the General Secretary, who shall transmit them to

all the other Contracting Parties and, in addition, to all other signatories in accordance with article 6. The Council, through the General Secretary, shall immediately following the meeting of signatories convene a special session of the General Conference to examine the proposals made, for the adoption of which a two-thirds majority of the Contracting Parties present and voting shall be required.

2. Amendments adopted shall enter into force as soon as the requirements set forth in article 28 of this Treaty have been complied with.

Duration and denunciation

Article 30

1. This Treaty shall be of a permanent nature and shall remain in force indefinitely, but any Party may denounce it by notifying the General Secretary of the Agency if, in the opinion of the denouncing State, there have arisen or may arise circumstances connected with the content of this Treaty or of the annexed Additional Protocols I and II which affect its supreme interests or the peace and security of one or more Contracting Parties.

2. The denunciation shall take effect three months after the delivery to the General Secretary of the Agency of the notification by the Government of the signatory State concerned. The General Secretary shall immediately communicate such notification to the other Contracting Parties and to the Secretary-General of the United Nations for the information of the United Nations Security Council and the General Assembly. He shall also communicate it to the Secretary-General of the Organization of American States.

Authentic texts and registration

Article 31

This Treaty, of which the Spanish, Chinese, English, French, Portuguese and Russian texts are equally authentic, shall be registered by the Depositary Government in accordance with article 102 of the United Nations Charter. The Depositary Government shall notify the Secretary-General of the United Nations of the signatures, ratifications and amendments relating to this Treaty and shall communicate them to the Secretary-General of the Organization of American States for its information.

Transitional Article

Denunciation of the declaration referred to in article 28, paragraph 2, shall be subject to the same procedures as the denunciation of this Treaty, except that it will take effect on the date of delivery of the respective notification.

IN WITNESS WHEREOF the undersigned Plenipotentiaries, having deposited their full powers, found in good and due form, sign this Treaty on behalf of their respective Governments.

DONE at Mexico, Distrito Federal, on the Fourteenth day of February, one thousand nine hundred and sixty-seven.

Additional Protocol I to the Treaty for the Prohibition of Nuclear Weapons in Latin America

Signed by the United States at Mexico City May 26, 1977

The undersigned Plenipotentiaries, furnished with full powers by their respective Governments,

Convinced that the Treaty for the Prohibition of Nuclear Weapons in Latin America, negotiated and signed in accordance with the recommendations of the General Assembly of the United Nations in Resolution 1911 (XVIII) of 27 November 1963, represents an important step towards ensuring the non-proliferation of nuclear weapons,

Aware that the non-proliferation of nuclear weapons is not an end in itself but, rather, a means of achieving general and complete disarmament at a later stage, and

Desiring to contribute, so far as lies in their power, towards ending the armaments race, especially in the field of nuclear weapons, and towards strengthening a world at peace, based on mutual respect and sovereign equality of States,

Have agreed as follows:

Article 1. To undertake to apply the statute of denuclearization in respect of warlike purposes as defined in articles 1, 3, 5 and 13 of the Treaty for the Prohibition of Nuclear Weapons in Latin America in territories for which, *de jure* or *de facto,* they are internationally responsible and which lie within the limits of the geographical zone established in that Treaty.

Article 2. The duration of this Protocol shall be the same as that of the Treaty for the Prohibition of Nuclear Weapons in Latin America of which this Protocol is an annex, and the provisions regarding ratification and denunciation contained in the Treaty shall be applicable to it.

Article 3. This Protocol shall enter into force, for the States which have ratified it, on the date of the deposit of their respective instruments of ratification.

IN WITNESS WHEREOF the undersigned Plenipotentiaries, having deposited their full powers, found in good and due form, sign this Protocol on behalf of their respective Governments.

Additional Protocol II to the Treaty for the Prohibition of Nuclear Weapons in Latin America

Signed by the United States at Mexico City April 1, 1968
Ratification advised by U.S. Senate April 19, 1971
Ratified by U.S. President May 8, 1971
U.S. ratification deposited at Mexico City May 12, 1971
Proclaimed by U.S. President June 11, 1971

The Undersigned Plenipotentiaries, furnished with full powers by their respective Governments,

Convinced that the Treaty for the Prohibition of Nuclear Weapons in Latin America, negotiated and signed in accordance with the recommendations of the General Assembly of the United Nations in Resolution 1911 (XVIII) of 27 November 1963, represents an important step towards ensuring the non-proliferation of nuclear weapons,

Aware that the non-proliferation of nuclear weapons is not an end in itself but, rather, a means of achieving general and complete disarmament at a later stage, and

Desiring to contribute, so far as lies in their power, towards ending the armaments race, especially in the field of nuclear weapons, and towards promoting and strengthening a world at peace, based on mutual respect and sovereign equality of States,

Have agreed as follows:

Article 1. The statute of denuclearization of Latin America in respect of warlike purposes, as defined, delimited and set forth in the Treaty for the Prohibition of Nuclear Weapons in Latin America of which this instrument is an annex, shall be fully respected by the Parties to this Protocol in all its express aims and provisions.

Article 2. The Governments represented by the undersigned Plenipotentiaries undertake, therefore, not to contribute in any way to the performance of acts involving a violation of the obligations of article 1 of the Treaty in the territories to which the Treaty applies in accordance with article 4 thereof.

Article 3. The Governments represented by the undersigned Plenipotentiaries also undertake not to use or threaten to use nuclear weapons against the Contracting Parties of the Treaty for the Prohibition of Nuclear Weapons in Latin America.

Article 4. The duration of this Protocol shall be the same as that of the Treaty for the Prohibition of Nuclear Weapons in Latin America of which this Protocol is an annex, and the definitions of territory and nuclear weapons set forth in articles 3 and 5 of the Treaty shall be applicable to this Protocol, as well as the provisions regarding ratification, reservations, denunciation, authentic texts and registration contained in articles 26, 27, 30 and 31 of the Treaty.

Article 5. This Protocol shall enter into force, for the States which have ratified it, on the date of the deposit of their respective instruments of ratification.

IN WITNESS WHEREOF the undersigned Plenipotentiaries, having deposited their full powers, found in good and due form, sign this Additional Protocol on behalf of their respective Governments.

Proclamation by President Nixon on Ratification of Additional Protocol II to the Treaty for the Prohibition of Nuclear Weapons in Latin America

BY THE PRESIDENT OF THE UNITED STATES OF AMERICA

A PROCLAMATION

Considering that:

Additional Protocol II to the Treaty for the Prohibition of Nuclear Weapons in Latin America, done at the City of Mexico on February 14, 1967, was signed on behalf of the United States of America on April 1, 1968, the text of which Protocol is word for word as follows:

[The text of the Protocol appears here.]

The Senate of the United States of America by its resolution of April 19, 1971, two-thirds of the Senators present concurring, gave its advice and consent to the ratification of Additional Protocol II, with the following understandings and declarations:

I

That the United States Government understands the reference in Article 3 of the treaty to "its own legislation" to relate only to such legislation as is compatible with the rules of international law and as involves an exercise of sovereignty consistent with those rules, and accordingly that ratification of Additional Protocol II by the United States Government could not be regarded as implying recognition, for the purposes of this treaty and its protocols or for any other purpose, of any legislation which did not, in the view of the United States, comply with the relevant rules of international law.

That the United States Government takes note of the Preparatory Commission's interpretation of the treaty, as set forth in the Final Act, that, governed by the principles and rules of international law, each of the Contracting Parties retains exclusive power and legal competence, unaffected by the terms of the treaty, to grant or deny non-Contracting Parties transit and transport privileges.

That as regards the undertaking in Article 3 of Protocol II not to use or threaten to use nuclear weapons against the Contracting Parties, the United States Government would have to consider that an armed attack by a Contracting Party, in which it was assisted by a nuclear-weapon state, would be incompatible with the Contracting Party's corresponding obligations under Article I of the Treaty.

II

That the United States Government considers that the technology of making nuclear explosive devices for peaceful purposes is indistinguishable from the technology of making nuclear weapons, and that nuclear weapons and nuclear explosive devices for peaceful purposes are both capable of releasing nuclear energy in an uncontrolled manner and have the common group of characteristics of large amounts of energy generated instantaneously from a compact source. Therefore, the United States

Government understands the definition contained in Article 5 of the treaty as necessarily encompassing all nuclear explosive devices. It is also understood that Articles 1 and 5 restrict accordingly the activities of the Contracting Parties under paragraph 1 of Article 18.

That the United States Government understands that paragraph 4 of Article 18 of the Treaty permits, and that United States adherence to Protocol II will not prevent, collaboration by the United States with Contracting Parties for the purpose of carrying out explosions of nuclear devices for peaceful purposes in a manner consistent with a policy of not contributing to the proliferation of nuclear weapons capabilities. In this connection, the United States Government notes Article V of the Treaty on the Non-Proliferation of Nuclerar Weapons, under which it joined in an undertaking to take appropriate measures to ensure that potential benefits of peaceful applications of nuclear explosions would be made available to non-nuclear-weapon states party to that treaty, and reaffirms its willingness to extend such undertaking, on the same basis, to states precluded by the present treaty from manufacturing or acquiring any nuclear explosive device.

III

That the United States Government also declares that, although not required by Protocol II, it will act with respect to such territories of Protocol I adherents as are within the geographical area defined in paragraph 2 of Article 4 of the treaty in the same manner as Protocol II requires it to act with respect to the territories of Contracting Parties.

The President ratified Additional Protocol II on May 8, 1971, with the above-recited understandings and declarations, in pursuance of the advice and consent of the Senate.

It is provided in Article 5 of Additional Protocol II that the Protocol shall enter into force, for the States which have ratified it, on the date of the deposit of their respective instruments of ratification.

The instrument of ratification of the United Kingdom of Great Britain and Northern Ireland was deposited on December 11, 1969 with understandings and a declaration, and the instrument of ratification of the United States of America was deposited on May 12, 1971 with the above-recited understandings and declarations.

In accordance with Article 5 of Additional Protocol II, the Protocol entered into force for the United States of America on May 12, 1971, subject to the above recited understandings and declarations.

NOW, THEREFORE, I, Richard Nixon, President of the United States of America, proclaim and make public Additional Protocol II to the Treaty for the Prohibition of Nuclear Weapons in Latin America to the end that it shall be observed and fulfilled with good faith, subject to the above-recited understandings and declarations, on and after May 12, 1971 by the United States of America and by the citizens of the United States of America and all other persons subject to the jurisdiction thereof.

IN TESTIMONY WHEREOF, I have signed this proclamation and caused the Seal of the United States of America to be affixed.

DONE at the city of Washington this eleventh day of June in the year of our Lord one thousand nine hundred seventy-one and of the Independence of the United States of America the one hundred ninety-fifth.

(SEAL)

Treaty for the Prohibition of Nuclear Weapons in Latin America.

Country	Date of Signature	Date of Deposit of Ratification
Argentina	9/27/67	
Bahamas, The		7/16/76[a]
Barbados	10/18/68	4/25/69
Bolivia	2/14/67	2/18/69
Brazil	5/ 9/67	1/29/68[b]
Chile	2/14/67	10/ 9/74[b]
Colombia	2/14/67	8/ 4/72
Costa Rica	2/14/67	8/25/69
Dominican Republic	7/29/67	6/14/68
Ecuador	2/14/67	2/11/69
El Salvador	2/14/67	4/22/68
Grenada	4/29/75	6/20/75
Guatemala	2/14/67	2/ 6/70
Haiti	2/14/67	5/23/69
Honduras	2/14/67	9/23/68
Jamaica	10/26/67	6/26/69
Mexico	2/14/67	9/20/67
Nicaragua	2/15/67	10/24/68
Panama	2/14/67	6/11/71
Paraguay	4/26/67	3/19/69
Peru	2/14/67	3/ 4/69
Suriname	2/13/76	6/10/77
Trinidad & Tobago	6/27/67	12/ 3/70[c]
Uruguay	2/14/67	8/20/68
Venezuela	2/14/67	3/23/70
Total	24	24

See footnotes on following page.

[a]This is date of notification of succession. The declaration of waiver was deposited 4/26/77, which is date of entry into force for The Bahamas.

[b]Not in force. No declaration of waiver under Art. 28, para. 2.

[c]The declaration of waiver was deposited 6/27/75, which is date of entry into force for Trinidad and Tobago.

Additional Protocol I to the Treaty for the Prohibition of Nuclear Weapons in Latin America

Country	Date of Signature	Date of Deposit of Ratification
France	3/2/79	
Netherlands	4/ 1/68	7/26/71
United Kingdom	12/20/67	12/11/69
United States	5/26/77	

Additional Protocol II to the Treaty for the Prohibition of Nuclear Weapons in Latin America

Country	Date of Signature	Date of Deposit of Ratification
China, People's Republic of	8/21/73	6/12/74
France	7/18/73	3/22/74
Union of Soviet Socialist Republics	5/18/78	1/ 8/79
United Kingdom	12/20/67	12/11/69
United States	4/ 1/68	5/12/71

Treaty on the Non-Proliferation of Nuclear Weapons

The need to prevent the spread of nuclear weapons was evident from the first days of the nuclear era. On November 15, 1945, the United States, the United Kingdom, and Canada proposed the establishment of a U.N. Atomic Energy Commission for the purpose of "entirely eliminating the use of atomic energy for destructive purposes." The Baruch plan of 1946, offered by the United States, sought to forestall nuclear arms proliferation by placing all nuclear resources under international ownership and control.

But the early postwar efforts to achieve agreement on nuclear disarmament failed. The Soviet Union in 1949, the United Kingdom in 1952, France in 1960, and the People's Republic of China in 1964, became nuclear-weapons states. And increasingly it was becoming apparent that earlier assumptions about the scarcity of nuclear materials and the difficulty of mastering nuclear technology were inaccurate.

Other developments and prospects further underscored the threat of nuclear proliferation. In the early 1960s the search for peaceful applications of nuclear energy had brought advances in the technology of nuclear reactors for the generation of electric power. By 1966 such nuclear reactors were operating or under construction in five countries. It was estimated that by 1985 more than 300 nuclear power reactors would be operating, under construction, or on order. Nuclear reactors produce not only power, but plutonium—a fissionable material which can be chemically separated and used in the manufacture of nuclear weapons. By 1985 the quantity of plutonium being produced would make possible the construction of 20 to 25 nuclear bombs daily, depending upon the level of the technology employed.

If the diversion of nuclear materials from peaceful purposes were not prevented by an international system of safeguards, and if a growing number of nations came to possess nuclear arsenals, the risks of nuclear war as a result of accident, unauthorized use, or escalation of regional conflicts would greatly increase. The possession of nuclear weapons by many countries would add a grave new dimension of threat to world security.

A succession of initiatives by both nuclear and nonnuclear powers sought to check proliferation. Indeed the effort to achieve a test ban—culminating in the treaty of 1963—had as one of its main purposes inhibiting the spread of nuclear weapons. But much before that, in August 1957, the Western powers (Canada, France, the United Kingdom, and the United States) submitted a "package" of measures, in the Subcommittee of the United Nations Disarmament Commission, which included a commitment "not to transfer out of its control any nuclear weapons, or to accept transfer to it of such weapons," except for self-defense.

Although the Soviet Union opposed proliferation, it claimed that this Western formula would allow an aggressor to judge his own actions, and to use nuclear weapons "under cover of the alleged right of self-defense." It sought to couple a ban on transfer of nuclear weapons to other states with a prohibition on stationing nuclear weapons in foreign countries.

In 1961 the General Assembly unanimously approved an Irish resolution calling on all states, particularly the nuclear powers, to conclude an international agreement to refrain from transfer or acquisition of nuclear weapons. Moreover, the general disarmament plans which had been submitted by the United States and the Soviet Union during the period 1960–62 included provisions banning the transfer and acquisition of nuclear weapons.

The United States, on January 21, 1964, outlined a program to halt the nuclear arms race in a message from President Johnson to the Eighteen-Nation Disarmament Committee (ENDC). This program, unlike the 1957 proposal, was not a "package." It included a nondissemination and nonacquisition proposal—based on the Irish resolution—and safeguards on international transfers of nuclear materials for peaceful purposes, combined with acceptance by the major nuclear powers that their peaceful nuclear activities undergo increasingly "the same inspection they recommend for other states."

An issue that was to be the principal stumbling block for the next 3 years was the proposed multilateral nuclear force (MLF) then under discussion by the United States and its NATO allies. The Soviet Union strongly objected to this plan and maintained that no agreement could be reached on non-proliferation so long as the United States held open the possibility of such nuclear-sharing arrangements in NATO. These would constitute proliferation, the Soviet Union contended, and were devices for giving the Federal Republic of Germany access to or control of nuclear weapons.

On August 17, 1965, the United States submitted a draft non-proliferation treaty to the ENDC. This draft would oblige the nuclear-weapons powers not to transfer nuclear weapons to the national control of any country not having them. Nonnuclear nations would undertake to facilitate the application of International Atomic Energy Agency or equivalent safeguards to their peaceful nuclear activities.

A Soviet draft treaty was submitted to the General Assembly on September 24. In an accompanying memorandum, the Soviet Union declared that the greatest danger of proliferation was posed by the MLF and the alternative British proposal for an Atlantic nuclear force (ANF). The Soviet draft prohibited the transfer of nuclear weapons "directly or indirectly, through third States or groups of States not possessing nuclear weapons." It would also bar nuclear powers from transferring "nuclear weapons, or control over them or their emplacement or use" to military units of nonnuclear allies, even if these were placed under joint command. The draft included no safeguards provisions.

In March 1966 the United States tabled amendments to its draft treaty in the ENDC, seeking to clarify and emphasize the Western view that collective defense arrangements would not violate the principle of non-proliferation. The U.S. representative stressed that the United States would not relinquish its veto over the use of U.S. weapons. The Soviet Union objected that the amendments did not prevent the transfer of nuclear weapons through such alliance arrangements as the MLF, the ANF, or units placed under joint command. The U.S. retention of a veto, the Soviet representative argued, did not provide security against dissemination.

Despite strong disagreement on the issue of collective defense arrangements, it was apparent that both sides recognized the desirability of an agreement on non-proliferation. Moreover, the interest of nonnuclear powers was increasingly manifest. It was shown in 1964 at the African summit conference and at the Cairo conference of nonaligned states and expressed in a series of resolutions in the General Assembly urging that non-proliferation receive priority attention. In May 1966 the U.S. Senate unanimously passed a resolution, sponsored by Senator Pastore of Rhode Island and 55 other Senators, commending efforts to reach a non-proliferation agreement and supporting continued efforts.

In the fall of 1966 the U.S. and Soviet co-chairmen of the ENDC began private talks, and by the end of the year they had reached tentative agreement on the basic nontransfer and nonacquisition provisions of a treaty, as well as on a number of other aspects.

There followed a long and arduous series of consultations between the United States and its allies. The allies raised a number of questions regarding the effect of the treaty on NATO nuclear defense arrangements, and the United States gave its interpretations. The United States considered that the treaty covered nuclear weapons or explosive devices but not delivery systems. It would not prohibit NATO consultation and planning on nuclear defense, nor ban deployment of U.S.-owned and -controlled nuclear weapons on the territory of nonnuclear NATO members. It would not "bar succession by a new federated European state to the nuclear status of one of its members." The allies' questions and the United States answers were provided to the Soviet Union, which did not challenge the U.S. interpretations.

On August 24, 1967, the United States and the Soviet Union were able to submit separate but identical texts of a draft treaty to the ENDC. Other ENDC members proposed numerous amendments, largely reflecting the concerns of the nonnuclear states. In response to these, the drafts underwent several revisions, and the co-chairmen tabled a joint draft on March 11, 1968. With additional revisions, the joint draft was submitted to the General Assembly, where it was extensively debated. Further suggestions for strengthening the treaty were made, and in the light of these the United States and the Soviet Union submitted a new revised version—the seventh—to the First Committee of the General Assembly on May 31. The General Assembly on June 12 approved a resolution commending the text and requesting the depositary governments to open it for signature. France abstained in the General Assembly vote, stating that while France would not sign the treaty, it "would behave in the future in this field exactly as the States adhering to the treaty."

In the course of these extended negotiations, the concerns of the nonnuclear powers centered particularly on three main issues:

Safeguards. There was general agreement that the treaty should include provisions designed to prevent the diversion of nuclear materials from peaceful to weapons use. Two problems were involved. One was to reconcile the Soviet insistence that all nonnuclear parties accept IAEA[1] safeguards with the desire of the nonnuclear members of EURATOM[2] (Belgium, the Federal Republic of Germany, Italy, Luxembourg, and the Netherlands) to preserve their regional system. To meet this concern, the final draft provided that nonnuclear parties could negotiate safeguards agreements with IAEA either individually or together with other states.[3]

The other problem was to satisfy the widespread concern among nonnuclear states that IAEA safeguards might place them at a commercial and industrial disadvantage in developing nuclear energy for peaceful use, since the nuclear powers would not be

---

[1]International Atomic Energy Agency, a U.N.-sponsored agency headquartered at Vienna.

[2]European Atomic Energy Community, an organization established by the original European Common Market partners for cooperation in nuclear energy matters.

[3]EURATOM and the IAEA began negotiations in 1971. An IAEA-EURATOM safeguards agreement was signed in April 1973 and entered into force on February 21, 1977.

required to accept safeguards. To help allay these misgivings, the United States offered, on December 2, 1967, to place all nuclear facilities in the United States under IAEA treaty safeguards when these became operative, excluding only those with "direct national security significance." The United Kingdom announced that it would take similar action. Its safeguards agreement with the IAEA was concluded in 1976 and is now in force. The U.S.-IAEA agreement, signed on November 18, 1977, was submitted by the President to the Senate for its advice and consent to ratification on February 9, 1978. In 1977, France opened negotiations with the IAEA, and a safeguards agreement has been approved by the IAEA Board of Governors. It has yet to be approved by the French Government. The Soviet Union, on the other hand, has not been willing to accept safeguards on its nuclear facilities.

Further, to meet objections about the possible discriminatory effects of safeguards, the treaty stipulated that parties were to participate in and have fullest access to materials and information for peaceful uses of nuclear energy. The treaty also provided that any potential benefits of nuclear explosions for peaceful purposes would be made available to nonnuclear weapons parties on a nondiscriminatory basis.

Balanced Obligations. Throughout the negotiations most nonnuclear states held that their renunciation of nuclear weapons should be accompanied by a commitment on the part of the nuclear powers to reduce their nuclear arsenals and to make progress on measures of comprehensive disarmament. General provisions were attached to the treaty affirming the intentions of the parties to negotiate in good faith to achieve a cessation of the nuclear arms race, nuclear disarmament, and general and complete disarmament.

Security Assurances. Nonnuclear-weapons states sought guarantees that renunciation of nuclear arms would not place them at a permanent military disadvantage and make them vulnerable to nuclear intimidation. But, it was argued, the security interests of the various states, and groups of states, were not identical; an effort to frame provisions within the treaty that would meet this diversity of requirements—for unforeseeable future contingencies—would create inordinate complexities. To resolve the issue, the United States, the Soviet Union, and the United Kingdom submitted in the ENDC, on March 7, 1968, a tripartite proposal that security assurances take the form of a U.N. Security Council resolution, supported by declarations of the three powers. The resolution, noting the security concerns of states wishing to subscribe to the Non-Proliferation Treaty, would recognize that nuclear aggression, or the threat of nuclear aggression, created a situation requiring immediate action by the Security Council, especially its permanent members.

Following submission of the treaty itself to the General Assembly, the tripartite resolution was submitted to the Security Council. In a formal declaration the United States asserted its intention to seek immediate Security Council actions to provide assistance to any nonnuclear-weapons state party to the treaty that was the object of nuclear aggression or threats. The Soviet Union and the United Kingdom made similar declarations. France abstained from voting on the Security Council resolution; the French representative said that France did not intend its abstention to be an obstacle to adoption of the tripartite proposal, but that France did not believe the nations would receive adequate security guarantees without nuclear disarmament.

The treaty was opened for signature on July 1, 1968, and signed on that date by the United States, the United Kingdom, the Soviet Union, and 59 other countries. On July 9, President Johnson transmitted it to the Senate, but prospects for early U.S. ratification dimmed after the Soviet invasion of Czechoslovakia in August. The Senate adjourned without voting on the Treaty. In February 1969 President Nixon requested Senate approval of the treaty, and in March the Senate gave its advice and consent to ratification. The treaty entered into force with the deposit of U.S. ratification on March 5, 1970.

In broadest outline, the basic provisions of the treaty are designed to

— prevent the spread of nuclear weapons (Articles I and II);
— provide assurance, through international safeguards, that the peaceful nuclear activities of states which have not already developed nuclear weapons will not be diverted to making such weapons (Article III);
— promote, to the maximum extent consistent with the other purposes of the treaty, the peaceful uses of nuclear energy through full cooperation—with the potential benefits of any peaceful application of nuclear explosion technology being made available to nonnuclear parties under appropriate international observation (Articles IV and V);
— express the determination of the parties that the treaty should lead to further progress in comprehensive arms control and nuclear disarmament measures (Article VI).

Article VIII provides for a conference "to review the operation of this Treaty with a view to assuring that the Purposes of the Preamble and the provisions of the Treaty are being realized." The NPT Review Conference, held in Geneva in May 1975, produced a number of significant recommendations. It expressed strong support for IAEA safeguards and called for greater efforts to make them universal and effective. There was general agreement that safeguards do not hamper peaceful nuclear activities. The final declaration of the conference, accepted by consensus, urged all states with peaceful nuclear activities to maintain effective accounting and control systems, noting the readiness of the International Atomic Energy Agency to assist them and the importance of such systems to effective IAEA monitoring. It recommended that safeguards be of adequate duration (which had not always been the case in the past); and that they preclude the diversion of safeguarded material to any nuclear explosive device, regardless of its stated purpose. It recommended that support be given to improving safeguards techniques, instrumentation, data handling, and implementation.

The conference urged common export requirements designed to extend safeguards, in all available ways, to all peaceful nuclear activities in importing states not party to the treaty, and urged all suppliers and recipients to accept these requirements.

The conference recommended better physical protection of nuclear materials, giving weight to NPT adherence in decisions on nuclear assistance and credit arrangements, and also recommended the study of the potential advantages of multinational fuel cycle centers.

The conference emphasized the need for further study of "peaceful" nuclear explosions (PNEs) by the IAEA (which subsequently established an international advisory group on this subject) and for considering arms control implications of PNEs by the Conference of the Committee on Disarmament (which subsequently held a meeting of experts on this aspect of the subject).

A second review conference is scheduled for August 1980, and in 1995 a conference is to be held to determine whether the treaty shall be extended indefinitely, or for an additional fixed period.

The following can be said about implementation of the Treaty Articles:

Articles I and II: No nuclear-weapon state party to the Treaty has transferred nuclear explosive devices or has assisted any nonnuclear-weapon state in acquiring or manufacturing a nuclear explosive device. No nonnuclear-weapon state party to the Treaty has acquired or manufactured a nuclear explosive device.

Article III: The IAEA has developed an extensive system of safeguards which ensures that nuclear materials located in nonnuclear-weapon states party to the Treaty are used solely for nonexplosive purposes. Safeguards agreements required by the NPT have entered into force for 68 countries. For 44 nonnuclear-weapon states party to the Treaty, the relevant safeguards agreements have not yet entered into force; however, none of these states has significant nuclear activities. In 1974 a number of NPT parties indicated which nuclear exports would require IAEA safeguards under Article III.2 of the NPT. Since then a total of 18 nuclear suppliers which are party to the NPT have expanded the list of items which trigger safeguards under this article.

Article IV: The United States has been in the forefront of nations which have provided technical assistance in the nuclear field. At the United Nations Special Session on Disarmament in 1978, the United States announced that it would be expanding technical assistance through the IAEA for NPT parties. In 1977 President Carter proposed the International Nuclear Fuel Cycle Evaluation to study how nuclear energy can be used in peaceful applications while minimizing the danger of proliferation. Over 40 nations participated in this 2-year study.

Article V: No nuclear explosions for peaceful purposes have been conducted under this Article. It is the view of the United States that there are no potential benefits to be derived from such explosions.

Article VI: Article VI is one of the most contentious articles of the NPT. The United States and the Soviet Union have pointed to the Strategic Arms Limitation Talks as evidence that they are implementing this Article. While the nonnuclear-weapon states have welcomed the SALT talks and agreements reached to date, they have noted that the number of nuclear weapons have increased on both sides since the NPT came into force. A Comprehensive Test Ban Treaty prohibiting the testing of nuclear explosives is viewed by many nonnuclear-weapon states as a *sine qua non* for preventing the emergence of additional nuclear-weapon states and for preserving the NPT regime.

Treaty on the Non-Proliferation of Nuclear Weapons

Signed at Washington, London, and Moscow July 1, 1968
Ratification advised by U.S. Senate March 13, 1969
Ratified by U.S. President November 24, 1969
U.S. ratification deposited at Washington, London, and Moscow March 5, 1970
Proclaimed by U.S. President March 5, 1970
Entered into force March 5, 1970

The States concluding this Treaty, hereinafter referred to as the "Parties to the Treaty",

Considering the devastation that would be visited upon all mankind by a nuclear war and the consequent need to make every effort to avert the danger of such a war and to take measures to safeguard the security of peoples,

Believing that the proliferation of nuclear weapons would seriously enhance the danger of nuclear war,

In conformity with resolutions of the United Nations General Assembly calling for the conclusion of an agreement on the prevention of wider dissemination of nuclear weapons,

Undertaking to cooperate in facilitating the application of International Atomic Energy Agency safeguards on peaceful nuclear activities,

Expressing their support for research, development and other efforts to further the application, within the framework of the International Atomic Energy Agency safeguards system, of the principle of safeguarding effectively the flow of source and special fissionable materials by use of instruments and other techniques at certain strategic points,

Affirming the principle that the benefits of peaceful applications of nuclear technology, including any technological by-products which may be derived by nuclear-weapon States from the development of nuclear explosive devices, should be available for peaceful purposes to all Parties of the Treaty, whether nuclear-weapon or non-nuclear weapon States,

Convinced that, in furtherance of this principle, all Parties to the Treaty are entitled to participate in the fullest possible exchange of scientific information for, and to contribute alone or in cooperation with other States to, the further development of the applications of atomic energy for peaceful purposes,

Declaring their intention to achieve at the earliest possible date the cessation of the nuclear arms race and to undertake effective measures in the direction of nuclear disarmament,

Urging the cooperation of all States in the attainment of this objective,

Recalling the determination expressed by the Parties to the 1963 Treaty banning nuclear weapon tests in the atmosphere, in outer space and under water in its Preamble to seek to achieve the discontinuance of all test explosions of nuclear weapons for all time and to continue negotiations to this end,

Desiring to further the easing of international tension and the strengthening of trust between States in order to facilitate the cessation of the manufacture of nuclear weapons, the liquidation of all their existing stockpiles, and the elimination from national arsenals of nuclear weapons and the means of their delivery pursuant to a treaty on general and complete disarmament under strict and effective international control,

Recalling that, in accordance with the Charter of the United Nations, States must refrain in their international relations from the threat or use of force against the territorial integrity or political independence of any State, or in any other manner inconsistent with the Purposes of the United Nations, and that the establishment and maintenance of international peace and security are to be promoted with the least diversion for armaments of the world's human and economic resources,

Have agreed as follows:

Article I

Each nuclear-weapon State Party to the Treaty undertakes not to transfer to any recipient whatsoever nuclear weapons or other nuclear explosive devices or control over such weapons or explosive devices directly, or indirectly; and not in any way to assist, encourage, or induce any non-nuclear-weapon State to manufacture or otherwise acquire nuclear weapons or other nuclear explosive devices, or control over such weapons or explosive devices.

Article II

Each non-nuclear-weapon State Party to the Treaty undertakes not to receive the transfer from any transfer or whatsoever of nuclear weapons or other nuclear explosive devices or of control over such weapons or explosive devices directly, or indirectly; not to manufacture or otherwise acquire nuclear weapons or other nuclear explosive devices; and not to seek or receive any assistance in the manufacture of nuclear weapons or other nuclear explosive devices.

Article III

1. Each non-nuclear-weapon State Party to the Treaty undertakes to accept safeguards, as set forth in an agreement to be negotiated and concluded with the International Atomic Energy Agency in accordance with the Statute of the International Atomic Energy Agency and the Agency's safeguards system, for the exclusive purpose of verification of the fulfillment of its obligations assumed under this Treaty with a view to preventing diversion of nuclear energy from peaceful uses to nuclear weapons or other nuclear explosive devices. Procedures for the safeguards required by this article shall be followed with respect to source or special fissionable material whether it is being produced, processed or used in any principal nuclear facility or is outside any such facility. The safeguards required by this article shall be applied to all source or special fissionable material in all peaceful nuclear activities within the territory of such State, under its jurisdiction, or carried out under its control anywhere.

2. Each State Party to the Treaty undertakes not to provide: (a) source or special fissionable material, or (b) equipment or material especially designed or prepared for the processing, use or production of special fissionable material, to any non-nuclear-weapon State for peaceful purposes, unless the source or special fissionable material shall be subject to the safeguards required by this article.

3. The safeguards required by this article shall be implemented in a manner designed to comply with article IV of this Treaty, and to avoid hampering the economic or technological development of the Parties or international cooperation in the field of peaceful nuclear activities, including the international exchange of nuclear material and equipment for the processing, use or production of nuclear material for peaceful purposes in accordance with the provisions of this article and the principle of safeguarding set forth in the Preamble of the Treaty.

4. Non-nuclear-weapon States Party to the Treaty shall conclude agreements with the International Atomic Energy Agency to meet the requirements of this article either

individually or together with other States in accordance with the Statute of the International Atomic Energy Agency. Negotiation of such agreements shall commence within 180 days from the original entry into force of this Treaty. For States depositing their instruments of ratification or accession after the 180-day period, negotiation of such agreements shall commence not later than the date of such deposit. Such agreements shall enter into force not later than eighteen months after the date of initiation of negotiations.

Article IV

1. Nothing in this Treaty shall be interpreted as affecting the inalienable right of all the Parties to the Treaty to develop research, production and use of nuclear energy for peaceful purposes without discrimination and in conformity with articles I and II of this Treaty.
2. All the Parties to the Treaty undertake to facilitate, and have the right to participate in, the fullest possible exchange of equipment, materials and scientific and technological information for the peaceful uses of nuclear energy. Parties to the Treaty in a position to do so shall also cooperate in contributing alone or together with other States or international organizations to the further development of the applications of nuclear energy for peaceful purposes, especially in the territories of non-nuclear-weapon States Party to the Treaty, with due consideration for the needs of the developing areas of the world.

Article V

Each party to the Treaty undertakes to take appropriate measures to ensure that, in accordance with this Treaty, under appropriate international observation and through appropriate international procedures, potential benefits from any peaceful applications of nuclear explosions will be made available to non-nuclear-weapon States Party to the Treaty on a nondiscriminatory basis and that the charge to such Parties for the explosive devices used will be as low as possible and exclude any charge for research and development. Non-nuclear-weapon States Party to the Treaty shall be able to obtain such benefits, pursuant to a special international agreement or agreements, through an appropriate international body with adequate representation of non-nuclear-weapon States. Negotiations on this subject shall commence as soon as possible after the Treaty enters into force. Non-nuclear-weapon States Party to the Treaty so desiring may also obtain such benefits pursuant to bilateral agreements.

Article VI

Each of the Parties to the Treaty undertakes to pursue negotiations in good faith on effective measures relating to cessation of the nuclear arms race at an early date and to nuclear disarmament, and on a treaty on general and complete disarmament under strict and effective international control.

Article VII

Nothing in this Treaty affects the right of any group of States to conclude regional treaties in order to assure the total absence of nuclear weapons in their respective territories.

Article VIII

1. Any Party to the Treaty may propose amendments to this Treaty. The text of any proposed amendment shall be submitted to the Depositary Governments which shall

circulate it to all Parties to the Treaty. Thereupon, if requested to do so by one-third or more of the Parties to the Treaty, the Depositary Governments shall convene a conference, to which they shall invite all the Parties to the Treaty, to consider such an amendment.

2. Any amendment to this Treaty must be approved by a majority of the votes of all the Parties to the Treaty, including the votes of all nuclear-weapon States Party to the Treaty and all other Parties which, on the date the amendment is circulated, are members of the Board of Governors of the International Atomic Energy Agency. The amendment shall enter into force for each Party that deposits its instrument of ratification of the amendment upon the deposit of such instruments of ratification by a majority of all the Parties, including the instruments of ratification of all nuclear-weapon States Party to the Treaty and all other Parties which, on the date the amendment is circulated, are members of the Board of Governors of the International Atomic Energy Agency. Thereafter, it shall enter into force for any other Party upon the deposit of its instrument of ratification of the amendment.

3. Five years after the entry into force of this Treaty, a conference of Parties to the Treaty shall be held in Geneva, Switzerland, in order to review the operation of this Treaty with a view to assuring that the purposes of the Preamble and the provisions of the Treaty are being realized. At intervals of five years thereafter, a majority of the Parties to the Treaty may obtain, by submitting a proposal to this effect to the Depositary Governments, the convening of further conferences with the same objective of reviewing the operation of the Treaty.

Article IX

1. This Treaty shall be open to all States for signature. Any State which does not sign the Treaty before its entry into force in accordance with paragraph 3 of this article may accede to it at any time.

2. This Treaty shall be subject to ratification by signatory States. Instruments of ratification and instruments of accession shall be deposited with the Governments of the United States of America, the United Kingdom of Great Britain and Northern Ireland and the Union of Soviet Socialist Republics, which are hereby designated the Depositary Governments.

3. This Treaty shall enter into force after its ratification by the States, the Governments of which are designated Depositaries of the Treaty, and forty other States signatory to this Treaty and the deposit of their instruments of ratification. For the purposes of this Treaty, a nuclear-weapon State is one which has manufactured and exploded a nuclear weapon or other nuclear explosive device prior to January 1, 1967.

4. For States whose instruments of ratification or accession are deposited subsequent to the entry into force of this Treaty, it shall enter into force on the date of the deposit of their instruments of ratification or accession.

5. The Depositary Governments shall promptly inform all signatory and acceding States of the date of each signature, the date of deposit of each instrument of ratification or of accession, the date of the entry into force of this Treaty, and the date of receipt of any requests for convening a conference or other notices.

6. This Treaty shall be registered by the Depositary Governments pursuant to article 102 of the Charter of the United Nations.

Article X

1. Each Party shall in exercising its national sovereignty have the right to withdraw from the Treaty if it decides that extraordinary events, related to the subject matter of this Treaty, have jeopardized the supreme interests of its country. It shall give notice of

such withdrawal to all other Parties to the Treaty and to the United Nations Security Council three months in advance. Such notice shall include a statement of the extraordinary events it regards as having jeopardized its supreme interests.

2. Twenty-five years after the entry into force of the Treaty, a conference shall be convened to decide whether the Treaty shall continue in force indefinitely, or shall be extended for an additional fixed period or periods. This decision shall be taken by a majority of the Parties to the Treaty.

Article XI

This Treaty, the English, Russian, French, Spanish and Chinese texts of which are equally authentic, shall be deposited in the archives of the Depositary Governments. Duly certified copies of this Treaty shall be transmitted by the Depositary Governments to the Governments of the signatory and acceding States.

Non-Proliferation Treaty

Country	Date of[1] Signature	Date of Deposit[1] of Ratification	Date of Deposit[1] of Accession
Afghanistan	7/1/68	2/4/70	
Australia	2/27/70	1/23/73	
Austria	7/1/68	6/27/69	
Bahamas, The			8/11/76
Bangladesh			8/31/79
Barbados	7/1/68	2/21/80	
Belgium	8/20/68	5/2/75	
Benin	7/1/68	10/31/72	
Bolivia	7/1/68	5/26/70	
Botswana	7/1/68	4/28/69	
Bulgaria	7/1/68	9/5/69	
Burundi			3/19/71
Cameroon	7/17/68	1/8/69	
Canada	7/23/68	1/8/69	
Cape Verde			10/24/79
Central African Republic			10/25/70
Chad	7/1/68	3/10/71	
China (Taiwan)	7/1/68	1/27/70	
Colombia	7/1/68		
Congo, People's Republic of (Brazzaville)			10/23/78
Costa Rica	7/1/68	3/3/70	
Cyprus	7/1/68	2/10/70	
Czechoslovakia	7/1/68	7/22/69	
Denmark	7/1/68	1/3/69	
Dominican Republic	7/1/68	7/24/71	
Ecuador	7/9/68	3/7/69	
Egypt	7/1/68		
El Salvador	7/1/68	7/11/72	
Ethiopia	9/5/68	2/5/70	
Fiji			7/14/72
Finland	7/1/68	2/5/69	
Gabon			2/19/74
Gambia, The	9/4/68	5/12/75	
German Democratic Republic	7/1/68	10/31/69	
Germany, Federal Republic of	11/28/69	5/2/75	
Ghana	7/1/68	5/4/70	

See footnotes on page 239.

Country	Date of[1] Signature	Date of Deposit[1] of Ratification	Date of Deposit[1] of Accession
Greece	7/1/68	3/11/70	
Grenada			9/2/75
Guatemala	7/26/68	9/22/70	
Guinea-Bissau			8/20/76
Haiti	7/1/68	6/2/70	
Holy See			2/25/71
Honduras	7/1/68	5/16/73	
Hungary	7/1/68	5/27/69	
Iceland	7/1/68	7/18/69	
Indonesia	3/2/70	7/12/79	
Iran	7/1/68	2/2/70	
Iraq	7/1/68	10/29/69	
Ireland	7/1/68	7/1/68	
Italy	1/28/69	5/2/75	
Ivory Coast	7/1/68	3/6/73	
Jamaica	4/14/69	3/5/70	
Japan	2/3/70	6/8/76	
Jordan	7/10/68	2/11/70	
Kampuchea			6/2/72
Kenya	7/1/68	6/11/70	
Korea, Republic of	7/1/68	4/23/75	
Kuwait	8/15/68		
Laos	7/1/68	2/20/70	
Lebanon	7/1/68	7/15/70	
Lesotho	7/9/68	5/20/70	
Liberia	7/1/68	3/5/70	
Libya	7/18/68	5/26/75	
Liechtenstein			4/20/78
Luxembourg	8/14/68	5/2/75	
Madagascar	8/22/68	10/8/70	
Malaysia	7/1/68	3/5/70	
Maldive Islands	9/11/68	4/7/70	
Mali	7/14/69	2/10/70	
Malta	4/17/69	2/6/70	
Mauritius	7/1/68	4/8/69	
Mexico	7/26/68	1/21/69	
Mongolia	7/1/68	5/14/69	
Morocco	7/1/68	11/27/70	
Nepal	7/1/68	1/5/70	

See footnotes on page 239.

Country	Date of[1] Signature	Date of Deposit[1] of Ratification	Date of Deposit[1] of Accession
Netherlands	8/20/68	5/2/75	
New Zealand	7/1/68	9/10/69	
Nicaragua	7/1/68	3/6/73	
Nigeria	7/1/68	9/27/68	
Norway	7/1/68	2/5/69	
Panama	7/1/68	1/13/77	
Paraguay	7/1/68	2/4/70	
Peru	7/1/68	3/3/70	
Philippines	7/1/68	10/5/72	
Poland	7/1/68	6/12/69	
Portugal			12/15/77
Romania	7/1/68	2/4/70	
Rwanda			5/20/75
San Marino	7/1/68	8/10/70	
St. Lucia			12/28/79
Senegal	7/1/68	12/17/70	
Sierra Leone			2/26/75
Singapore	2/5/70	3/10/76	
Somalia	7/1/68	3/5/70	
Sri Lanka	7/1/68	3/5/79	
Sudan	12/24/68	10/31/73	
Suriname			6/30/76[a]
Swaziland	6/24/69	12/11/69	
Sweden	8/19/68	1/9/70	
Switzerland	11/27/69	3/9/77	
Syrian Arab Republic	7/1/68	9/24/69	
Thailand			12/2/72
Togo	7/1/68	2/26/70	
Tonga			7/7/71[1]
Trinidad and Tobago	8/20/68		
Tunisia	7/1/68	2/26/70	
Turkey	1/28/69	4/17/80	
Tuvalu			1/19/79[1]
Union of Soviet Socialist Republics	7/1/68	3/5/70	
United Kingdom	7/1/68	11/27/68	
United States	7/1/68	3/5/70	
Upper Volta	11/25/68	3/3/70	
Uruguay	7/1/68	8/31/70	
Venezuela	7/1/68	9/25/75	

See footnotes on page 239.

[a] Effective 11/25/75.

Country	Date of[1] Signature	Date of Deposit[1] of Ratification	Date of Deposit[1] of Accession
Western Samoa			3/17/75
Yemen Arab Republic (Sana)	9/23/68		
Yemen, People's Democratic Republic of (Aden)	11/14/68	6/1/79	
Yugoslavia	7/10/68	3/4/70	
Zaire	7/22/68	8/4/70	
Total[3]	97	92	22

See footnotes on page 239.

Treaty on the Prohibition of the Emplacement of Nuclear Weapons and Other Weapons of Mass Destruction on the Seabed and the Ocean Floor and in the Subsoil Thereof

Like the Antarctic Treaty, the Outer Space Treaty, and the Latin American Nuclear-Free Zone, the Seabed Treaty sought to prevent the introduction of international conflict and nuclear weapons into an area hitherto free of them. Reaching agreement on the seabed, however, involved problems not met in framing the other two agreements.

In the 1960s advances in the technology of oceanography and greatly increased interest in the vast and virtually untapped resources of the ocean floor led to concern that the absence of clearly established rules of law might lead to strife. And there were concurrent fears that nations might use the seabed as a new environment for military installations, including those capable of launching nuclear weapons.

In keeping with a proposal submitted to the U.N. Secretary General by Ambassador Pardo of Malta in August 1967, the U.N. General Assembly, on December 18, 1967, established an *ad hoc* committee to study ways of reserving the seabed for peaceful purposes, with the objective of assuring "that the exploration and use of the seabed and the ocean floor should be conducted in accordance with the principles and purposes of the Charter of the United Nations, in the interests of maintaining international peace and security and for the benefit of all mankind." The Committee was given permanent status the following year. At the same time, seabed-related military and arms control issues were referred to the ENDC and its successor, the CCD.[1] In a message of March 18, 1969, President Nixon said the American delegation to the ENDC should seek discussion of the factors necessary for an international agreement prohibiting the emplacement of weapons of mass destruction on the seabed and ocean floor and pointed out that an agreement of this kind would, like the Antarctic and outer space treaties, "prevent an arms race before it has a chance to start."

On March 18, 1969, the Soviet Union presented a draft treaty that provided for the complete demilitarization of the seabed beyond a 12-

---

[1]As noted elsewhere, the Geneva-based ENDC (Eighteen-Nation Disarmament Committee) became known as the CCD (Conference of the Committee on Disarmament) after its enlargement in 1969.

mile limit and making all seabed installations open to treaty parties on the basis of reciprocity. The U.S. draft treaty, submitted on May 22, prohibited the emplacement of nuclear weapons and other weapons of mass destruction on the seabed and ocean floor beyond a 3-mile band. This, the United States held, was the urgent problem, and complete demilitarization would not be verifiable.

As can be seen, the two drafts differed importantly on what was to be prohibited. The Soviet draft would have banned *all* military uses of the seabed. It would have precluded, for example, submarine surveillance systems that were fixed to the ocean floor. The United States regarded these as essential to its defense.

The two drafts also differed on the issue of verification. Using as a model the provisions for verification in the Outer Space Treaty, the Soviets proposed that all installations and structures be open to inspection, provided that reciprocal rights to inspect were granted. The United States contended that on the moon no claims of national jurisdiction existed and that provisions suitable for the moon would not be adequate for the seabed, where many claims of national jurisdiction already existed and many kinds of activities were in progress or possible. Moreover, the United States felt that to attempt to inspect for the emplacement of *all* kinds of weapons would make the problems connected with verification virtually insuperable.

On the other hand, the United States stated the case that any structure capable of handling nuclear devices would necessarily be large and elaborate; their installation would require extensive activity, difficult to conceal; and there would probably be a number of devices involved, as it would not be worth violating the treaty simply to install one or two weapons. Violations, therefore, would be readily observed and evoke the appropriate steps—first an effort to deal directly with the problem through consultations with the country violating the treaty; if that failed, recourse to cooperative action; and, as a last resort, appeal to the Security Council.

Comments on the two drafts in the ENDC, U.S. consultations with its NATO allies, and private U.S.-Soviet talks at the ENDC eventually led to the framing of a joint draft by the United States and the Soviet Union, submitted on October 7, 1969, to the CCD. This joint draft underwent intensive discussion and was three times revised in response to suggestions made in the CCD and at the United Nations.

Discussion centered on a few difficult issues. In international law there is much confusion about how territorial waters are to be defined. Some countries claim up to 200 miles, and even international conventions on the subject contain ambiguities. In its final form the treaty adopted a 12-mile limit to define the seabed area.

The verification provisions also were a subject of intensive discussion. Coastal states were concerned about whether their rights would be protected. Smaller states had doubts as to their ability to check on violations. Some felt that the United Nations should play a larger role. Some wondered whether the verification procedures would really be effective. Reassurances were given to the coastal states. Smaller states could apply for assistance to another state to help it in case of a suspected violation.

The verification procedures are set forth in Article III. Parties may undertake verification using their own means, with the assistance of other parties, or through appropriate international procedures within the framework of the United Nations and in accordance with its Charter. These provisions permit parties to assure themselves the treaty obligations are being fulfilled without interfering with legitimate seabed activities.

After more than 2 years of negotiation, the final draft was approved by the U.N. General Assembly on December 7, 1970, by a vote of 104 to 2 (El Salvador, Peru), with 2 abstentions (Ecuador and France).

Article I sets forth the principal obligation of the treaty. It prohibits parties from omplacing nuclear weapons or weapons of mass destruction on the seabed and the ocean floor beyond a 12-mile coastal zone. Article II provides that the "seabed zone" is to be measured in accordance with the provisions of the 1958 Convention on the Territorial Sea and the Contiguous Zone. To make clear that none of the treaty's provisions should be interpreted as supporting or prejudicing the positions of any party regarding law-of-the-sea issues, a broad disclaimer provision to this effect was included as Article IV.

In recognition of the feeling that efforts to achieve a more comprehensive agreement should continue, Article V of the treaty bound parties to work for further measures to prevent an arms race on the seabed.

The Seabed Arms Control Treaty was opened for signature in Washington, London, and Moscow on February 11, 1971. It entered into force May 18, 1972, when the United States, the United Kingdom, the U.S.S.R., and more than 22 nations had deposited instruments of ratification.

Article VII included a provision for a review conference to be held in 5 years. The Seabed Arms Control Treaty Review Conference was held in Geneva June 20–July 1, 1977. The Conference concluded that the first 5 years in the life of the treaty had demonstrated its effectiveness. It decided that a further review conference should be held in Geneva in 1982, unless a majority of the treaty parties wanted it postponed for up to 2 years.

Treaty on the Prohibition of the Emplacement of Nuclear Weapons and Other Weapons of Mass Destruction on the Seabed and the Ocean Floor and in the Subsoil Thereof

Signed at Washington, London, and Moscow February 11, 1971
Ratification advised by U.S. Senate February 15, 1972
Ratified by U.S. President April 26, 1972
U.S. ratification deposited at Washington, London, and Moscow May 18, 1972
Proclaimed by U.S. President May 18, 1972
Entered into force May 18, 1972

The States Parties to this Treaty,

Recognizing the common interest of mankind in the progress of the exploration and use of the seabed and the ocean floor for peaceful purposes,

Considering that the prevention of a nuclear arms race on the seabed and the ocean floor serves the interests of maintaining world peace, reduces international tensions and strengthens friendly relations among States,

Convinced that this Treaty constitutes a step towards the exclusion of the seabed, the ocean floor and the subsoil thereof from the arms race,

Convinced that this Treaty constitutes a step towards a treaty on general and complete disarmament under strict and effective international control, and determined to continue negotiations to this end,

Convinced that this Treaty will further the purposes and principles of the Charter of the United Nations, in a manner consistent with the principles of international law and without infringing the freedoms of the high seas,

Have agreed as follows:

Article I

1. The States Parties to this Treaty undertake not to emplant or emplace on the seabed and the ocean floor and in the subsoil thereof beyond the outer limit of a seabed zone, as defined in article II, any nuclear weapons or any other types of weapons of mass destruction as well as structures, launching installations or any other facilities specifically designed for storing, testing or using such weapons.

2. The undertakings of paragraph 1 of this article shall also apply to the seabed zone referred to in the same paragraph, except that within such seabed zone, they shall not apply either to the coastal State or to the seabed beneath its territorial waters.

3. The States Parties to this Treaty undertake not to assist, encourage or induce any State to carry out activities referred to in paragraph 1 of this article and not to participate in any other way in such actions.

Article II

For the purpose of this Treaty, the outer limit of the seabed zone referred to in article I shall be coterminous with the twelve-mile outer limit of the zone referred to in part II of the Convention on the Territorial Sea and the Contiguous Zone, signed at Geneva on

April 29, 1958, and shall be measured in accordance with the provisions of part I, section II, of that Convention and in accordance with international law.

Article III

1. In order to promote the objectives of and insure compliance with the provisions of this Treaty, each State Party to the Treaty shall have the right to verify through observations the activities of other States Parties to the Treaty on the seabed and the ocean floor and in the subsoil thereof beyond the zone referred to in article I, provided that observation does not interfere with such activities.

2. If after such observation reasonable doubts remain concerning the fulfillment of the obligations assumed under the Treaty, the State Party having such doubts and the State Party that is responsible for the activities giving rise to the doubts shall consult with a view to removing the doubts. If the doubts persist, the State Party having such doubts shall notify the other States Parties, and the Parties concerned shall cooperate on such further procedures for verification as may be agreed, including appropriate inspection of objects, structures, installations or other facilities that reasonably may be expected to be of a kind described in article I. The Parties in the region of the activities, including any coastal State, and any other Party so requesting, shall be entitled to participate in such consultation and cooperation. After completion of the further procedures for verification, an appropriate report shall be circulated to other Parties by the Party that initiated such procedures.

3. If the State responsible for the activities giving rise to the reasonable doubts is not identifiable by observation of the object, structure, installation or other facility, the State Party having such doubts shall notify and make appropriate inquiries of States Parties in the region of the activities and of any other State Party. If it is ascertained through these inquiries that a particular State Party is responsible for the activities, that State Party shall consult and cooperate with other Parties as provided in paragraph 2 of this article. If the identity of the State responsible for the activities cannot be ascertained through these inquiries, then further verification procedures, including inspection, may be undertaken by the inquiring State Party, which shall invite the participation of the Parties in the region of the activities, including any coastal State, and of any other Party desiring to cooperate.

4. If consultation and cooperation pursuant to paragraphs 2 and 3 of this article have not removed the doubts concerning the activities and there remains a serious question concerning fulfillment of the obligations assumed under this Treaty, a State Party may, in accordance with the provisions of the Charter of the United Nations, refer the matter to the Security Council, which may take action in accordance with the Charter.

5. Verification pursuant to this article may be undertaken by any State Party using its own means, or with the full or partial assistance of any other State Party, or through appropriate international procedures within the framework of the United Nations and in accordance with its Charter.

6. Verification activities pursuant to this Treaty shall not interfere with activities of other States Parties and shall be conducted with due regard for rights recognized under international law, including the freedoms of the high seas and the rights of coastal States with respect to the exploration and exploitation of their continental shelves.

Article IV

Nothing in this Treaty shall be interpreted as supporting or prejudicing the position of any State Party with respect to existing international conventions, including the 1958

Convention on the Territorial Sea and the Contiguous Zone, or with respect to rights or claims which such State Party may assert, or with respect to recognition or non-recognition of rights or claims asserted by any other State, related to waters off its coasts, including, *inter alia,* territorial seas and contiguous zones, or to the seabed and the ocean floor, including continental shelves.

Article V

The Parties to this Treaty undertake to continue negotiations in good faith concerning further measures in the field of disarmament for the prevention of an arms race on the seabed, the ocean floor and the subsoil thereof.

Article VI

Any State Party may propose amendments to this Treaty. Amendments shall enter into force for each State Party accepting the amendments upon their acceptance by a majority of the States Parties to the Treaty and, thereafter, for each remaining State Party on the date of acceptance by it.

Article VII

Five years after the entry into force of this Treaty, a conference of Parties to the Treaty shall be held at Geneva, Switzerland, in order to review the operation of this Treaty with a view to assuring that the purposes of the preamble and the provisions of the Treaty are being realized. Such review shall take into account any relevant technological developments. The review conference shall determine, in accordance with the views of a majority of those Parties attending, whether and when an additional review conference shall be convened.

Article VIII

Each State Party to this Treaty shall in exercising its national sovereignty have the right to withdraw from this Treaty if it decides that extraordinary events related to the subject matter of this Treaty have jeopardized the supreme interests of its country. It shall give notice of such withdrawal to all other States Parties to the Treaty and to the United Nations Security Council three months in advance. Such notice shall include a statement of the extraordinary events it considers to have jeopardized its supreme interests.

Article IX

The provisions of this Treaty shall in no way affect the obligations assumed by States Parties to the Treaty under international instruments establishing zones free from nuclear weapons.

Article X

1. This Treaty shall be open for signature to all States. Any State which does not sign the Treaty before its entry into force in accordance with paragraph 3 of this article may accede to it at any time.

2. This Treaty shall be subject to ratification by signatory States. Instruments of ratification and of accession shall be deposited with the Governments of the United States of America, the United Kingdom of Great Britain and Northern Ireland, and the Union of Soviet Socialist Republics, which are hereby designated the Depositary Governments.

3. This Treaty shall enter into force after the deposit of instruments of ratification by twenty-two Governments, including the Governments designated as Depositary Governments of this Treaty.

4. For states whose instruments of ratification or accession are deposited after the entry into force of this Treaty, it shall enter into force on the date of the deposit of their instruments of ratification or accession.

5. The Depositary Governments shall promptly inform the Governments of all signatory and acceding States of the date of each signature, of the date of deposit of each instrument of ratification or of accession, of the date of the entry into force of this Treaty, and of the receipt of other notices.

6. This Treaty shall be registered by the Depositary Governments pursuant to Article 102 of the Charter of the United Nations.

Article XI

This Treaty, the English, Russian, French, Spanish and Chinese texts of which are equally authentic, shall be deposited in the archives of the Depositary Governments. Duly certified copies of this Treaty shall be transmitted by the Depositary Governments to the Governments of the States signatory and acceding thereto.

IN WITNESS WHEREOF the undersigned, being duly authorized thereto, have signed this Treaty.

DONE in triplicate, at the cities of Washington, London and Moscow, this eleventh day of February, one thousand nine hundred seventy-one.

Seabed Arms Control Treaty

Country	Date of[1] Signature	Date of Deposit[1] of Ratification	Date of Deposit[1] of Accession
Afghanistan	2/11/71	4/22/71	
Argentina	9/3/71		
Australia	2/11/71	1/23/73	
Austria	2/11/71	8/10/72	
Belgium	2/11/71	11/20/72	
Benin	3/18/71		
Bolivia	2/11/71		
Botswana	2/11/71	11/10/72	
Brazil	9/3/71		
Bulgaria	2/11/71	4/16/71	
Burma	2/11/71		
Burundi	2/11/71		
Byelorussian S.S.R.[2]	3/3/71	9/14/71	
Cameroon	11/11/71		
Canada	2/11/71	5/17/72	
Cape Verde			10/24/79
Central African Republic	2/11/71		
China (Taiwan)	2/11/71	2/22/72	
Colombia	2/11/71		
Congo, People's Republic of (Brazzaville)			10/23/78
Costa Rica	2/11/71		
Cyprus	2/11/71	11/17/71	
Czechoslovakia	2/11/71	1/11/72	
Denmark	2/11/71	6/15/71	
Dominican Republic	2/11/71	2/11/72	
Equatorial Guinea	6/4/71		
Ethiopia	2/11/71	7/14/77	
Finland	2/11/71	6/8/71	
Gambia, The	5/18/71		
German Democratic Republic	2/11/71	7/27/71	
Germany, Federal Republic of	6/8/71	11/18/75	
Ghana	2/11/71	8/9/72	
Greece	2/11/71		
Guatemala	2/11/71		
Guinea	2/11/71		
Guinea-Bissau			8/20/76

See footnotes on page 239.

Country	Date of[1] Signature	Date of Deposit[1] of Ratification	Date of Deposit[1] of Accession
Honduras	2/11/71		
Hungary	2/11/71	8/13/71	
Iceland	2/11/71	5/30/72	
India			7/20/73
Iran	2/11/71	8/26/71	
Iraq	2/22/71	9/13/72	
Ireland	2/11/71	8/19/71	
Italy	2/11/71	9/3/74	
Ivory Coast			1/14/72
Jamaica	10/11/71		
Japan	2/11/71	6/21/71	
Jordan	2/11/71	8/17/71	
Kampuchea	2/11/71		
Korea, Republic of	2/11/71		
Laos	2/11/71	10/19/71	
Lebanon	2/11/71		
Lesotho	9/8/71	4/3/73	
Liberia	2/11/71		
Luxembourg	2/11/71		
Madagascar	9/14/71		
Malaysia	5/20/71	6/21/72	
Mali	2/11/71		
Malta	2/11/71	5/4/71	
Mauritius	2/11/71	4/23/71	
Mongolia	2/11/71	10/8/71	
Morocco	2/11/71	7/26/71	
Nepal	2/11/71	7/6/71	
Netherlands	2/11/71	1/14/76	
New Zealand	2/11/71	2/24/72	
Nicaragua	2/11/71	2/7/73	
Niger	2/11/71	8/9/71	
Norway	2/11/71	6/28/71	
Panama	2/11/71	3/20/74	
Paraguay	2/23/71		
Poland	2/11/71	11/15/71	
Portugal			6/24/75
Qatar			11/12/74

See footnotes on page 239.

Country	Date of[1] Signature	Date of Deposit[1] of Ratification	Date of Deposit[1] of Accession
Romania	2/11/71	7/10/72	
Rwanda	2/11/71	5/20/75	
São Tome and Principe			8/24/79
Saudi Arabia	1/7/72	6/23/72	
Senegal	3/17/71		
Seychelles			6/29/76[1]
Sierra Leone	2/11/71		
Singapore	5/5/71	9/10/76	
South Africa	2/11/71	11/14/73	
Sudan	2/11/71		
Swaziland	2/11/71	8/9/71	
Sweden	2/11/71	4/28/72	
Switzerland	2/11/71	5/4/76	
Tanzania	2/11/71		
Togo	4/2/71	6/28/71	
Tunisia	2/11/71	10/22/71	
Turkey	2/25/71	10/19/72	
Ukrainian S.S.R.[2]	3/3/71	9/3/71	
Union of Soviet Socialist Republics	2/11/71	5/18/72	
United Kingdom	2/11/71	5/18/72	
United States	2/11/71	5/18/72	
Uruguay	2/11/71		
Yemen Arab Republic (Sana)	2/23/71		
Yemen, People's Democratic Republic of (Aden)	2/23/71	6/1/79	
Yugoslavia	3/2/71	10/25/73	
Zambia			10/9/72
Total[3]	87	56	10

See footnotes on page 239.

Agreement on Measures To Reduce the Risk of Outbreak of Nuclear War Between the United States of America and the Union of Soviet Socialist Republics

The very existence of nuclear-weapons systems, even under the most sophisticated command-and-control procedures, obviously is a source of constant concern. Despite the most elaborate precautions, it is conceivable that technical malfunction or human failure, a misinterpreted incident or unauthorized action, could trigger a nuclear disaster or nuclear war. In the course of the Strategic Arms Limitation Talks (SALT), the United States and the Soviet Union reached two agreements that manifest increasing recognition of the need to reduce such risks, and that complement the central goal of the negotiations.

In early sessions, discussions parallel to the main SALT negotiations showed a degree of mutual concern regarding the problem of accidental war that indicated encouraging prospects of accord. These preliminary explorations resulted in the establishment of two special working groups under the direction of the two SALT delegations. One group focused on arrangements for exchanging information to reduce uncertainties and prevent misunderstandings in the event of a nuclear incident. The other addressed a related topic—ways to improve the direct communications link between Washington and Moscow. By the summer of 1971, major substantive issues had been resolved, and draft international agreements were referred by the SALT delegations to their governments. Both agreements were signed in Washington on September 30, 1971, and came into force on that date.

The "Agreement on Measures To Reduce the Risk of Outbreak of Nuclear War between the United States of America and the Union of Soviet Socialist Republics" covers three main areas:

— A pledge by both sides to take measures each considers necessary to maintain and improve its organizational and technical safeguards against accidental or unauthorized use of nuclear weapons.

— Arrangements for immediate notification should a risk of nuclear war arise from such incidents, from detection of unidentified objects on early warning systems, or from any accidental, unauthorized, or other unexplained incident involving a possible detonation of a nuclear weapon.

— Advance notification of any planned missile launches beyond the territory of the launching party and in the direction of the other party.

The agreement provides that for urgent communication "in situations requiring prompt clarification" the "Hot Line" will be used. The duration of the agreement is not limited, and the parties undertake to consult on questions that may arise and to discuss possible amendments aimed at further reduction of risks.

Agreement on Measures To Reduce the Risk of Outbreak of Nuclear War Between the United States of America and the Union of Soviet Socialist Republics

Signed at Washington September 30, 1971
Entered into force September 30, 1971

The United States of America and the Union of Soviet Socialist Republics, hereinafter referred to as the Parties:

Taking into account the devastating consequences that nuclear war would have for all mankind, and recognizing the need to exert every effort to avert the risk of outbreak of such a war, including measures to guard against accidental or unauthorized use of nuclear weapons,

Believing that agreement on measures for reducing the risk of outbreak of nuclear war serves the interests of strengthening international peace and security, and is in no way contrary to the interests of any other country,

Bearing in mind that continued efforts are also needed in the future to seek ways of reducing the risk of outbreak of nuclear war,

Have agreed as follows:

Article 1

Each Party undertakes to maintain and to improve, as it deems necessary, its existing organizational and technical arrangements to guard against the accidental or unauthorized use of nuclear weapons under its control.

Article 2

The Parties undertake to notify each other immediately in the event of an accidental, unauthorized or any other unexplained incident involving a possible detonation of a nuclear weapon which could create a risk of outbreak of nuclear war. In the event of such an incident, the Party whose nuclear weapon is involved will immediately make every effort to take necessary measures to render harmless or destroy such weapon without its causing damage.

Article 3

The Parties undertake to notify each other immediately in the event of detection by missile warning systems of unidentified objects, or in the event of signs of interference with these systems or with related communications facilities, if such occurrences could create a risk of outbreak of nuclear war between the two countries.

Article 4

Each Party undertakes to notify the other Party in advance of any planned missile launches if such launches will extend beyond its national territory in the direction of the other Party.

Article 5

Each Party, in other situations involving unexplained nuclear incidents, undertakes to act in such a manner as to reduce the possibility of its actions being misinterpreted by the other Party. In any such situation, each Party may inform the other Party or request information when, in its view, this is warranted by the interests of averting the risk of outbreak of nuclear war.

Article 6

For transmission of urgent information, notifications and requests for information in situations requiring prompt clarification, the Parties shall make primary use of the Direct Communications Link between the Governments of the United States of America and the Union of Soviet Socialist Republics.

For transmission of other information, notifications and requests for information, the Parties, at their own discretion, may use any communications facilities, including diplomatic channels, depending on the degree of urgency.

Article 7

The Parties undertake to hold consultations, as mutually agreed, to consider questions relating to implementation of the provisions of this Agreement, as well as to discuss possible amendments thereto aimed at further implementation of the purposes of this Agreement.

Article 8

This Agreement shall be of unlimited duration.

Article 9

This Agreement shall enter into force upon signature.

DONE at Washington on September 30, 1971, in two copies, each in the English and Russian languages, both texts being equally authentic.

**FOR THE UNITED STATES
OF AMERICA:**

**FOR THE UNION OF SOVIET
SOCIALIST REPUBLICS:**

Agreement Between the United States of America and the Union of Soviet Socialist Republics on Measures To Improve the USA-USSR Direct Communications Link (With Annex, Supplementing and Modifying the Memorandum of Understanding With Annex, of June 20,1963)

The United States and the Soviet Union had agreed in 1963 to establish, for use in time of emergency, a direct communications link between the two governments. The original "Hot Line" (see "Hot Line" section) agreement provided for a wire telegraph circuit, routed Washington-London-Copenhagen-Stockholm-Helsinki-Moscow, and as a backup system a radio telegraph circuit routed Washington-Tangier-Moscow. These circuits had one terminal in the United States and one in the U.S.S.R.

Concern about the risk that nuclear accidents, ambiguous incidents, or unauthorized actions might lead to the outbreak of nuclear war contributed to concern about the reliability and survivability of the "Hot Line," which had shown its value in emergency situations. The advances in satellite communications technology that had occurred since 1963, moveover, offered the possibility of greater reliability than the arrangements originally agreed upon. Hence, when the SALT delegations established a special working group under their direction to work on "accidents measures," a similar group was established to consider ways to improve the Washington-Moscow direct communications link.

The understandings reached by this group were reported to the SALT delegations in the summer of 1971 and became a formal agreement to improve the "Hot Line" at the same time that the related agreement on steps to reduce the risks of accidental war was concluded.

The terms of the agreement, with its annex detailing the specifics of operation, equipment, and allocation of costs, provided for establishment of two satellite communications circuits between the United States and the U.S.S.R., with a system of multiple terminals in each country. The United States was to provide one circuit via the Intelsat system, and the Soviet Union a circuit via its Molniya II system. The agreement of 1963 was to remain in force "except to the extent that its provisions are modified by this Agreement and Annex thereto." The original circuits were to be maintained until it was agreed that the operation of the satellite circuits made them no longer necessary.

On September 30, 1971, the agreement was signed in Washington. The two satellite communications circuits became operational in January 1978. The radio circuit provided for in the 1963 agreement was then terminated, but the wire telegraph circuit has been retained as a backup.

Agreement Between the United States of America and the Union of Soviet Socialist Republics on Measures To Improve the USA-USSR Direct Communications Link

Signed at Washington September 30, 1971
Entered into force September 30, 1971

The United States of America and the Union of Soviet Socialist Republics, hereinafter referred to as the Parties,

Noting the positive experience gained in the process of operating the existing Direct Communications Link between the United States of America and the Union of Soviet Socialist Republics, which was established for use in time of emergency pursuant to the Memorandum of Understanding Regarding the Establishment of a Direct Communications Link, signed on June 20, 1963,

Having examined, in a spirit of mutual understanding, matters relating to the improvement and modernization of the Direct Communications Link,

Having agreed as follows:

Article 1

1. For the purpose of increasing the reliability of the Direct Communications Link, there shall be established and put into operation the following:

(a) two additional circuits between the United States of America and the Union of Soviet Socialist Republics each using a satellite communications system, with each Party selecting a satellite communications system of its own choice.

(b) a system of terminals (more than one) in the territory of each Party for the Direct Communications Link, with the locations and number of terminals in the United States of America to be determined by the United States side, and the locations and number of terminals in the Union of Soviet Socialist Republics to be determined by the Soviet side.

2. Matters relating to the implementation of the aforementioned improvements of the Direct Communications Link are set forth in the Annex which is attached hereto and forms an integral part hereof.

Article 2

Each Party confirms its intention to take all possible measures to assure the continuous and reliable operation of the communications circuits and the system of terminals of the Direct Communications Link for which it is responsible in accordance with this Agreement and the Annex hereto, as well as to communicate to the head of its Government any messages received via the Direct Communications Link from the head of Government of the other Party.

Article 3

The Memorandum of Understanding Between the United States of America and the Union of Soviet Socialist Republics Regarding the Establishment of a Direct Communications Link, signed on June 20, 1963, with the Annex thereto, shall remain in force, except to the extent that its provisions are modified by this Agreement and Annex hereto.

Article 4

The undertakings of the Parties hereunder shall be carried out in accordance with their respective Constitutional processes.

Article 5

This Agreement, including the Annex hereto, shall enter into force upon signature.

DONE at Washington on September 30, 1971, in two copies, each in the English and Russian languages, both texts being equally authentic.

**FOR THE UNITED STATES
OF AMERICA:**

**FOR THE UNION OF SOVIET
SOCIALIST REPUBLICS:**

Annex to the Agreement Between the United States of America and the Union of Soviet Socialist Republics on Measures To Improve the USA-USSR Direct Communications Link

Improvements to the USA-USSR Direct Communications Link shall be implemented in accordance with the provisions set forth in this Annex.

I. CIRCUITS

(a) Each of the original circuits established pursuant to paragraph 1 of the Annex to the Memorandum of Understanding, dated June 20, 1963, shall continue to be maintained and operated as part of the Direct Communications Link until such time, after the satellite communications circuits provided for herein become operational, as the agencies designated pursuant to paragraph III (hereinafter referred to as the "designated agencies") mutually agree that such original circuit is no longer necessary. The provisions of paragraph 7 of the Annex to the Memorandum of Understanding, dated June 20, 1963, shall continue to govern the allocation of the costs of maintaining and operating such original circuits.

(b) Two additional circuits shall be established using two satellite communications systems. Taking into account paragraph I (e) below, the United States side shall provide one circuit via the Intelsat system and the Soviet side shall provide one circuit via the Molniya II system. The two circuits shall be duplex telephone band-width circuits conforming to CCITT standards, equipped for secondary telegraphic multiplexing. Transmission and reception of messages over the Direct Communications Link shall be effected in accordance with applicable recommendations of international communications regulations, as well as with mutually agreed instructions.

(c) When the reliability of both additional circuits has been established to the mutual satisfaction of the designated agencies, they shall be used as the primary circuits of the Direct Communications Link for transmission and reception of teleprinter messages between the United States and the Soviet Union.

(d) Each satellite communications circuit shall utilize an earth station in the territory of the United States, a communications satellite transponder, and an earth station in the territory of the Soviet Union. Each Party shall be responsible for linking the earth stations in its territory to its own terminals of the Direct Communications Link.

(e) For the circuits specified in paragraph I (b):

—The Soviet side will provide and operate at least one earth station in its territory for the satellite communications circuit in the Intelsat system, and will also arrange for the use of suitable earth station facilities in its territory for the satellite communications circuit in the Molniya II system. The United States side, through a governmental agency or other United States legal entity, will make appropriate arrangements with Intelsat with regard to access for the Soviet Intelsat earth station to the Intelsat space segment, as well as for the use of the applicable portion of the Intelsat space segment.

—The United States side will provide and operate at least one earth station in its territory for the satellite communications circuit in the Molniya II system, and will also arrange for the use of suitable earth station facilities in its territory for the satellite communications circuit in the Intelsat system.

(f) Each earth station shall conform to the performance specifications and operating procedures at the corresponding satellite communications system and the ratio of antenna gain to the equivalent noise temperature should be no less than 31 decibels. Any deviation from these specifications and procedures which may be required in any unusual situation shall be worked out and mutually agreed upon by the designated agencies of both Parties after consultation.

(g) The operational commissioning dates for the satellite communications circuits based on the Intelsat and Molniya II systems shall be as agreed upon by the designated agencies of the Parties through consultations.

(h) The United States side shall bear the costs of: (1) providing and operating the Molniya II earth station in its territory; (2) the use of the Intelsat earth station in its territory; and (3) the transmission of messages via the Intelsat system. The Soviet side shall bear the costs of: (1) providing and operating the Intelsat earth station in its territory; (2) the use of the Molniya II earth station in its territory; and (3) the transmission of messages via the Molniya II system. Payment of the costs of the satellite communications circuits shall be effected without any transfer of payments between the Parties.

(i) Each Party shall be responsible for providing to the other Party notification of any proposed modification or replacement of the communications satellite system containing the circuit provided by it that might require accommodation by earth stations using that system or otherwise affect the maintenance or operation of the Direct Communications Link. Such notification should be given sufficiently in advance to enable the designated agencies to consult and to make, before the modification or replacement is effected, such preparation as may be agreed upon for accommodation by the affected earth stations.

II. TERMINALS

(a) Each Party shall establish a system of terminals in its territory for the exchange of messages with the other Party, and shall determine the locations and number of terminals in such a system. Terminals of the Direct Communications Link shall be designated "USA" and "USSR."

(b) Each Party shall take necessary measures to provide for rapidly switching circuits among terminal points in such a manner that only one terminal location is connected to the circuits at any one time.

(c) Each Party shall use teleprinter equipment from its own sources to equip the additional terminals for the transmission and reception of messages from the United States to the Soviet Union in the English language and from the Soviet Union to the United States in the Russian language.

(d) The terminals of the Direct Communications Link shall be provided with encoding equipment. One-time tape encoding equipment shall be used for transmissions via the Direct Communications Link. A mutually agreed quantity of encoding equipment of a modern and reliable type selected by the United States side, with spares, test equipment, technical literature and operating supplies, shall be furnished by the United States side to the Soviet side against payment of the cost thereof by the Soviet side; additional spares for the encoding equipment supplied will be furnished as necessary.

(e) Keying tapes shall be supplied in accordance with the provisions set forth in paragraph 4 of the Annex to the Memorandum of Understanding, dated June 20, 1963. Each Party shall be responsible for reproducing and distributing additional keying tapes for its system of terminals and for implementing procedures which ensure that the required synchronization of encoding equipment can be effected from any one terminal at any time.

III. OTHER MATTERS

Each Party shall designate the agencies responsible for arrangements regarding the establishment of the additional circuits and the systems of terminals provided for in this Agreement and Annex, for their operation and for their continuity and reliability. These agencies shall, on the basis of direct contacts:

(a) arrange for the exchange of required performance specifications and operating procedures for the earth stations of the communications systems using Intelsat and Molniya II satellites;

(b) arrange for testing, acceptance and commissioning of the satellite circuits and for operation of these circuits after commissioning; and,

(c) decide matters and develop instructions relating to the operation of the secondary teleprinter multiplex system used on the satellite circuits.

Convention on the Prohibition of the Development, Production and Stockpiling of Bacteriological (Biological) and Toxin Weapons and on Their Destruction

Biological and chemical weapons have generally been associated in the public mind, and the extensive use of poison gas in World War I (resulting in over a million casualties and over 100,000 deaths) led to the Geneval Protocol of 1925 prohibiting the use of both poison gas *and* bacteriological methods in warfare. At the 1932–1937 Disarmament Conference, unsuccessful attempts were made to work out an agreement that would prohibit the production and stockpiling of biological and chemical weapons. During World War II, new and more toxic nerve gases were developed, and research and development was begun on biological weapons. Neither side used such weapons. President Roosevelt, in a statement warning the Axis powers against the use of chemical weapons, declared:

> Use of such weapons has been outlawed by the general opinion of civilized mankind. This country has not used them, and I hope we never will be compelled to use them. I state categorically that we shall under no circumstances resort to the use of such weapons unless they are first used by our enemies.

In the postwar negotiations on general disarmament, biological and chemical weapons were usually considered together with nuclear and conventional weapons. Both the United States and Soviet Union, in the 1962 sessions of the Eighteen-Nation Disarmament Committee (ENDC), offered plans for general and complete disarmament that included provisions for eliminating chemical and biological weapons.

An issue that long hindered progress was whether chemical and biological weapons should continue to be linked. A British draft convention submitted to the ENDC on July 10, 1969, concentrated on the elimination of biological weapons only. A draft convention proposed in the General Assembly by the Soviet Union and its allies on September 19 dealt with both chemical and biological weapons. The Soviet representative argued that they had been treated together in the Geneva Protocol and in the General Assembly resolutions and report, and should continue to be dealt with in the same instrument. A separate biological weapons convention, he warned, might serve to intensify the chemical arms race.

The United States supported the British position and stressed the difference between the two kinds of weapons. Unlike biological weapons, chemical weapons had actually been used in modern warfare. Many states maintained chemical weapons in their arsenals to deter the use of this type of weapons against them, and to provide a retaliatory capability if deterrence failed. Many of these nations, the United States pointed out, would be reluctant to give up this capability without reliable assurance that other nations were not developing, producing, and stockpiling chemical weapons.

While the United States did not consider prohibition of one of these classes of weapons less urgent or important than the other, it held that biological weapons presented less intractable problems, and an agreement on banning them should not be delayed until agreement on reliable prohibition of chemical weapons could be reached.

Shortly after President Nixon took office, he ordered a review of U.S. policy and programs regarding biological and chemical warfare. On November 25, 1969, the President declared that the United States unilaterally renounced first use of lethal or incapacitating chemical agents and weapons and unconditionally renounced all methods of biological warfare. Henceforth the U.S. biological program would be confined to research on strictly defined measures of defense, such as immunization. The Department of Defense was ordered to draw up a plan for the disposal of existing stocks of biological agents and weapons. On February 14, 1970, the White House announced extension of the ban to cover toxins (substances falling between biologicals and chemicals in that they act like chemicals but are ordinarily produced by biological or microbic processes).

The American action was widely welcomed internationally, and the example was followed by others. Canada, Sweden, and the United Kingdom stated that they had no biological weapons and did not intend to produce any. It was generally recognized, however, that unilateral actions could not take the place of a binding international commitment. A number of nations, including the Soviet Union and its allies, continued to favor a comprehensive agreement covering both chemical and biological weapons.

Discussion throughout 1970 in the General Assembly and the Conference of the Committee on Disarmament (CCD)—as the ENDC was named after its enlargement to 26 members in August 1969—produced no agreement. A breakthrough came on March 30, 1971, however, when the Soviet Union and its allies changed their position and introduced a revised draft convention limited to biological weapons and toxins. It then became possible for the co-chairmen of the CCD—the U.S. and Soviet representatives—to work out an agreed draft, as they had done with the non-proliferation and the seabed treaties. On

August 5, the United States and the Soviet Union submitted separate but identical texts.

On December 16, the General Assembly approved a resolution, adopted by a vote of 110 to 0, commending the convention and expressing hope for the widest possible adherence.

The French representative abstained, explaining that the convention, though a step forward, might weaken the Geneval Protocol ban on the use of chemical weapons, and he did not consider that adequate international controls were provided. He announced, however, that France would enact domestic legislation prohibiting biological weapons, and this was done in June of the next year.

The People's Republic of China did not participate in the negotiations on the convention and did not sign it. At the 1972 General Assembly its representative attacked the convention as a "sham," and criticized it for not prohibiting chemical weapons.

The convention was opened for signature at Washington, London, and Moscow on April 10, 1972. President Nixon submitted it to the Senate on August 10, calling it "the first international agreement since World War II to provide for the actual elimination of an entire class of weapons from the arsenals of nations." The Senate Foreign Relations Committee delayed action on the convention, however, holding it for consideration after resolution of the herbicide and riot-control issues involved in the Geneva Protocol (see section on the Geneva Protocol).

In the latter part of 1974 the Ford Administration undertook a new initiative to obtain Senate consent to ratification of both the Geneva Protocol and the Biological Weapons Convention, and ACDA Director Fred Ikle testified with respect to both instruments before the Senate Foreign Relations Committee on December 10. Soon thereafter the Committee voted unanimously to send the two measures to the Senate floor, and on December 16 the Senate voted its approval, also unanimously.

President Ford signed instruments of ratification for the two measures on January 22, 1975.

Under the terms of the convention, the parties undertake not to develop, produce, stockpile, or acquire biological agents or toxins "of types and in quantities that have no justification for prophylactic, protective, and other peaceful purposes," as well as weapons and means of delivery. All such materiel is to be destroyed within 9 months of the convention's entry into force. In January 1976, all heads of Federal departments and agencies certified to the President that as of December 26, 1975, their respective departments and agencies were in full compliance with the convention.

The parties are to consult and cooperate in solving any problems that arise. Complaints of a breach of obligations may be lodged with the Security Council, and parties undertake to cooperate with any investigation the Council initiates. If the Security Council finds that a state has been endangered by a violation, the parties are to provide any assistance requested.

Nothing in the convention is to be interpreted as lessening the obligations imposed by the Geneva Protocol, and the parties undertake to pursue negotiations for a ban on chemical weapons.

In addition, articles provide for exchange of information on peaceful uses, amendment and review, and accession and withdrawal. The convention is of unlimited duration.

Convention on the Prohibition of the Development, Production and Stockpiling of Bacteriological (Biological) and Toxin Weapons and on Their Destruction

Signed at Washington, London, and Moscow April 10, 1972
Ratification advised by U.S. Senate December 16, 1974
Ratified by U.S. President January 22, 1975
U.S. ratification deposited at Washington, London, and Moscow March 26, 1975
Proclaimed by U.S. President March 26, 1975
Entered into force March 26, 1975

The States Parties to this Convention,

Determined to act with a view to achieving effective progress towards general and complete disarmament, including the prohibition and elimination of all types of weapons of mass destruction, and convinced that the prohibition of the development, production and stockpiling of chemical and bacteriological (biological) weapons and their elimination, through effective measures, will facilitate the achievement of general and complete disarmament under strict and effective international control,

Recognizing the important significance of the Protocol for the Prohibition of the Use in War of Asphyxiating, Poisonous or Other Gases, and of Bacteriological Methods of Warfare, signed at Geneva on June 17, 1925, and conscious also of the contribution which the said Protocol has already made, and continues to make, to mitigating the horrors of war,

Reaffirming their adherence to the principles and objectives of that Protocol and calling upon all States to comply strictly with them,

Recalling that the General Assembly of the United Nations has repeatedly condemned all actions contrary to the principles and objectives of the Geneva Protocol of June 17, 1925,

Desiring to contribute to the strengthening of confidence between peoples and the general improvement of the international atmosphere,

Desiring also to contribute to the realization of the purposes and principles of the Charter of the United Nations,

Convinced of the importance and urgency of eliminating from the arsenals of States, through effective measures, such dangerous weapons of mass destruction as those using chemical or bacteriological (biological) agents,

Recognizing that an agreement on the prohibition of bacteriological (biological) and toxin weapons represents a first possible step towards the achievement of agreement on effective measures also for the prohibition of the development, production and stockpiling of chemical weapons, and determined to continue negotiations to that end,

Determined, for the sake of all mankind, to exclude completely the possibility of bacteriological (biological) agents and toxins being used as weapons,

Convinced that such use would be repugnant to the conscience of mankind and that no effort should be spared to minimize this risk,

Have agreed as follows:

Article I

Each State Party to this Convention undertakes never in any circumstances to develop, produce, stockpile or otherwise acquire or retain:

(1) Microbial or other biological agents, or toxins whatever their origin or method of production, of types and in quantities that have no justification for prophylactic, protective or other peaceful purposes;

(2) Weapons, equipment or means of delivery designed to use such agents or toxins for hostile purposes or in armed conflict.

Article II

Each State Party to this Convention undertakes to destroy, or to divert to peaceful purposes, as soon as possible but not later than nine months after the entry into force of the Convention, all agents, toxins, weapons, equipment and means of delivery specified in article I of the Convention, which are in its possession or under its jurisdiction or control. In implementing the provisions of this article all necessary safety precautions shall be observed to protect populations and the environment.

Article III

Each State Party to this Convention undertakes not to transfer to any recipient what-soever, directly or indirectly, and not in any way to assist, encourage, or induce any State, group of States or international organizations to manufacture or otherwise acquire any of the agents, toxins, weapons, equipment or means of delivery specified in article I of the Convention.

Article IV

Each State Party to this Convention shall, in accordance with its constitutional processes, take any necessary measures to prohibit and prevent the development, production, stockpiling, acquisition, or retention of the agents, toxins, weapons, equipment and means of delivery specified in article I of the Convention, within the territory of such State, under its jurisdiction or under its control anywhere.

Article V

The States Parties to this Convention undertake to consult one another and to cooperate in solving any problems which may arise in relation to the objective of, or in the application of the provisions of, the Convention. Consultation and cooperation pursuant to this article may also be undertaken through appropriate international procedures within the framework of the United Nations and in accordance with its Charter.

Article VI

(1) Any State Party to this Convention which finds that any other State Party is acting in breach of obligations deriving from the provisions of the Convention may lodge a complaint with the Security Council of the United Nations. Such a complaint should include all possible evidence confirming its validity, as well as a request for its consideration by the Security Council.

(2) Each State Party to this Convention undertakes to cooperate in carrying out any investigation which the Security Council may initiate, in accordance with the provisions of the Charter of the United Nations, on the basis of the complaint received

by the Council. The Security Council shall inform the States Parties to the Convention of the results of the investigation.

Article VII

Each State Party to this Convention undertakes to provide or support assistance, in accordance with the United Nations Charter, to any Party to the Convention which so requests, if the Security Council decides that such Party has been exposed to danger as a result of violation of the Convention.

Article VIII

Nothing in this Convention shall be interpreted as in any way limiting or detracting from the obligations assumed by any State under the Protocol for the Prohibition of the Use in War of Asphyxiating, Poisonous or Other Gases, and of Bacteriological Methods of Warfare, signed at Geneva on June 17, 1925.

Article IX

Each State Party to this Convention affirms the recognized objective of effective prohibition of chemical weapons and, to this end, undertakes to continue negotiations in good faith with a view to reaching early agreement on effective measures for the prohibition of their development, production and stockpiling and for their destruction, and on appropriate measures concerning equipment and means of delivery specifically designed for the production or use of chemical agents for weapons purposes.

Article X

(1) The States Parties to this Convention undertake to facilitate, and have the right to participate in, the fullest possible exchange of equipment, materials and scientific and technological information for the use of bacteriological (biological) agents and toxins for peaceful purposes. Parties to the Convention in a position to do so shall also cooperate in contributing individually or together with other States or international organizations to the further development and application of scientific discoveries in the field of bacteriology (biology) for prevention of disease, or for other peaceful purposes.

(2) This Convention shall be implemented in a manner designed to avoid hampering the economic or technological development of States Parties to the Convention or international cooperation in the field of peaceful bacteriological (biological) activities, including the international exchange of bacteriological (biological) agents and toxins and equipment for the processing, use or production of bacteriological (biological) agents and toxins for peaceful purposes in accordance with the provisions of the Convention.

Article XI

Any State Party may propose amendments to this Convention. Amendments shall enter into force for each State Party accepting the amendments upon their acceptance by a majority of the States Parties to the Convention and thereafter for each remaining State Party on the date of acceptance by it.

Article XII

Five years after the entry into force of this Convention, or earlier if it is requested by a majority of Parties to the Convention by submitting a proposal to this effect to the

Depositary Governments, a conference of States Parties to the Convention shall be held at Geneva, Switzerland, to review the operation of the Convention, with a view to assuring that the purposes of the preamble and the provisions of the Convention, including the provisions concerning negotiations on chemical weapons, are being realized. Such review shall take into account any new scientific and technological developments relevant to the Convention.

Article XIII

(1) This Convention shall be of unlimited duration.

(2) Each State Party to this Convention shall in exercising its national sovereignty have the right to withdraw from the Convention if it decides that extraordinary events, related to the subject matter of the Convention, have jeopardized the supreme interests of its country. It shall give notice of such withdrawal to all other States Parties to the Convention and to the United Nations Security Council three months in advance. Such notice shall include a statement of the extraordinary events it regards as having jeopardized its supreme interests.

Article XIV

(1) This Convention shall be open to all States for signature. Any State which does not sign the Convention before its entry into force in accordance with paragraph (3) of this Article may accede to it at any time.

(2) This Convention shall be subject to ratification by signatory States. Instruments of ratification and instruments of accession shall be deposited with the Governments of the United States of America, the United Kingdom of Great Britain and Northern Ireland and the Union of Soviet Socialist Republics, which are hereby designated the Depositary Governments.

(3) This Convention shall enter into force after the deposit of instruments of ratification by twenty-two Governments, including the Governments designated as Depositaries of the Convention.

(4) For States whose instruments of ratification or accession are deposited subsequent to the entry into force of this Convention, it shall enter into force on the date of the deposit of their instruments of ratification or accession.

(5) The Depositary Governments shall promptly inform all signatory and acceding States of the date of each signature, the date of deposit of each instrument of ratification or of accession and the date of the entry into force of this Convention, and of the receipt of other notices.

(6) This Convention shall be registered by the Depositary Governments pursuant to Article 102 of the Charter of the United Nations.

Article XV

This Convention, the English, Russian, French, Spanish and Chinese texts of which are equally authentic, shall be deposited in the archives of the Depositary Governments. Duly certified copies of the Convention shall be transmitted by the Depositary Governments to the Governments of the signatory and acceding states.

Biological Weapons Convention

Country	Date of[1] Signature	Date of Deposit[1] of Ratification	Date of Deposit[1] of Accession
Afghanistan	4/10/72	3/26/75	
Argentina	8/1/72	11/27/79	
Australia	4/10/72	10/5/77	
Austria	4/10/72	8/10/73	
Barbados	2/16/73	2/16/73	
Belgium	4/10/72	3/15/79	
Benin	4/10/72	4/25/75	
Bhutan			6/8/78
Bolivia	4/10/72	10/30/75	
Botswana	4/10/72		
Brazil	4/10/72	2/27/73	
Bulgaria	4/10/72	8/2/72	
Burma	4/10/72		
Burundi	4/10/72		
Byelorussian S.S.R.[2]	4/10/72	3/26/75	
Canada	4/10/72	9/18/72	
Cape Verde			10/20/77
Central African Republic	4/10/72		
Chile	4/10/72		
China (Taiwan)	4/10/72	2/9/73	
Colombia	4/10/72		
Congo, People's Republic of (Brazzaville)			10/23/78
Costa Rica	4/10/72	12/17/73	
Cuba	4/12/72	4/21/76	
Cyprus	4/10/72	11/6/73	
Czechoslovakia	4/10/72	4/30/73	
Denmark	4/10/72	3/1/73	
Dominican Republic	4/10/72	2/23/73	
Ecuador	6/14/72	3/12/75	
Egypt	4/10/72		
El Salvador	4/10/72		
Ethiopia	4/10/72	6/26/75	
Fiji	2/22/73	9/4/73	
Finland	4/10/72	2/4/74	
Gabon	4/10/72		
Gambia, The	6/2/72		
German Democratic Republic	4/10/72	11/28/72	

See footnotes on page 239.

Country	Date of[1] Signature	Date of Deposit[1] of Ratification	Date of Deposit[1] of Accession
Germany, Federal Republic of	4/10/72		
Ghana	4/10/72	6/6/75	
Greece	4/10/72	12/10/75	
Guatemala	5/9/72	9/19/73	
Guinea-Bissau			8/20/76
Guyana	1/3/73		
Haiti	4/10/72		
Honduras	4/10/72	3/14/79	
Hungary	4/10/72	12/27/72	
Iceland	4/10/72	2/15/73	
India	1/15/73	7/15/74	
Indonesia	6/20/72		
Iran	4/10/72	8/22/73	
Iraq	5/11/72		
Ireland	4/10/72	10/27/72	
Italy	4/10/72	5/30/75	
Ivory Coast	5/23/72		
Jamaica			8/13/75
Japan	4/10/72		
Jordan	4/10/72	6/2/75	
Kampuchea	4/10/72		
Korea, Republic of	4/10/72		
Kuwait	4/14/72	7/18/72	
Laos	4/10/72	3/20/73	
Lebanon	4/10/72	6/13/75	
Lesotho	4/10/72		
Liberia	4/10/72		
Luxembourg	4/10/72	3/23/76	
Madagascar	10/13/72		
Malawi	4/10/72		
Malaysia	4/10/72		
Mali	4/10/72		
Malta	9/11/72	4/7/75	
Mauritania		1/15/73	
Mauritius	4/10/72	8/7/72	
Mexico	4/10/72	4/8/74	
Mongolia	4/10/72	9/5/72	
Morocco	5/2/72		
Nepal	4/10/72		
Netherlands	4/10/72		

See footnotes on page 239.

Country	Date of[1] Signature	Date of Deposit[1] of Ratification	Date of Deposit[1] of Accession
New Zealand	4/10/72	12/13/72	
Nicaragua	4/10/72	8/7/75	
Niger	4/21/72	6/23/72	
Nigeria	7/3/72	7/3/73	
Norway	4/10/72	8/1/73	
Pakistan	4/10/72	9/25/74	
Panama	5/2/72	3/20/74	
Paraguay			6/9/76
Peru	4/10/72		
Philippines	4/10/72	5/21/73	
Poland	4/10/72	1/25/73	
Portugal	6/29/72	5/15/75	
Qatar	11/14/72	4/17/75	
Romania	4/10/72	7/25/79	
Rwanda	4/10/72	5/20/75	
San Marino	9/12/72	3/11/75	
São Tome and Principe			8/24/79
Saudi Arabia	4/12/72	5/24/72	
Senegal	4/10/72	3/26/75	
Sierra Leone	11/7/72	6/29/76	
Seychelles			10/24/79
Singapore	6/19/72	12/2/75	
Somalia	7/3/72		
South Africa	4/10/72	11/3/75	
Spain	4/10/72	6/20/79	
Sri Lanka	4/10/72		
Sweden	2/27/75	2/5/76	
Switzerland	4/10/72	5/4/76	
Syrian Arab Republic	4/14/72		
Tanzania	8/16/72		
Thailand	1/17/73	5/28/75	
Togo	4/10/72	11/10/76	
Tunisia	4/10/72	5/18/73	
Turkey	4/10/72	11/5/74	
Ukrainian S.S.R.[2]	4/10/72	3/26/75	
Union of Soviet Socialist Republics	4/10/72	3/26/75	
United Arab Emirates	9/28/72		
United Kingdom	4/10/72	3/26/75	
United States	4/10/72	3/26/75	

See footnotes on page 239.

Country	Date of[1] Signature	Date of Deposit[1] of Ratification	Date of Deposit[1] of Accession
Venezuela	4/10/72	10/18/78	
Yemen Arab Republic (Sana)	4/10/72		
Yemen, People's Democratic Republic of (Aden)	4/26/72	6/1/79	
Yugoslavia	4/10/72	10/25/73	
Zaire	4/10/72	9/16/75	
Total[3]	111	76	8

See footnotes on page 239.

Strategic Arms Limitation Talks (SALT I)

SALT I, the first series of Strategic Arms Limitation Talks, extended from November 1969 to May 1972. During that period the United States and the Soviet Union negotiated the first agreements to place limits and restraints on some of their central and most important armaments. In a "Treaty...on the Limitation of Anti-Ballistic Missile Systems," they moved to end an emerging competition in defensive systems that threatened to spur offensive competition to still greater heights. In an "Interim Agreement...on Certain Measures With Respect to the Limitation of Strategic Offensive Arms," the two nations took the first steps to check the rivalry in their most powerful land- and submarine-based offensive nuclear weapons.

The earliest efforts to halt the growth in strategic arms had met with no success. Strategic weapons had been included in the U.S. and Soviet proposals for general and complete disarmament. But the failure of these comprehensive schemes left strategic arms unrestrained. The United States was the first to suggest dissociating them from comprehensive disarmament plans—proposing, at the Geneva-based Eighteen-Nation Disarmament Committee in January 1964, that the two sides should "explore a verified freeze of the number and characteristics of their strategic nuclear offensive and defensive vehicles."

The competition in offensive and defensive armaments continued. By 1966 the Soviet Union had begun to deploy an antiballistic missile defense around Moscow; and that year the People's Republic of China successfully tested a nuclear missile. In the United States, research and development were leading to U.S. deployment of its own ABM system.

In March 1967, after an exchange of communications with Soviet leaders, President Johnson announced that Premier Kosygin had indicated a willingness to begin discussions. Attempts to get talks underway, however, were not successful.

On September 18, 1967, the United States announced that it would begin deployment of a "thin" antiballistic missile (ABM) system. The Administration emphasized that the deployment was intended to meet a possible limited Chinese ICBM threat, to underscore U.S. security assurances to its allies by reinforcing the U.S. deterrent, and to add protection against "the improbable but possible accidental launch of an intercontinental missile by one of the nuclear powers." This program for limited ABM defense brought sharply divided views in public and congressional debate regarding the efficacy and desirability of an ABM system and its possible effects on the arms race.

In announcing the U.S. decision, Secretary of Defense McNamara said,

> Let me emphasize—and I cannot do so too strongly—that our decision to go ahead with a limited ABM deployment in no way indicates that we feel an agreement with the Soviet Union on the limitation of strategic nuclear offensive and defensive forces is in any way less urgent or desirable.

Through diplomatic channels in Washington and Moscow, discussions with Soviet representatives in the ENDC, and exchanges at the highest levels of the two governments, the United States continued to press for a Soviet commitment to discuss strategic arms limitation. But it was not until the following year that evidence of a Soviet reassessment of its position emerged. On July 1, 1968, President Johnson announced, at the signing of the Non-Proliferation Treaty, that agreement had been reached with the Soviet Union to begin discussions on limiting and reducing both strategic nuclear weapons delivery systems and defenses against ballistic missiles. The date and place for the talks had not yet been announced, when, on August 20, the Soviet Union began its invasion of Czechoslovakia, and the talks were indefinitely postponed.

On January 20, 1969, the day that President Nixon assumed office, a statement by the Soviet Foreign Ministry expressed willingness to discuss strategic arms limitations. The new President promptly voiced his support for talks, and initiated, under the aegis of the National Security Council, an extensive and detailed review of the strategic, political, and verification aspects of the problem.

In October, the White House and the Kremlin announced that the Strategic Arms Limitation Talks would begin in Helsinki on November 17, 1969, "for preliminary discussion of the questions involved." The Director of ACDA, Gerard Smith, was named to head the U.S. delegation and led it throughout the 2½-year series of SALT I negotiations.

In the first session of the talks, from November 17 to December 22, each side gained a better understanding of the other's views and of the range of questions to be considered. It was agreed that the talks would be private, to encourage a free and frank exchange, and the stage was set for the main negotiations, which opened in Vienna in April 1970. Sessions thereafter alternated between Helsinki and Vienna until the first accords were reached in May 1972. (When SALT II began, in November 1972, to reduce the administrative burdens involved in shifting sites it was agreed to hold them henceforth in one place—Geneva.)

Soviet and American weapons systems were far from symmetrical. The Soviet Union had continued its development and deployment of heavy ballistic missiles and had overtaken the U.S. lead in land-based ICBMs. During the SALT I years alone its ICBMs rose from around 1,000 to around 1,500, and they were being deployed at the rate of some 200 annually. Soviet submarine-based launchers had quadrupled. The huge payload capacity of some Soviet missiles ("throw-weight") was seen as a possible threat to U.S. land-based strategic missiles even in heavily protected ("hardened") launch-sites.

The United States had not increased its deployment of strategic missiles since 1967, when its ICBMs numbered 1,054 and its SLBMs, 656, but it was conducting a vigorous program of substituting missiles with "Multiple Independently-targeted Re-entry Vehicles" (MIRV). These MIRVs permit an individual missile to carry a number of warheads directed at separate targets. MIRVs gave the United States a lead in numbers of warheads, and the United States retained a lead in long-range bombers. The Soviet Union had a limited ABM system around Moscow; the United States had shifted from its earlier plan for a "thin" ABM defense of certain American cities and had begun to deploy ABMs at two land-based (ICBM) missile sites to protect its retaliatory forces. (The full program envisaged 12 ABM complexes.)

Besides these asymmetries in their strategic forces, the defense needs and commitments of the two parties differed materially. The United States had obligations for the defense of allies overseas, such as Western Europe and Japan, while the Soviet Union's allies were its near neighbors. All these circumstances made for difficulties in equating specific weapons, or categories of weapons, and in defining overall strategic equivalence.

Two initial disagreements presented obstacles. The Soviet representatives sought to define as "strategic"—i.e., negotiable in SALT—any U.S. or Soviet weapons system capable of reaching the territory of the other side. This would have included U.S. "forward-based systems," chiefly short-range or medium-range bombers on aircraft carriers or based in Europe, but it would have excluded, for example, Soviet intermediate-range missiles aimed at Western Europe. The United States held that weapons to be negotiated in SALT comprised intercontinental systems. Its forward-based forces served to counter Soviet medium-range missiles and aircraft aimed at U.S. allies. To accept the Soviet approach would have prejudiced alliance commitments.

After initial attempts to reach a comprehensive agreement failed, the Soviets sought to restrict negotiations to antiballistic missile systems, maintaining that limitation on offensive systems should be deferred. The U.S. position was that to limit ABM systems but allow the unrestricted growth of offensive weapons would be incompatible with the basic objectives of SALT and that it was essential to make at least a beginning at limiting offensive systems as well. A long deadlock on the question was finally broken by exchanges at the highest levels of both governments. On May 20, 1971, Washington and Moscow announced that an understanding had been reached to concentrate on a permanent treaty to limit ABM systems, but at the same time to work out certain limitations on offensive systems, and to continue negotiations for a more comprehensive and long-term agreement on the latter.

In a summit meeting in Moscow, after 2½ years of negotiation, the first round of SALT was brought to a conclusion on May 26, 1972, when President Nixon and General Secretary Brezhnev signed the ABM Treaty and the Interim Agreement on strategic offensive arms.

Intensive research had gone into finding ways of verifying possible agreements without requiring access to the territory of the other side. Both the ABM Treaty and the Interim Agreement stipulate that compliance is to be assured by "national technical means of verification." Moreover, the agreements include provisions that are important steps to strengthen assurance against violations: both sides undertake not to interfere with national technical means of verification. In addition, both countries agree not to use deliberate concealment measures to impede verification.

The basic provisions of each SALT I agreement are briefly reviewed in sections that follow. The two accords differ in their duration and inclusiveness. The ABM Treaty "shall be of unlimited duration," but each party has the right to withdraw on 6 months' notice if it decides that its supreme interests are jeopardized by "extraordinary events related to the subject matter of this Treaty." The Interim Agreement was for a 5-year span, and covered only certain major aspects of strategic weaponry. The agreements are linked not only in their strategic effects, but in their relationship to future negotiations for limitations on strategic offensive arms. A formal statement by the United States stressed the critical importance it attaches to achieving more complete limitations on strategic offensive arms.

The two agreements were accompanied by a number of "Agreed Statements" that were agreed upon and initialed by the Heads of the Delegations. When the two agreements were submitted to the U.S. Congress, they were also accompanied by common understandings reached and unilateral statements made during the negotiations.

These were intended to clarify specific provisions of the agreements or parts of the negotiating record. The three groups of items are reproduced here with the texts of the agreements.

Treaty Between the United States of America and the Union of Soviet Socialist Republics on the Limitation of Anti-Ballistic Missile Systems

In the Treaty on the Limitation of Anti-Ballistic Missile Systems the United States and the Soviet Union agree that each may have only two ABM deployment areas,[1] so restricted and so located that they cannot provide a nationwide ABM defense or become the basis for developing one. Each country thus leaves unchallenged the penetration capability of the other's retaliatory missile forces.

The treaty permits each side to have one limited ABM system to protect its capital and another to protect an ICBM launch area. The two sites defended must be at least 1,300 kilometers apart, to prevent the creation of any effective regional defense zone or the beginnings of a nationwide system.

Precise quantitative and qualitative limits are imposed on the ABM systems that may be deployed. At each site there may be no more than 100 interceptor missiles and 100 launchers. Agreement on the number and characteristics of radars to be permitted had required extensive and complex technical negotiations, and the provisions governing these important components of ABM systems are spelled out in very specific detail in the treaty and further clarified in the "Agreed Statements" accompanying it.

Both parties agreed to limit qualitative improvement of their ABM technology, e.g., not to develop, test, or deploy ABM launchers capable of launching more than one interceptor missile at a time or modify existing launchers to give them this capability, and systems for rapid reload of launchers are similarly barred. These provisions, the Agreed Statements clarify, also ban interceptor missiles with more than one independently guided warhead.

There had been some concern over the possibility that surface-to-air missiles (SAMs) intended for defense against aircraft might be improved, along with their supporting radars, to the point where they could effectively be used against ICBMs and SLBMs, and the treaty prohibits this. While further deployment of radars intended to give early warning of strategic ballistic missile attack is not prohibited, they must be located along the territorial boundaries of each country

---

[1]Subsequently reduced to one area (see section on ABM Protocol).

and oriented outward, so that they do not contribute to an effective ABM defense of points in the interior.

Further, to decrease the pressures of technological change and its unsettling impact on the strategic balance, both sides agree to prohibit development, testing, or deployment of sea-based, air-based, or space-based ABM systems and their components, along with mobile land-based ABM systems. Should future technology bring forth new ABM systems "based on other physical principles" than those employed in current systems, it was agreed that limiting such systems would be discussed, in accordance with the treaty's provisions for consultation and amendment.

The treaty also provides for a U.S.-Soviet Standing Consultative Commission to promote its objectives and implementation. The commission was established during the first negotiating session of SALT II, by a Memorandum of Understanding dated December 21, 1972. Since then both the United States and the Soviet Union have raised a number of questions in the Commission relating to each side's compliance with the SALT I agreements. In each case raised by the United States, the Soviet activity in question has either ceased or additional information has allayed U.S. concern.

Article XIV of the treaty calls for review of the treaty 5 years after its entry into force, and at 5-year intervals thereafter. The first such review was conducted by the Standing Consultative Commission at its special session in the fall of 1977. At this session, the United States and the Soviet Union agreed that the treaty had operated effectively during its first 5 years, that it had continued to serve national security interests, and that it did not need to be amended at that time.

Treaty Between the United States of America and the Union of Soviet Socialist Republics on the Limitation of Anti-Ballistic Missile Systems

Signed at Moscow May 26, 1972
Ratification advised by U.S. Senate August 3, 1972
Ratified by U.S. President September 30, 1972
Proclaimed by U.S. President October 3, 1972
Instruments of ratification exchanged October 3, 1972
Entered into force October 3, 1972

The United States of America and the Union of Soviet Socialist Republics, hereinafter referred to as the Parties,

Proceeding from the premise that nuclear war would have devastating consequences for all mankind,

Considering that effective measures to limit anti-ballistic missile systems would be a substantial factor in curbing the race in strategic offensive arms and would lead to a decrease in the risk of outbreak of war involving nuclear weapons,

Proceeding from the premise that the limitation of anti-ballistic missile systems, as well as certain agreed measures with respect to the limitation of strategic offensive arms, would contribute to the creation of more favorable conditions for further negotiations on limiting strategic arms,

Mindful of their obligations under Article VI of the Treaty on the Non-Proliferation of Nuclear Weapons,

Declaring their intention to achieve at the earliest possible date the cessation of the nuclear arms race and to take effective measures toward reductions in strategic arms, nuclear disarmament, and general and complete disarmament,

Desiring to contribute to the relaxation of international tension and the strengthening of trust between States,

Have agreed as follows:

Article I

1. Each party undertakes to limit anti-ballistic missile (ABM) systems and to adopt other measures in accordance with the provisions of this Treaty.

2. Each Party undertakes not to deploy ABM systems for a defense of the territory of its country and not to provide a base for such a defense, and not to deploy ABM systems for defense of an individual region except as provided for in Article III of this Treaty.

Article II

1. For the purpose of this Treaty an ABM system is a system to counter strategic ballistic missiles or their elements in flight trajectory, currently consisting of:

(a) ABM interceptor missiles, which are interceptor missiles constructed and deployed for an ABM role, or of a type tested in an ABM mode;

(b) ABM launchers, which are launchers constructed and deployed for launching ABM interceptor missiles; and

(c) ABM radars, which are radars constructed and deployed for an ABM role, or of a type tested in an ABM mode.

2. The ABM system components listed in paragraph 1 of this Article include those which are:

(a) operational;
(b) under construction;
(c) undergoing testing;
(d) undergoing overhaul, repair or conversion; or
(e) mothballed.

Article III

Each Party undertakes not to deploy ABM systems or their components except that:

(a) within one ABM system deployment area having a radius of one hundred and fifty kilometers and centered on the Party's national capital, a Party may deploy: (1) no more than one hundred ABM launchers and no more than one hundred ABM interceptor missiles at launch sites, and (2) ABM radars within no more than six ABM radar complexes, the area of each complex being circular and having a diameter of no more than three kilometers; and

(b) within one ABM system deployment area having a radius of one hundred and fifty kilometers and containing ICBM silo launchers, a Party may deploy: (1) no more than one hundred ABM launchers and no more than one hundred ABM interceptor missiles at launch sites, (2) two large phased-array ABM radars comparable in potential to corresponding ABM radars operational or under construction on the date of signature of the Treaty in an ABM system deployment area containing ICBM silo launchers, and (3) no more than eighteen ABM radars each having a potential less than the potential of the smaller of the above-mentioned two large phased-array ABM radars.

Article IV

The limitations provided for in Article III shall not apply to ABM systems or their components used for development or testing, and located within current or additionally agreed test ranges. Each Party may have no more than a total of fifteen ABM launchers at test ranges.

Article V

1. Each Party undertakes not to develop, test, or deploy ABM systems or components which are sea-based, air-based, space-based, or mobile land-based.

2. Each Party undertakes not to develop, test, or deploy ABM launchers for launching more than one ABM interceptor missile at a time from each launcher, not to modify deployed launchers to provide them with such a capability, not to develop, test, or deploy automatic or semi-automatic or other similar systems for rapid reload of ABM launchers.

Article VI

To enhance assurance of the effectiveness of the limitations on ABM systems and their components provided by the Treaty, each Party undertakes:

(a) not to give missiles, launchers, or radars, other than ABM interceptor missiles, ABM launchers, or ABM radars, capabilities to counter strategic ballistic missiles or their elements in flight trajectory, and not to test them in an ABM mode; and

(b) not to deploy in the future radars for early warning of strategic ballistic missile attack except at locations along the periphery of its national territory and oriented outward.

Article VII

Subject to the provisions of this Treaty, modernization and replacement of ABM systems or their components may be carried out.

Article VIII

ABM systems or their components in excess of the numbers or outside the areas specified in this Treaty, as well as ABM systems or their components prohibited by this Treaty, shall be destroyed or dismantled under agreed procedures within the shortest possible agreed period of time.

Article IX

To assure the viability and effectiveness of this Treaty, each Party undertakes not to transfer to other States, and not to deploy outside its national territory, ABM systems or their components limited by this Treaty.

Article X

Each Party undertakes not to assume any international obligations which would conflict with this Treaty.

Article XI

The Parties undertake to continue active negotiations for limitations on strategic offensive arms.

Article XII

1. For the purpose of providing assurance of compliance with the provisions of this Treaty, each Party shall use national technical means of verification at its disposal in a manner consistent with generally recognized principles of international law.

2. Each Party undertakes not to interfere with the national technical means of verification of the other Party operating in accordance with paragraph 1 of this Article.

3. Each Party undertakes not to use deliberate concealment measures which impede verification by national technical means of compliance with the provisions of this Treaty. This obligation shall not require changes in current construction, assembly, conversion, or overhaul practices.

Article XIII

1. To promote the objectives and implementation of the provisions of this Treaty, the Parties shall establish promptly a Standing Consultative Commission, within the framework of which they will:

(a) consider questions concerning compliance with the obligations assumed and related situations which may be considered ambiguous;

(b) provide on a voluntary basis such information as either Party considers necessary to assure confidence in compliance with the obligations assumed;

(c) consider questions involving unintended interference with national technical means of verification;

(d) consider possible changes in the strategic situation which have a bearing on the provisions of this Treaty;

(e) agree upon procedures and dates for destruction or dismantling of ABM systems or their components in cases provided for by the provisions of this Treaty;

(f) consider, as appropriate, possible proposals for further increasing the viability of this Treaty; including proposals for amendments in accordance with the provisions of this Treaty;

(g) consider, as appropriate, proposals for further measures aimed at limiting strategic arms.

2. The Parties through consultation shall establish, and may amend as appropriate, Regulations for the Standing Consultative Commission governing procedures, composition and other relevant matters.

Article XIV

1. Each Party may propose amendments to this Treaty. Agreed amendments shall enter into force in accordance with the procedures governing the entry into force of this Treaty.

2. Five years after entry into force of this Treaty, and at five-year intervals thereafter, the Parties shall together conduct a review of this Treaty.

Article XV

1. This Treaty shall be of unlimited duration.

2. Each Party shall, in exercising its national sovereignty, have the right to withdraw from this Treaty if it decides that extraordinary events related to the subject matter of this Treaty have jeopardized its supreme interests. It shall give notice of its decision to the other Party six months prior to withdrawal from the Treaty. Such notice shall include a statement of the extraordinary events the notifying Party regards as having jeopardized its supreme interests.

Article XVI

1. This Treaty shall be subject to ratification in accordance with the constitutional procedures of each Party. The Treaty shall enter into force on the day of the exchange of instruments of ratification.

2. This Treaty shall be registered pursuant to Article 102 of the Charter of the United Nations.

DONE at Moscow on May 26, 1972, in two copies, each in the English and Russian languages, both texts being equally authentic.

FOR THE UNITED STATES OF AMERICA

FOR THE UNION OF SOVIET SOCIALIST REPUBLICS

President of the United States of America

General Secretary of the Central Committee of the CPSU

Agreed Statements, Common Understandings, and Unilateral Statements Regarding the Treaty Between the United States of America and the Union of Soviet Socialist Republics on the Limitation of Anti-Ballistic Missiles

1. Agreed Statements

The document set forth below was agreed upon and initialed by the Heads of the Delegations on May 26, 1972 (letter designations added);

AGREED STATEMENTS REGARDING THE TREATY BETWEEN THE UNITED STATES OF AMERICA AND THE UNION OF SOVIET SOCIALIST REPUBLICS ON THE LIMITATION OF ANTI-BALLISTIC MISSILE SYTEMS

[A]

The Parties understand that, in addition to the ABM radars which may be deployed in accordance with subparagraph (a) of Article III of the Treaty, those non-phased-array ABM radars operational on the date of signature of the Treaty within the ABM system deployment area for defense of the national capital may be retained.

[B]

The Parties understand that the potential (the product of mean emitted power in watts and antenna area in square meters) of the smaller of the two large phased-array ABM radars referred to in subparagraph (b) of Article III of the Treaty is considered for purposes of the Treaty to be three million.

[C]

The Parties understand that the center of the ABM system deployment area centered on the national capital and the center of the ABM system deployment area containing ICBM silo launchers for each Party shall be separated by no less than thirteen hundred kilometers.

[D]

In order to insure fulfillment of the obligation not to deploy ABM systems and their components except as provided in Article III of the Treaty, the Parties agree that in the event ABM systems based on other physical principles and including components capable of substituting for ABM interceptor missiles, ABM launchers, or ABM radars are created in the future, specific limitations on such systems and their components would be subject to discussion in accordance with Article XIII and agreement in accordance with Article XIV of the Treaty.

143

[E]

The Parties understand that Article V of the Treaty includes obligations not to develop, test or deploy ABM interceptor missiles for the delivery by each ABM interceptor missile of more than one independently guided warhead.

[F]

The Parties agree not to deploy phased-array radars having a potential (the product of mean emitted power in watts and antenna area in square meters) exceeding three million, except as provided for in Articles III, IV and VI of the Treaty, or except for the purposes of tracking objects in outer space or for use as national technical means of verification.

[G]

The Parties understand that Article IX of the Treaty includes the obligation of the US and the USSR not to provide to other States technical descriptions or blue prints specially worked out for the construction of ABM systems and their components limited by the Treaty.

2. Common Understandings

Common understanding of the Parties on the following matters was reached during the negotiations:

A. Location of ICBM Defenses

The U.S. Delegation made the following statement on May 26, 1972:

Article III of the ABM Treaty provides for each side one ABM system deployment area centered on its national capital and one ABM system deployment area containing ICBM silo launchers. The two sides have registered agreement on the following statement: "The Parties understand that the center of the ABM system deployment area centered on the national capital and the center of the ABM system deployment area containing ICBM silo launchers for each Party shall be separated by no less than thirteen hundred kilometers." In this connection, the U.S. side notes that its ABM system deployment area for defense of ICBM silo launchers, located west of the Mississippi River, will be centered in the Grand Forks ICBM silo launcher deployment area. (See Agreed Statement [C].)

B. ABM Test Ranges

The U.S. Delegation made the following statement on April 26, 1972:

Article IV of the ABM Treaty provides that "the limitations provided for in Article III shall not apply to ABM systems or their components used for development or testing, and located within current or additionally agreed test ranges." We believe it would be useful to assure that there is no misunderstanding as to current ABM test ranges. It is our understanding that ABM test ranges encompass the area within which ABM components are located for test purposes. The current U.S. ABM test ranges are at White Sands, New Mexico, and at Kwajalein Atoll, and the current Soviet ABM test range is near Sary Shagan in Kazakhstan. We consider that non-phased array radars of types used for range safety or instrumentation purposes may be located outside of ABM test ranges. We interpret the reference in Article IV to "additionally agreed test ranges" to mean that ABM components will not be located at any other test ranges without prior agreement between our Governments that there will be such additional ABM test ranges.

On May 5, 1972, the Soviet Delegation stated that there was a common understanding on what ABM test ranges were, that the use of the types of non-ABM radars for range safety or instrumentation was not limited under the Treaty, that the reference in Article IV to "additionally agreed" test ranges was sufficiently clear, and that national means permitted identifying current test ranges.

C. Mobile ABM Systems

On January 29, 1972, the U.S. Delegation made the following statement:

Article V(1) of the Joint Draft Text of the ABM Treaty includes an undertaking not to develop, test, or deploy mobile land-based ABM systems and their components. On May 5, 1971, the U.S. side indicated that, in its view, a prohibition on deployment of mobile ABM systems and components would rule out the deployment of ABM launchers and radars which were not permanent fixed types. At that time, we asked for the Soviet view of this interpretation. Does the Soviet side agree with the U.S. side's interpretation put forward on May 5, 1971?

On April 13, 1972, the Soviet Delegation said there is a general common understanding on this matter.

D. Standing Consultative Commission

Ambassador Smith made the following statement on May 22, 1972:

The United States proposes that the sides agree that, with regard to initial implementation of the ABM Treaty's Article XIII on the Standing Consultative Commission (SCC) and of the consultation Articles to the Interim Agreement on offensive arms and the Accidents Agreement,[1] agreement establishing the SCC will be worked out early in the follow-on SALT negotiations; until that is completed, the following arrangements will prevail: when SALT is in session, any consultation desired by either side under these Articles can be carried out by the two SALT Delegations; when SALT is not in session, *ad hoc* arrangements for any desired consultations under these Articles may be made through diplomatic channels.

Minister Semenov replied that, on an *ad referendum* basis, he could agree that the U.S. statement corresponded to the Soviet understanding.

E. Standstill

On May 6, 1972, Minister Semenov made the following statement:

In an effort to accommodate the wishes of the U.S. side, the Soviet Delegation is prepared to proceed on the basis that the two sides will in fact observe the obligations of both the Interim Agreement and the ABM Treaty beginning from the date of signature of these two documents.

In reply, the U.S. Delegation made the following statement on May 20, 1972:

---

[1]See Article 7 of Agreement to Reduce the Risk of Outbreak of Nuclear War Between the United States of America and the Union of Soviet Socialist Republics, signed Sept. 30, 1971.

The U.S. agrees in principle with the Soviet statement made on May 6 concerning observance of obligations beginning from date of signature but we would like to make clear our understanding that this means that, pending ratification and acceptance, neither side would take any action prohibited by the agreements after they had entered into force. This understanding would continue to apply in the absence of notification by either signatory of its intention not to proceed with ratification or approval.

The Soviet Delegation indicated agreement with the U.S. statement.

3. Unilateral Statements

The following noteworthy unilateral statements were made during the negotiations by the United States Delegation:

A. Withdrawal from the ABM Treaty

On May 9, 1972, Ambassador Smith made the following statement:

The U.S. Delegation has stressed the importance the U.S. Government attaches to achieving agreement on more complete limitations on strategic offensive arms, following agreement on an ABM Treaty and on an Interim Agreement on certain measures with respect to the limitation of strategic offensive arms. The U.S. Delegation believes that an objective of the follow-on negotiations should be to constrain and reduce on a long-term basis threats to the survivability of our respective strategic retaliatory forces. The USSR Delegation has also indicated that the objectives of SALT would remain unfulfilled without the achievement of an agreement providing for more complete limitations on strategic offensive arms. Both sides recognize that the initial agreements would be steps toward the achievement of more complete limitations on strategic arms. If an agreement providing for more complete strategic offensive arms limitations were not achieved within five years, U.S. supreme interests could be jeopardized. Should that occur, it would constitute a basis for withdrawal from the ABM Treaty. The U.S. does not wish to see such a situation occur, nor do we believe that the USSR does. It is because we wish to prevent such a situation that we emphasize the importance the U.S. Government attaches to achievement of more complete limitations on strategic offensive arms. The U.S. Executive will inform the Congress, in connection with Congressional consideration of the ABM Treaty and the Interim Agreement, of this statement of the U.S. position.

B. Tested in ABM Mode

On April 7, 1972, the U.S. Delegation made the following statement:

Article II of the Joint Text Draft uses the term "tested in an ABM mode," in defining ABM components, and Article VI includes certain obligations concerning such testing. We believe that the sides should have a common understanding of this phrase. First, we would note that the testing provisions of the ABM Treaty are intended to apply to testing which occurs after the date of signature of the Treaty, and not to any testing which may have occurred in the past. Next, we would amplify the remarks we have made on this subject during the previous Helsinki phase by setting forth the objectives which govern the U.S. view on the subject, namely, while prohibiting testing of non-ABM components for ABM purposes: not to prevent testing of ABM components, and not to prevent testing of non-ABM components for non-ABM purposes. To clarify our interpretation of "tested in an ABM mode," we note that we would consider a launcher, missile or radar to be "tested in an ABM mode" if, for example, any of the following events occur: (1) a launcher is used to launch an ABM interceptor missile, (2) an interceptor missile is flight tested against a target vehicle which has a flight trajectory with characteristics of a strategic ballistic missile flight trajectory, or is flight tested in conjunction with the test of an ABM interceptor missile or an ABM radar at the same test range, or is flight tested to an altitude inconsistent with interception of targets against which air defenses are deployed, (3) a radar makes measurements on a cooperative target vehicle of the kind referred to in item (2) above during the reentry portion of its trajectory or makes measurements in conjunction with the test of an ABM interceptor missile or an ABM radar at the same test range. Radars used for purposes such as range safety or instrumentation would be exempt from application of these criteria.

C.   No-Transfer Article of ABM Treaty

On April 18, 1972, the U.S. Delegation made the following statement:

In regard to this Article [IX], I have a brief and I believe self-explanatory statement to make. The U.S. side wishes to make clear that the provisions of this Article do not set a precedent for whatever provision may be considered for a Treaty on Limiting Strategic Offensive Arms. The question of transfer of strategic offensive arms is a far more complex issue, which may require a different solution.

D.   No Increase in Defense of Early Warning Radars

On July 28, 1970, the U.S. Delegation made the following statement:

Since Hen House radars [Soviet ballistic missile early warning radars] can detect and track ballistic missile warheads at great distances, they have a significant ABM potential. Accordingly, the U.S. would regard any increase in the defenses of such radars by surface-to-air missiles as inconsistent with an agreement.

Interim Agreement Between the United States of America and the Union of Soviet Socialist Republics on Certain Measures With Respect to the Limitation of Strategic Offensive Arms

As its title suggests, the "Interim Agreement Between the United States and the Union of Soviet Socialist Republics on Certain Measures With Respect to the Limitation of Offensive Arms" was limited in duration and scope. It was intended to remain in force for 5 years. (See preceding section on SALT.) Both countries undertook to continue negotiations for a more comprehensive agreement as soon as possible, and the scope and terms of any new agreement were not to be prejudiced by the provisions of the 1972 accord.

Thus the Interim Agreement was set essentially as a holding action, designed to complement the ABM Treaty by limiting competition in offensive strategic arms and to provide time for further negotiations. The agreement essentially freezes at existing levels the number of strategic ballistic missile launchers, operational or under construction, on each side, and permits an increase in SLBM launchers up to an agreed level for each party only with the dismantling or destruction of a corresponding number of older ICBM or SLBM launchers.

In view of the many asymmetries in the two countries' forces, imposing equivalent limitations required rather complex and precise provisions. At the date of signing, the United States had 1,054 operational land-based ICBMs, and none under construction; the Soviet Union had an estimated 1,618, operational and under construction. Launchers under construction could be completed. Neither side would start construction of additional fixed land-based ICBM launchers during the period of the agreement—this, in effect, also bars relocation of existing launchers. Launchers for light or older ICBMs cannot be converted into launchers for modern heavy ICBMs. This prevents the U.S.S.R. from replacing older missiles with missiles such as the SS-9, which in 1972 was the largest and most powerful missile in the Soviet inventory and a source of particular concern to the United States.

Within these limitations, modernization and replacement are permitted, but in the process of modernizing, the dimensions of silo launchers cannot be significantly increased.

Mobile ICBMs are not covered. The Soviet Union held that since neither side had such systems, a freeze should not apply to them; it also opposed banning them in a future comprehensive agreement. The United States held they should be banned because of the verification difficulties they presented. In a formal statement, the U.S. delegation declared that the United States would consider deployment of land-mobile ICBMs during the period of the agreement as inconsistent with its objectives.

Article III and the protocol limit launchers for submarine-launched ballistic missiles (SLBMs) and modern ballistic missile submarines. The United States is permitted to reach a ceiling of 710 SLBM launchers on 44 submarines, from its base level of 656 SLBM launchers on 41 ballistic missile submarines, by replacing 54 older ICBM launchers. The Soviet Union, beyond the level of 740 SLBM launchers on modern nuclear-powered submarines, may increase to 950. But these additional launchers are permitted only as replacements for older ICBM or SLBM launchers, which must be dismantled or destroyed under agreed procedures.

In a unilateral statement, the Soviet Union asserted that if U.S. NATO allies increased the number of their modern submarines, the Soviet Union would have a right to increase the number of its submarines correspondingly. The United States declared that it did not accept this claim.

Interim Agreement Between the United States of America and the Union of Soviet Socialist Republics on Certain Measures With Respect to the Limitation of Strategic Offensive Arms

Signed at Moscow May 26, 1972
Approval authorized by U.S. Congress September 30, 1972
Approved by U.S. President September 30, 1972
Notices of acceptance exchanged October 3, 1972
Entered into force October 3, 1972

The United States of America and the Union of Soviet Socialist Republics, hereinafter referred to as the Parties,

Convinced that the Treaty on the Limitation of Anti-Ballistic Missile Systems and this Interim Agreement on Certain Measures with Respect to the Limitation of Strategic Offensive Arms will contribute to the creation of more favorable conditions for active negotiations on limiting strategic arms as well as to the relaxation of international tension and the strengthening of trust between States,

Taking into account the relationship between strategic offensive and defensive arms,

Mindful of their obligations under Article VI of the Treaty on the Non-Proliferation of Nuclear Weapons,

Have agreed as follows:

Article I

The Parties undertake not to start construction of additional fixed land-based intercontinental ballistic missile (ICBM) launchers after July 1, 1972.

Article II

The Parties undertake not to convert land-based launchers for light ICBMs, or for ICBMs of older types deployed prior to 1964, into land-based launchers for heavy ICBMs of types deployed after that time.

Article III

The Parties undertake to limit submarine-launched ballistic missile (SLBM) launchers and modern ballistic missile submarines to the numbers operational and under construction on the date of signature of this Interim Agreement, and in addition to launchers and submarines constructed under procedures established by the Parties as replacements for an equal number of ICBM launchers of older types deployed prior to 1964 or for launchers on older submarines.

Article IV

Subject to the provisions of this Interim Agreement, modernization and replacement of strategic offensive ballistic missiles and launchers covered by this Interim Agreement may be undertaken.

Article V

1. For the purpose of providing assurance of compliance with the provisions of this Interim Agreement, each Party shall use national technical means of verification at its disposal in a manner consistent with generally recognized principles of international law.

2. Each party undertakes not to interfere with the national technical means of verification of the other Party operating in accordance with paragraph 1 of this Article.

3. Each Party undertakes not to use deliberate concealment measures which impede verification by national technical means of compliance with the provisions of this Interim Agreement. This obligation shall not require changes in current construction, assembly, conversion, or overhaul practices.

Article VI

To promote the objectives and implementation of the provisions of this Interim Agreement, the Parties shall use the Standing Consultative Commission established under Article XIII of the Treaty on the Limitation of Anti-Ballistic Missile Systems in accordance with the provisions of that Article.

Article VII

The Parties undertake to continue active negotiations for limitations on strategic offensive arms. The obligations provided for in this Interim Agreement shall not prejudice the scope or terms of the limitations on strategic offensive arms which may be worked out in the course of further negotiations.

Article VIII

1. This Interim Agreement shall enter into force upon exchange of written notices of acceptance by each Party, which exchange shall take place simultaneously with the exchange of instruments of ratification of the Treaty on the Limitation of Anti-Ballistic Missile Systems.

2. This Interim Agreement shall remain in force for a period of five years unless replaced earlier by an agreement on more complete measures limiting strategic offensive arms. It is the objective of the Parties to conduct active follow-on negotiations with the aim of concluding such an agreement as soon as possible.

3. Each Party shall, in exercising its national sovereignty, have the right to withdraw from this Interim Agreement if it decides that extraordinary events related to the subject matter of this Interim Agreement have jeopardized its supreme interests. It shall give notice of its decision to the other Party six months prior to withdrawal from this Interim Agreement. Such notice shall include a statement of the extraordinary events the notifying Party regards as having jeopardized its supreme interests.

DONE at Moscow on May 26, 1972, in two copies, each in the English and Russian languages, both texts being equally authentic.

**FOR THE UNITED STATES OF
AMERICA**

**FOR THE UNION OF SOVIET SOCIALIST
REPUBLICS**

*President of the United States
of America*

*General Secretary of the Central Committee
of the CPSU*

Protocol to the Interim Agreement Between the United States of America and the Union of Soviet Socialist Republics on Certain Measures With Respect to the Limitation of Strategic Offensive Arms

The United States of America and the Union of Soviet Socialist Republics, hereinafter referred to as the Parties,

Having agreed on certain limitations relating to submarine-launched ballistic missile launchers and modern ballistic missile submarines, and to replacement procedures, in the Interim Agreement,

Have agreed as follows:

The Parties understand that, under Article III of the Interim Agreement, for the period during which that Agreement remains in force:

The U.S. may have no more than 710 ballistic missile launchers on submarines (SLBMs) and no more than 44 modern ballistic missile submarines. The Soviet Union may have no more than 950 ballistic missile launchers on submarines and no more than 62 modern ballistic missile submarines.

Additional ballistic missile launchers on submarines up to the above-mentioned levels, in the U.S.—over 656 ballistic missile launchers on nuclear-powered submarines, and in the U.S.S.R.—over 740 ballistic missile launchers on nuclear-powered submarines, operational and under construction, may become operational as replacements for equal numbers of ballistic missile launchers of older types deployed prior to 1964 or of ballistic missile launchers on older submarines.

The deployment of modern SLBMs on any submarine, regardless of type, will be counted against the total level of SLBMs permitted for the U.S. and the U.S.S.R.

This Protocol shall be considered an integral part of the Interim Agreement.

DONE at Moscow this 26th day of May, 1972

FOR THE UNITED STATES OF AMERICA

FOR THE UNION OF SOVIET SOCIALIST REPUBLICS

President of the
United States of America

General Secretary of the
Central Committee of the CPSU

Agreed Statements, Common Understandings, and Unilateral Statements Regarding the Interim Agreement Between the United States of America and the Union of Soviet Socialist Republics on Certain Measures With Respect to the Limitation of Strategic Offensive Arms

1. Agreed Statements

The document set forth below was agreed upon and initialed by the Heads of the Delegations on May 26, 1972 (letter designations added):

AGREED STATEMENTS REGARDING THE INTERIM AGREEMENT BETWEEN THE UNITED STATES OF AMERICA AND THE UNION OF SOVIET SOCIALIST REPUBLICS ON CERTAIN MEASURES WITH RESPECT TO THE LIMITATION OF STRATEGIC OFFENSIVE ARMS

[A]

The Parties understand that land-based ICBM launchers referred to in the Interim Agreement are understood to be launchers for strategic ballistic missiles capable of ranges in excess of the shortest distance between the northeastern border of the continental U.S. and the northwestern border of the continental USSR.

[B]

The Parties understand that fixed land-based ICBM launchers under active construction as of the date of signature of the Interim Agreement may be completed.

[C]

The Parties understand that in the process of modernization and replacement the dimensions of land-based ICBM silo launchers will not be significantly increased.

[D]

The Parties understand that during the period of the Interim Agreement there shall be no significant increase in the number of ICBM or SLBM test and training launchers, or in the number of such launchers for modern land-based heavy ICBMs. The Parties further understand that construction or conversion of ICBM launchers at test ranges shall be undertaken only for purposes of testing and training.

[E]

The Parties understand that dismantling or destruction of ICBM launchers of older types deployed prior to 1964 and ballistic missile launchers on older submarines being replaced by new SLBM launchers on modern submarines will be initiated at the time of the beginning of sea trials of a replacement submarine, and will be completed in the

154

shortest possible agreed period of time. Such dismantling or destruction, and timely notification thereof, will be accomplished under procedures to be agreed in the Standing Consultative Commission.

2. Common Understandings

Common understanding of the Parties on the following matters was reached during the negotiations:

A. Increase in ICBM Silo Dimensions

Ambassador Smith made the following statement on May 26, 1972:

The Parties agree that the term "significantly increased" means that an increase will not be greater than 10–15 percent of the present dimensions of land-based ICBM silo launchers.

Minister Semenov replied that this statement corresponded to the Soviet understanding.

B. Standing Consultative Commission

Ambassador Smith made the following statement on May 22, 1972:

The United States proposes that the sides agree that, with regard to initial implementation of the ABM Treaty's Article XIII on the Standing Consultative Commission (SCC) and of the consultation Articles to the Interim Agreement on offensive arms and the Accidents Agreement,[1] agreement establishing the SCC will be worked out early in the follow-on SALT negotiations; until that is completed, the following arrangements will prevail: when SALT is in session, any consultation desired by either side under these Articles can be carried out by the two SALT Delegations; when SALT is not in session, ad hoc arrangements for any desired consultations under these Articles may be made through diplomatic channels.

Minister Semenov replied that, on an ad referendum basis, he could agree that the U.S. statement corresponded to the Soviet understanding.

C. Standstill

On May 6, 1972, Minister Semenov made the following statement.

In an effort to accommodate the wishes of the U.S. side, the Soviet Delegation is prepared to proceed on the basis that the two sides will in fact observe the obligations of both the Interim Agreement and the ABM Treaty beginning from the date of signature of these two documents.

In reply, the U.S. Delegation made the following statement on May 20, 1972:

The U.S. agrees in principle with the Soviet statement made on May 6 concerning observance of obligations beginning from date of signature but we would like to make clear our understanding that this means that, pending ratification and acceptance, neither side would take any action prohibited by the agreements after

---

[1] See Article 7 of Agreement to Reduce the Risk of Outbreak of Nuclear War Between the United States of America and the Union of Soviet Socialist Republics, signed Sept. 30, 1971.

they had entered into force. This understanding would continue to apply in the absence of notification by either signatory of its intention not to proceed with ratification or approval.

The Soviet Delegation indicated agreement with the U.S. statement.

3. Unilateral Statements

(a) The following noteworthy unilateral statements were made during the negotiations by the United States Delegation:

A. Withdrawal from the ABM Treaty

On May 9, 1972, Ambassador Smith made the following statement:

The U.S. Delegation has stressed the importance the U.S. Government attaches to achieving agreement on more complete limitations on strategic offensive arms, following agreement on an ABM Treaty and on an Interim Agreement on certain measures with respect to the limitation of strategic offensive arms. The U.S. Delegation believes that an objective of the follow-on negotiations should be to constrain and reduce on a long-term basis threats to the survivability of our respective strategic retaliatory forces. The USSR Delegation has also indicated that the objectives of SALT would remain unfulfilled without the achievement of an agreement providing for more complete limitations on strategic offensive arms. Both sides recognize that the initial agreements would be steps toward the achievement of more complete limitations on strategic arms. If an agreement providing for more complete strategic offensive arms limitations were not achieved within five years, U.S. supreme interests could be jeopardized. Should that occur, it would constitute a basis for withdrawal from the ABM Treaty. The U.S. does not wish to see such a situation occur, nor do we believe that the USSR does. It is because we wish to prevent such a situation that we emphasize the importance the U.S. Government attaches to achievement of more complete limitations on strategic offensive arms. The U.S. Executive will inform the Congress, in connection with Congressional consideration of the ABM Treaty and the Interim Agreement, of this statement of the U.S. position.

B. Land-Mobile ICBM Launchers

The U.S. Delegation made the following statement on May 20, 1972:

In connection with the important subject of land-mobile ICBM launchers, in the interest of concluding the Interim Agreement the U.S. Delegation now withdraws its proposal that Article I or an agreed statement explicitly prohibit the deployment of mobile land-based ICBM launchers. I have been instructed to inform you that, while agreeing to defer the question of limitation of operational land-mobile ICBM launchers to the subsequent negotiations on more complete limitations on strategic offensive arms, the U.S. would consider the deployment of operational land-mobile ICBM launchers during the period of the Interim Agreement as inconsistent with the objectives of that Agreement.

C. Covered Facilities

The U.S. Delegation made the following statement on May 20, 1972:

I wish to emphasize the importance that the United States attaches to the provisions of Article V, including in particular their application to fitting out or berthing submarines.

D. "Heavy" ICBM's

The U.S. Delegation made the following statement on May 26, 1972:

The U.S. Delegation regrets that the Soviet Delegation has not been willing to agree on a common definition of a heavy missile. Under these circumstances, the U.S. Delegation believes it necessary to state the following: The United States would consider any ICBM having a volume significantly greater than that of the largest light ICBM now operational on either side to be a heavy ICBM. The U.S. proceeds on the premise that the Soviet side will give due account to this consideration.

(b) The following noteworthy unilateral statement was made by the Delegation of the U.S.S.R. and is shown here with the U.S. reply:

On May 17, 1972, Minister Semenov made the following unilateral "Statement of the Soviet Side":

Taking into account that modern ballistic missile submarines are presently in the possession of not only the U.S., but also of its NATO allies, the Soviet Union agrees that for the period of effectiveness of the Interim 'Freeze' Agreement the U.S. and its NATO allies have up to 50 such submarines with a total of up to 800 ballistic missile launchers thereon (including 41 U.S. submarines with 656 ballistic missile launchers). However, if during the period of effectiveness of the Agreement U.S. allies in NATO should increase the number of their modern submarines to exceed the numbers of submarines they would have operational or under construction on the date of signature of the Agreement, the Soviet Union will have the right to a corresponding increase in the number of its submarines. In the opinion of the Soviet side, the solution of the question of modern ballistic missile submarines provided for in the Interim Agreement only partially compensates for the strategic imbalance in the deployment of the nuclear-powered missile submarines of the USSR and the U.S. Therefore, the Soviet side believes that this whole question, and above all the question of liquidating the American missile submarine bases outside the U.S., will be appropriately resolved in the course of follow-on negotiations.

On May 24, Ambassador Smith made the following reply to Minister Semenov:

The United States side has studied the "statement made by the Soviet side" of May 17 concerning compensation for submarine basing and SLBM submarines belonging to third countries. The United States does not accept the validity of the considerations in that statement.

On May 26 Minister Semenov repeated the unilateral statement made on May 17. Ambassador Smith also repeated the U.S. rejection on May 26.

Agreement Between the United States of America and the Union of Soviet Socialist Republics on the Prevention of Nuclear War

From the onset of the SALT negotiations between the United States and the Soviet Union, the two countries began the process of reshaping their relations on the basis of peaceful cooperation. One of the primary goals in this relationship was the prevention of war, especially nuclear war. During the last session of the Moscow summit meeting in May 1972, the countries exchanged some general ideas on how to accomplish this objective. These discussions were continued throughout the next year and were concluded in a formal agreement during General Secretary Brezhnev's visit to the United States on June 18-25, 1973.

In the Agreement on the Prevention of Nuclear War, signed in Washington on June 22, 1973, the United States and the Soviet Union agreed to make the removal of the danger of nuclear war and the use of nuclear weapons an "objective of their policies," to practice restraint in their relations toward each other and toward all countries, and to pursue a policy dedicated toward stability and peace. It was viewed as a preliminary step toward preventing the outbreak of nuclear war or military conflict by adopting an attitude of international cooperation.

The agreement basically covers two main areas:

1. It outlines the general conduct of both countries toward each other and toward third countries regarding the avoidance of nuclear war. In this respect it is a bilateral agreement with multilateral implications.

2. The parties agreed that in a situation in which the two great nuclear countries find themselves in a nuclear confrontation or in which, either as a result of their policies toward each other or as the result of developments elsewhere in the world, there is a danger of a nuclear confrontation between them or any other country, they are committed to consult with each other in order to avoid this risk.

The agreement further provides that these consultations may be communicated to the United Nations and to other countries, a clause the United States, of course, applies to its allies. Article VI stipulates that nothing in the agreement shall affect formal alliance obligations or the inherent right of countries to defend themselves.

Agreement Between the United States of America and the Union of Soviet Socialist Republics on the Prevention of Nuclear War

Signed at Washington June 22, 1973
Entered into force June 22, 1973

The United States of America and the Union of Soviet Socialist Republics, herein-after referred to as the Parties,

Guided by the objectives of strengthening world peace and international security,

Conscious that nuclear war would have devastating consequences for mankind,

Proceeding from the desire to bring about conditions in which the danger of an outbreak of nuclear war anywhere in the world would be reduced and ultimately eliminated,

Proceeding from their obligations under the Charter of the United Nations regarding the maintenance of peace, refraining from the threat or use of force, and the avoidance of war, and in conformity with the agreements to which either Party has subscribed,

Proceeding from the Basic Principles of Relations between the United States of America and the Union of Soviet Socialist Republics signed in Moscow on May 29, 1972,

Reaffirming that the development of relations between the United States of America and the Union of Soviet Socialist Republics is not directed against other countries and their interests,

Have agreed as follows:

Article I

The United States and the Soviet Union agree that an objective of their policies is to remove the danger of nuclear war and of the use of nuclear weapons.

Accordingly, the Parties agree that they will act in such a manner as to prevent the development of situations capable of causing a dangerous exacerbation of their relations, as to avoid military confrontations, and as to exclude the outbreak of nuclear war between them and between either of the Parties and other countries.

Article II

The Parties agree, in accordance with Article I and to realize the objective stated in that Article, to proceed from the premise that each Party will refrain from the threat or use of force against the other Party, against the allies of the other Party and against other countries, in circumstances which may endanger international peace and security. The Parties agree that they will be guided by these considerations in the formulation of their foreign policies and in their actions in the field of international relations.

Article III

The Parties undertake to develop their relations with each other and with other countries in a way consistent with the purposes of this Agreement.

Article IV

If at any time relations between the Parties or between either Party and other countries appear to involve the risk of a nuclear conflict, or if relations between countries not parties to this Agreement appear to involve the risk of nuclear war between the United States of America and the Union of Soviet Socialist Republics or between either Party and other countries, the United States and the Soviet Union, acting in accordance with the provisions of this Agreement, shall immediately enter into urgent consultations with each other and make every effort to avert this risk.

Article V

Each Party shall be free to inform the Security Council of the United Nations, the Secretary General of the United Nations and the Governments of allied or other countries of the progress and outcome of consultations initiated in accordance with Article IV of this Agreement.

Article VI

Nothing in this Agreement shall affect or impair:

(a) the inherent right of individual or collective self-defense as envisaged by Article 51 of the Charter of the United Nations,*
(b) the provisions of the Charter of the United Nations, including those relating to the maintenance or restoration of international peace and security, and
(c) the obligations undertaken by either Party towards its allies or other countries in treaties, agreements, and other appropriate documents.

Article VII

This Agreement shall be of unlimited duration.

Article VIII

This Agreement shall enter into force upon signature.

DONE at Washington on June 22, 1973, in two copies, each in the English and Russian languages, both texts being equally authentic.

FOR THE UNITED STATES OF AMERICA: **FOR THE UNION OF SOVIET SOCIALIST REPUBLICS:**

President of the United States of America   *General Secretary of the Central Committee, CPSU*

---

*TS 993; 59 Stat. 1044.

Protocol to the Treaty Between the United States of America and the Union of Soviet Socialist Republics on the Limitation of Anti-Ballistic Missile Systems

At the 1974 Summit meeting, the United States and the Soviet Union signed a protocol that further restrained deployment of strategic defensive armaments. The 1972 ABM Treaty had permitted each side two ABM deployment areas, one to defend its national capital and another to defend an ICBM field. The 1974 ABM Protocol limits each side to one site only.

The Soviet Union had chosen to maintain its ABM defense of Moscow, and the United States chose to maintain defense of its ICBM emplacements near Grand Forks, North Dakota. To allow some flexibility, the protocol allows each side to reverse its original choice of an ABM site. That is, the United States may dismantle or destroy its ABM system at Grand Forks and deploy an ABM defense of Washington. The Soviet Union, similarly, can decide to shift to an ABM defense of a missile field rather than of Moscow. Each side can make such a change only once. Advance notice must be given, and this may be done only during a year in which a review of the ABM Treaty is scheduled. The treaty prescribes reviews every 5 years; the first year for such a review began October 3, 1977.

Upon entry into force, the protocol became an integral part of the 1972 ABM Treaty, of which the verification and other provisions continue to apply. Thus the deployments permitted are governed by the treaty limitations on number and characteristics of interceptor missiles, launchers, and supporting radars.

Protocol to the Treaty Between the United States of America and the Union of Soviet Socialist Republics on the Limitation of Anti-Ballistic Missile Systems

Signed at Moscow July 3, 1974
Ratification advised by U.S. Senate November 10, 1975
Ratified by U.S. President March 19, 1976
Instruments of ratification exchanged May 24, 1976
Proclaimed by U.S. President July 6, 1976
Entered into force May 24, 1976

The United States of America and the Union of Soviet Socialist Republics, hereinafter referred to as the Parties,

Proceeding from the Basic Principles of Relations between the United States of America and the Union of Soviet Socialist Republics signed on May 29, 1972,

Desiring to further the objectives of the Treaty between the United States of America and the Union of Soviet Socialist Republics on the Limitation of Anti-Ballistic Missile Systems signed on May 26, 1972, hereinafter referred to as the Treaty,

Reaffirming their conviction that the adoption of further measures for the limitation of strategic arms would contribute to strengthening international peace and security,

Proceeding from the premise that further limitation of anti-ballistic missile systems will create more favorable conditions for the completion of work on a permanent agreement on more complete measures for the limitation of strategic offensive arms,

Have agreed as follows:

Article I

1. Each Party shall be limited at any one time to a single area out of the two provided in Article III of the Treaty for deployment of anti-ballistic missile (ABM) systems or their components and accordingly shall not exercise its right to deploy an ABM system or its components in the second of the two ABM system deployment areas permitted by Article III of the Treaty, except as an exchange of one permitted area for the other in accordance with Article II of this Protocol.

2. Accordingly, except as permitted by Article II of this Protocol: the United States of America shall not deploy an ABM system or its components in the area centered on its capital, as permitted by Article III(a) of the Treaty, and the Soviet Union shall not deploy an ABM system or its components in the deployment area of intercontinental ballistic missile (ICBM) silo launchers as permitted by Article III(b) of the Treaty.

Article II

1. Each Party shall have the right to dismantle or destroy its ABM system and the components thereof in the area where they are presently deployed and to deploy an ABM system or its components in the alternative area permitted by Article III of the Treaty, provided that prior to initiation of construction, notification is given in accord

with the procedure agreed to in the Standing Consultative Commission, during the year beginning October 3, 1977 and ending October 2, 1978, or during any year which commences at five year intervals thereafter, those being the years for periodic review of the Treaty, as provided in Article XIV of the Treaty. This right may be exercised only once.

2. Accordingly, in the event of such notice, the United States would have the right to dismantle or destroy the ABM system and its components in the deployment area of ICBM silo launchers and to deploy an ABM system or its components in an area centered on its capital, as permitted by Article III(a) of the Treaty, and the Soviet Union would have the right to dismantle or destroy the ABM system and its components in the area centered on its capital and to deploy an ABM system or its components in an area containing ICBM silo launchers, as permitted by Article III(b) of the Treaty.

3. Dismantling or destruction and deployment of ABM systems or their components and the notification thereof shall be carried out in accordance with Article VIII of the ABM Treaty and procedures agreed to in the Standing Consultative Commission.

Article III

The rights and obligations established by the Treaty remain in force and shall be complied with by the Parties except to the extent modified by this Protocol. In particular, the deployment of an ABM system or its components within the area selected shall remain limited by the levels and other requirements established by the Treaty.

Article IV

This Protocol shall be subject to ratification in accordance with the constitutional procedures of each Party. It shall enter into force on the day of the exchange of instruments of ratification and shall thereafter be considered an integral part of the Treaty.

DONE at Moscow on July 3, 1974, in duplicate, in the English and Russian languages, both texts being equally authentic.

For the United States of America:

RICHARD NIXON

President of the United States of America

For the Union of Soviet Socialist Republics:

L. I. BREZHNEV

General Secretary of the Central Committee of the CPSU

Treaty Between the United States of America and the Union of Soviet Socialist Republics on the Limitation of Underground Nuclear Weapon Tests (and Protocol Thereto)

The Treaty on the Limitation of Underground Nuclear Weapon Tests, also known as the Threshold Test Ban Treaty (TTBT), was signed in July 1974. It establishes a nuclear "threshold," by prohibiting tests having a yield exceeding 150 kilotons (equivalent to 150,000 tons of TNT).

The threshold is militarily important since it removes the possibility of testing new or existing nuclear weapons going beyond the fractional-megaton range. In the past decade, many tests above 150 kilotons have been conducted by both countries. The mutual restraint undertaken will significantly reduce the explosive force of new nuclear warheads and bombs which could otherwise be tested for weapon systems. Of particular significance is the relationship between explosive power of reliable, tested warheads and first-strike capability.

The task of negotiating a comprehensive test ban remains on the agenda of the U.S. Government, and, in Article I, the parties to the Threshold Test Ban Treaty undertook an obligation to continue negotiations toward that goal.

The first proposal for stopping nuclear weapon tests was made in 1955, and the first major negotiations with the Soviet Union for an effectively controlled test ban began in Geneva in 1958, with the United Kingdom also participating. The Conference on the Discontinuance of Nuclear Weapon Tests produced no agreement. The problem of working out verification procedures to insure compliance with a complete ban on nuclear weapon tests in all environments proved to be intractable at that time. The procedures deemed necessary by the United States and the United Kingdom were not acceptable to the Soviet Union.

In 1963 the Limited Test Ban Treaty (LTBT) was signed by the Soviet Union, the United States, and the United Kingdom. This treaty prohibits nuclear weapon testing in the atmosphere, in outer space and under water. The parties also agreed not to carry out any nuclear weapon test, or any other nuclear explosion, in any other environment—i.e., underground—that would cause radioactive debris to be present beyond the borders of the country in which the explosion took place.

Underground nuclear explosions were not prohibited by the 1963 treaty, although both in the treaty preamble and Article I, the LTBT parties pledged to seek "the discontinuance of all test explosions of nuclear weapons for all time...."

The United States and the Soviet Union agreed in the spring of 1974 to pursue the possibilities of further restrictions on nuclear testing. Accordingly, a team of U.S. experts was sent to Moscow for technical talks.

Agreement on the Threshold Test Ban Treaty was reached during the summit meeting in Moscow in July 1974. The test ban treaty includes a protocol which details technical data to be exchanged and which limits weapon testing to specific designated test sites to assist verification. The data to be exchanged include information on the geographical boundaries and geology of the testing areas. Geological data—including such factors as density of rock formation, water saturation, and depth of the water table—are useful in verifying test yields because the seismic signal produced by a given underground nuclear explosion varies with these factors at the test location. After an actual test has taken place, the geographic coordinates of the test location are to be furnished to the other party, to help in placing the test in the proper geological setting and thus in assessing the yield. Other information available to the United States will be used to cross-check the data provided.

The treaty also stipulates that data will be exchanged on a certain number of tests for calibration purposes. By establishing the correlation between stated yields of explosions at the specified sites and the seismic signals produced, this exchange will help improve assessments by both parties of the yields of explosions based primarily on the measurements derived from their seismic instruments. The tests used for calibration purposes may be tests which have been conducted in the past or may be new tests.

Agreement to exchange the detailed data described above represents a significant degree of direct cooperation by the two major nuclear powers in the effort to control nuclear weapons. For the first time, each party will make available to the other data relating to its nuclear weapons test program.

The technical problems associated with a yield threshold were recognized by the sides in the spring of 1974 during the negotiation of the TTB Treaty. In this context the U.S.S.R. mentioned the idea of some kind of a "mistakes" understanding concerning occasional, minor, unintended breaches. Discussions on the subject of such an understanding took place in the autumn of 1974 and in the spring of 1976. The U.S.S.R. was informed by the United States that the understanding reached would be included as part of the public record associated with submitting the TTB Treaty to the Senate for advice and consent to ratification. The entire understanding is as follows:

Both Parties will make every effort to comply fully with all the provisions of the TTB Treaty. However, there are technical uncertainties associated with predicting the precise yields of nuclear weapon tests. These uncertainties may result in slight, unintended breaches of the 150 kiloton threshold. Therefore, the two sides have discussed this problem and agreed that: (1) One or two slight, unintended breaches per year would not be considered a violation of the Treaty; (2) such breaches would be a cause for concern, however, and, at the request of either Party, would be the subject for consultations.

The U.S.S.R. was also informed that while the United States would not consider such a slight, unintentional breach a violation, the United States would carefully review each such breach to insure that it is not part of a general attempt to exceed the confines of the Treaty.

The understanding in its entirety was included in the transmittal documents which accompanied the TTB Treaty and the PNE Treaty when they were submitted to the Senate for advice and consent to ratification on July 29, 1976.

Although the TTBT was signed in 1974, it was not sent to the U.S. Senate for ratification until July 1976. Submission for ratification was held in abeyance until the companion treaty on underground nuclear explosions for peaceful purposes had been successfully negotiated in accordance with Article III of the TTBT. Both treaties are currently awaiting Senate action.

Treaty Between the United States of America and the Union of Soviet Socialist Republics on the Limitation of Underground Nuclear Weapon Tests

Signed at Moscow July 3, 1974

The United States of America and the Union of Soviet Socialist Republics, hereinafter referred to as the Parties,

Declaring their intention to achieve at the earliest possible date the cessation of the nuclear arms race and to take effective measures toward reductions in strategic arms, nuclear disarmament, and general and complete disarmament under strict and effective international control,

Recalling the determination expressed by the Parties to the 1963 Treaty Banning Nuclear Weapon Tests in the Atmosphere, in Outer Space and Under Water in its Preamble to seek to achieve the discontinuance of all test explosions of nuclear weapons for all time, and to continue negotiations to this end,

Noting that the adoption of measures for the further limitation of underground nuclear weapon tests would contribute to the achievement of these objectives and would meet the interests of strengthening peace and the further relaxation of international tension,

Reaffirming their adherence to the objectives and principles of the Treaty Banning Nuclear Weapon Tests in the Atmosphere, in Outer Space and Under Water and of the Treaty on the Non-Proliferation of Nuclear Weapons,

Have agreed as follows:

Article I

1. Each Party undertakes to prohibit, to prevent, and not to carry out any underground nuclear weapon test having a yield exceeding 150 kilotons at any place under its jurisdiction or control, beginning March 31, 1976.

2. Each Party shall limit the number of its underground nuclear weapon tests to a minimum.

3. The Parties shall continue their negotiations with a view toward achieving a solution to the problem of the cessation of all underground nuclear weapon tests.

Article II

1. For the purpose of providing assurance of compliance with the provisions of this Treaty, each Party shall use national technical means of verification at its disposal in a manner consistent with the generally recognized principles of international law.

2. Each Party undertakes not to interfere with the national technical means of verification of the other Party operating in accordance with paragraph 1 of this Article.

3. To promote the objectives and implementation of the provisions of this Treaty the Parties shall, as necessary, consult with each other, make inquiries and furnish information in response to such inquiries.

Article III

The provisions of this Treaty do not extend to underground nuclear explosions carried out by the Parties for peaceful purposes. Underground nuclear explosions for peaceful purposes shall be governed by an agreement which is to be negotiated and concluded by the Parties at the earliest possible time.

Article IV

This Treaty shall be subject to ratification in accordance with the constitutional procedures of each Party. This Treaty shall enter into force on the day of the exchange of instruments of ratification.

Article V

1. This Treaty shall remain in force for a period of five years. Unless replaced earlier by an agreement in implementation of the objectives specified in paragraph 3 of Article I of this Treaty, it shall be extended for successive five-year periods unless either Party notifies the other of its termination no later than six months prior to the expiration of the Treaty. Before the expiration of this period the Parties may, as necessary, hold consultations to consider the situation relevant to the substance of this Treaty and to introduce possible amendments to the text of the Treaty.

2. Each Party shall, in exercising its national sovereignty, have the right to withdraw from this Treaty if it decides that extraordinary events related to the subject matter of this Treaty have jeopardized its supreme interests. It shall give notice of its decision to the other Party six months prior to withdrawal from this Treaty. Such notice shall include a statement of the extraordinary events the notifying Party regards as having jeopardized its supreme interests.

3. This Treaty shall be registered pursuant to Article 102 of the Charter of the United Nations.

DONE at Moscow on July 3, 1974, in duplicate, in the English and Russian languages, both texts being equally authentic.

For the United States of America:

RICHARD NIXON,

> *The President of the United States of America*

For the Union of Soviet Socialist Republics:

L. BREZHNEV,

> *General Secretary of the Central Committee of the CPSU.*

Protocol to the Treaty Between the United States of America and the Union of Soviet Socialist Republics on the Limitation of Underground Nuclear Weapon Tests

The United States of America and the Union of Soviet Socialist Republics, hereinafter referred to as the Parties,
Having agreed to limit underground nuclear weapon tests,

Have agreed as follows:

1. For the Purpose of ensuring verification of compliance with the obligations of the Parties under the Treaty by national technical means, the Parties shall, on the basis of reciprocity, exchange the following data:

   a. The geographic coordinates of the boundaries of each test site and of the boundaries of the geophysically distinct testing areas therein.
   b. Information on the geology of the testing areas of the sites (the rock characteristics of geological formations and the basic physical properties of the rock, i.e., density, seismic velocity, water saturation, porosity and the depth of water table).
   c. The geographic coordinates of underground nuclear weapon tests, after they have been conducted.
   d. Yield, date, time, depth and coordinates for two nuclear weapon tests for calibration purposes from each geophysically distinct testing area where underground nuclear weapon tests have been and are to be conducted. In this connection the yield of such explosions for calibration purposes should be as near as possible to the limit defined in Article I of the Treaty and not less than one-tenth of that limit. In the case of testing areas where data are not available on two tests for calibration purposes, the data pertaining to one such test shall be exchanged, if available, and the data pertaining to the second test shall be exchanged as soon as possible after the second test having a yield in the above-mentioned range. The provisions of this Protocol shall not require the Parties to conduct tests solely for calibration purposes.

2. The Parties agree that the exchange of data pursuant to subparagraphs a, b, and d of paragraph 1 shall be carried out simultaneously with the exchange of instruments of ratification of the Treaty, as provided in Article IV of the Treaty, having in mind that the Parties shall, on the basis of reciprocity, afford each other the opportunity to familiarize themselves with these data before the exchange of instruments of ratification.

3. Should a Party specify a new test site or testing area after the entry into force of the Treaty, the data called for by subparagraphs a and b of paragraph 1 shall be transmitted to the other Party in advance of use of that site or area. The data called for by subparagraph d of paragraph 1 shall also be transmitted in advance of use of that site or area if they are available; if they are not available, they shall be transmitted as soon as possible after they have been obtained by the transmitting Party.

4. The Parties agree that the test sites of each Party shall be located at places under its jurisdiction or control and that all nuclear weapon tests shall be conducted solely within the testing areas specified in accordance with paragraph 1.

5. For the purposes of the Treaty, all underground nuclear explosions at the specified test sites shall be considered nuclear weapon tests and shall be subject to all the provisions of the Treaty relating to nuclear weapon tests. The provisions of Article III of the Treaty apply to all underground nuclear explosions conducted outside of the specified test sites, and only to such explosions.

This Protocol shall be considered an integral part of the Treaty.

DONE at Moscow on July 3, 1974.

For the United States of America:

RICHARD M. NIXON,

The President of the United States of America

For the Union of Soviet Socialist Republics:

L. BREZHNEV,

General Secretary of the Central Committee of the CPSU.

Treaty Between the United States of America and the Union of Soviet Socialist Republics on Underground Nuclear Explosions for Peaceful Purposes (and Protocol Thereto)

In preparing the Threshold Test Ban Treaty (TTBT) in July 1974, the United States and the Soviet Union recognized the need to establish an appropriate agreement to govern underground nuclear explosions for peaceful purposes (PNEs). There is no essential distinction between the technology of a nuclear explosive device which would be used as a weapon and the technology of a nuclear explosive device used for a peaceful purpose.

Negotiations on the PNE agreement contemplated in Article III of the TTBT began in Moscow on October 7, 1974, and after six negotiating sessions over a period of 18 months, resulted in the Treaty on Underground Nuclear Explosions for Peaceful Purposes in April 1976. The agreement consists of a treaty, a detailed protocol to the treaty, and an agreed statement delineating certain important activities which do not constitute a peaceful application as that term is used in the treaty.

The PNE Treaty will govern all nuclear explosions carried out at locations outside the weapons test sites specified under the Threshold Test Ban Treaty.

The two nations agreed: not to carry out any individual nuclear explosions having a yield exceeding 150 kilotons; not to carry out any group explosion (consisting of a number of individual explosions) having an aggregate yield exceeding 1,500 kilotons; and not to carry out any group explosion having an aggregate yield exceeding 150 kilotons unless the individual explosions in the group could be identified and measured by agreed verification procedures. The parties also reaffirmed their obligations to comply fully with the Limited Test Ban Treaty of 1963.

The parties reserve the right to carry out nuclear explosions for peaceful purposes in the territory of another country if requested to do so, but only in full compliance with the yield limitations and other provisions of the PNE Treaty and in accord with the Non-Proliferation Treaty.

Articles IV and V of the PNE Treaty set forth the agreed verification arrangements. In addition to the use of national technical means, the treaty states that information and access to sites of explosions will be provided by each side, and includes a commitment not to interfere with verification means and procedures.

The protocol to the PNE Treaty sets forth the specific agreed arrangements for assuring that no weapon-related benefits precluded by the Threshold Test Ban Treaty are derived by carrying out a nuclear explosion for peaceful purposes, including provisions for both detailed information and the rights and functions of observers.

The central problem to be solved through observation procedures is that of ensuring that no single nuclear device will be exploded with a yield exceeding 150 kilotons. Special procedures are required when the aggregate yield of a group explosion is larger than 150 kilotons. It is necessary for observers, using appropriate equipment, at the site of a group explosion to determine the yield of each of the individual explosive devices making up the group explosion.

The protocol spells out the procedures to be followed during the observation process, including such specifics as the number of observers, the geographical extent of their access, and the provision of certain information, such as maps of the area of the explosion, to assist in the planning of their activities.

In addition, the protocol provides for certain necessary privileges and immunities to be granted to observer personnel and their equipment, and for housing and working facilities to assure their freedom to carry out their rights and functions effectively.

The agreed statement that accompanies the treaty specifies that a "peaceful application" of an underground nuclear explosion would not include the developmental testing of any nuclear explosive. Such testing must be carried out at the nuclear weapon test sites specified by the terms of the TTBT, and therefore, is treated as the testing of a nuclear weapon.

The provisions of the PNE Treaty, together with those of the TTBT, establish a comprehensive system of regulations which will govern all underground nuclear explosions of the United States and the Soviet Union. The interrelationship of the TTBT and the PNE Treaty is further recognized by their identical 5-year durations, and by the provision that neither party may withdraw from the PNE Treaty while the TTBT remains in force. Conversely, either party may withdraw from the PNE Treaty upon termination of the TTBT.

A Joint Consultative Commission will be established to discuss any questions of compliance, to develop further details of the on-site inspection process as needed, and to facilitate cooperation in various areas related to PNEs which might be mutually beneficial.

Both treaties were submitted to the Senate on July 29, 1976, for advice and consent to ratification.

Treaty Between the United States of America and the Union of Soviet Socialist Republics on Underground Nuclear Explosions for Peaceful Purposes

Signed at Washington and Moscow May 28, 1976

The United States of America and the Union of Soviet Socialist Republics, hereinafter referred to as the Parties,

Proceeding from a desire to implement Article III of the Treaty between the United States of America and the Union of Soviet Socialist Republics on the Limitation of Underground Nuclear Weapon Tests, which calls for the earliest possible conclusion of an agreement on underground nuclear explosions for peaceful purposes,

Reaffirming their adherence to the objectives and principles of the Treaty Banning Nuclear Weapon Tests in the Atmosphere, in Outer Space and Under Water, the Treaty on Non-Proliferation of Nuclear Weapons, and the Treaty on the Limitation of Underground Nuclear Weapon Tests, and their determination to observe strictly the provisions of these international agreements,

Desiring to assure that underground nuclear explosions for peaceful purposes shall not be used for purposes related to nuclear weapons,

Desiring that utilization of nuclear energy be directed only toward peaceful purposes,

Desiring to develop appropriately cooperation in the field of underground nuclear explosions for peaceful purposes,

Have agreed as follows:

Article I

1. The Parties enter into this Treaty to satisfy the obligations in Article III of the Treaty on the Limitation of Underground Nuclear Weapon Tests, and assume additional obligations in accordance with the provisions of this Treaty.

2. This Treaty shall govern all underground nuclear explosions for peaceful purposes conducted by the Parties after March 31, 1976.

Article II

For the purposes of this Treaty:

(a) "explosion" means any individual or group underground nuclear explosion for peaceful purposes;

(b) "explosive" means any device, mechanism or system for producing an individual explosion;

(c) "group explosion" means two or more individual explosions for which the time interval between successive individual explosions does not exceed five seconds and for which the emplacement points of all explosives can be interconnected by straight line segments, each of which joins two emplacement points and each of which does not exceed 40 kilometers.

173

Article III

1. Each Party, subject to the obligations assumed under this Treaty and other international agreements, reserves the right to:

(a) carry out explosions at any place under its jurisdiction or control outside the geographical boundaries of test sites specified under the provisions of the Treaty on the Limitation of Underground Nuclear Weapon Tests; and

(b) carry out, participate or assist in carrying out explosions in the territory of another State at the request of such other State.

2. Each Party undertakes to prohibit, to prevent and not to carry out at any place under its jurisdiction or control, and further undertakes not to carry out, participate or assist in carrying out anywhere:

(a) any individual explosion having a yield exceeding 150 kilotons;

(b) any group explosion:

(1) having an aggregate yield exceeding 150 kilotons except in ways that will permit identification of each individual explosion and determination of the yield of each individual explosion in the group in accordance with the provisions of Article IV of and the Protocol to this Treaty;

(2) having an aggregate yield exceeding one and one-half megatons;

(c) any explosion which does not carry out a peaceful application;

(d) any explosion except in compliance with the provisions of the Treaty Banning Nuclear Weapon Tests in the Atmosphere, in Outer Space and Under Water, the Treaty on the Non-Proliferation of Nuclear Weapons, and other international agreements entered into by that Party.

3. The question of carrying out any individual explosion having a yield exceeding the yield specified in paragraph 2(a) of this article will be considered by the Parties at an appropriate time to be agreed.

Article IV

1. For the purpose of providing assurance of compliance with the provisions of this Treaty, each Party shall:

(a) use national technical means of verification at its disposal in a manner consistent with generally recognized principles of international law; and

(b) provide to the other Party information and access to sites of explosions and furnish assistance in accordance with the provisions set forth in the Protocol to this Treaty.

2. Each Party undertakes not to interfere with the national technical means of verification of the other Party operating in accordance with paragraph 1(a) of this article, or with the implementation of the provisions of paragraph 1(b) of this article.

Article V

1. To promote the objectives and implementation of the provisions of this Treaty, the Parties shall establish promptly a Joint Consultative Commission within the framework of which they will:

(a) consult with each other, make inquiries and furnish information in response to such inquiries, to assure confidence in compliance with the obligations assumed;

(b) consider questions concerning compliance with the obligations assumed and related situations which may be considered ambiguous;

(c) consider questions involving unintended interference with the means for assuring compliance with the provisions of this Treaty;

(d) consider changes in technology or other new circumstances which have a bearing on the provisions of this Treaty; and

(e) consider possible amendments to provisions governing underground nuclear explosions for peaceful purposes.

2. The Parties through consultation shall establish, and may amend as appropriate, Regulations for the Joint Consultative Commission governing procedures, composition and other relevant matters.

Article VI

1. The Parties will develop cooperation on the basis of mutual benefit, equality, and reciprocity in various areas related to carrying out underground nuclear explosions for peaceful purposes.

2. The Joint Consultative Commission will facilitate this cooperation by considering specific areas and forms of cooperation which shall be determined by agreement between the Parties in accordance with their constitutional procedures.

3. The Parties will appropriately inform the International Atomic Energy Agency of results of their cooperation in the field of underground nuclear explosions for peaceful purposes.

Article VII

1. Each Party shall continue to promote the development of the international agreement or agreements and procedures provided for in Article V of the Treaty on the Non-Proliferation of Nuclear Weapons, and shall provide appropriate assistance to the International Atomic Energy Agency in this regard.

2. Each Party undertakes not to carry out, participate or assist in the carrying out of any explosion in the territory of another State unless that State agrees to the implementation in its territory of the international observation and procedures contemplated by Article V of the Treaty on the Non-Proliferation of Nuclear Weapons and the provisions of Article IV of and the Protocol to this Treaty, including the provision by that State of the assistance necessary for such implementation and of the privileges and immunities specified in the Protocol.

Article VIII

1. This Treaty shall remain in force for a period of five years, and it shall be extended for successive five-year periods unless either Party notifies the other of its termination no later than six months prior to its expiration. Before the expiration of this period the Parties may, as necessary, hold consultations to consider the situation relevant to the substance of this Treaty. However, under no circumstances shall either Party be entitled to terminate this Treaty while the Treaty on the Limitation of Underground Nuclear Weapon Tests remains in force.

2. Termination of the Treaty on the Limitation of Underground Nuclear Weapon Tests shall entitle either Party to withdraw from this Treaty at any time.

3. Each Party may propose amendments to this Treaty. Amendments shall enter into force on the day of the exchange of instruments of ratification of such amendments.

Article IX

1. This Treaty including the Protocol which forms an integral part hereof, shall be subject to ratification in accordance with the constitutional procedures of each Party. This Treaty shall enter into force on the day of the exchange of instruments of ratification which exchange shall take place simultaneously with the exchange of instruments of ratification of the Treaty on the Limitation of Underground Nuclear Weapon Tests.

2. This Treaty shall be registered pursuant to Article 102 of the Charter of the United Nations.

DONE at Washington and Moscow, on May 28, 1976, in duplicate, in the English and Russian languages, both texts being equally authentic.

For the United States of America:

GERALD R. FORD,

The President of the United States of America.

For the Union of Soviet Socialist Republics:

L. BREZHNEV,

General Secretary of the Central Committee of the CPSU.

Protocol to the Treaty Between the United States of America and the Union of Soviet Socialist Republics on Underground Nuclear Explosions for Peaceful Purposes

The United States of America and the Union of Soviet Socialist Republics, hereinafter referred to as the Parties,

Having agreed to the provisions in the Treaty on Underground Nuclear Explosions for Peaceful Purposes, hereinafter referred to as the Treaty,

Have agreed as follows:

Article I

1. No individual explosion shall take place at a distance, in meters, from the ground surface which is less than 30 times the 3.4 root of its planned yield in kilotons.

2. Any group explosion with a planned aggregate yield exceeding 500 kilotons shall not include more than five individual explosions, each of which has a planned yield not exceeding 50 kilotons.

Article II

1. For each explosion, the Party carrying out the explosion shall provide the other Party:

(a) not later than 90 days before the beginning of emplacement of the explosives when the planned aggregate yield of the explosion does not exceed 100 kilotons, or not later than 180 days before the beginning of emplacement of the explosives when the planned aggregate yield of the explosion exceeds 100 kilotons, with the following information to the extent and degree of precision available when it is conveyed:

(1) the purpose of the planned explosion;

(2) the location of the explosion expressed in geographical coordinates with a precision of four or less kilometers, planned date and aggregate yield of the explosion;

(3) the type or types of rock in which the explosion will be carried out, including the degree of liquid saturation of the rock at the point of emplacement of each explosive; and

(4) a description of specific technological features of the project, of which the explosion is a part, that could influence the determination of its yield and confirmation of purpose; and

(b) not later than 60 days before the beginning of emplacement of the explosives the information specified in subparagraph 1(a) of this article to the full extent and with the precision indicated in that subparagraph.

2. For each explosion with a planned aggregate yield exceeding 50 kilotons, the Party carrying out the explosion shall provide the other Party, not later than 60 days before the beginning of emplacement of the explosives, with the following information:

(a) the number of explosives, the planned yield of each explosive, the location of each explosive to be used in a group explosion relative to all other explosives in the group with a precision of 100 or less meters, the depth of emplacement of each explosive with a precision of one meter and the time intervals between individual explosions in any group explosion with a precision of one-tenth second; and

(b) a description of specific features of geological structure or other local conditions that could influence the determination of the yield.

3. For each explosion with a planned aggregate yield exceeding 75 kilotons, the Party carrying out the explosion shall provide the other Party, not later than 60 days before the beginning of emplacement of the explosives, with a description of the geological and geophysical characteristics of the site of each explosion which could influence determination of the yield, which shall include: the depth of the water table; a stratigraphic column above each emplacement point; the position of each emplacement point relative to nearby geological and other features which influenced the design of the project of which the explosion is a part; and the physical parameters of the rock, including density, seismic velocity, porosity, degree of liquid saturation, and rock strength, within the sphere centered on each emplacement point and having a radius, in meters, equal to 30 times the cube root of the planned yield in kilotons of the explosive emplaced at that point.

4. For each explosion with a planned aggregate yield exceeding 100 kilotons, the Party carrying out the explosion shall provide the other Party, not later than 60 days before the beginning of emplacement of the explosives, with:

(a) information on locations and purposes of facilities and installations which are associated with the conduct of the explosion;

(b) information regarding the planned date of the beginning of emplacement of each explosive; and

(c) a topographic plan in local coordinates of the areas specified in paragraph 7 of Article IV, at a scale of 1 : 24,000 or 1 : 25,000 with a contour interval of 10 meters or less.

5. For application of an explosion to alleviate the consequences of an emergency situation involving an unforeseen combination of circumstances which calls for immediate action for which it would not be practicable to observe the timing requirements of paragraphs 1, 2 and 3 of this article, the following conditions shall be met:

(a) the Party deciding to carry out an explosion for such purposes shall inform the other Party of that decision immediately after it has been made and describe such circumstances;

(b) the planned aggregate yield of an explosion for such purpose shall not exceed 100 kilotons; and

(c) the Party carrying out an explosion for such purpose shall provide to the other Party the information specified in paragraph 1 of this article, and the information specified in paragraphs 2 and 3 of this article if applicable, after the decision to conduct the explosion is taken, but not later than 30 days before the beginning of emplacement of the explosives.

6. For each explosion, the Party carrying out the explosion shall inform the other Party, not later than two days before the explosion, of the planned time of detonation of each explosive with a precision of one second.

7. Prior to the explosion, the Party carrying out the explosion shall provide the other Party with timely notification of changes in the information provided in accordance with this article.

8. The explosion shall not be carried out earlier than 90 days after notification of any change in the information provided in accordance with this article which requires more extensive verification procedures than those required on the basis of the original information, unless an earlier time for carrying out the explosion is agreed between the Parties.

9. Not later than 90 days after each explosion the Party carrying out the explosion shall provide the other Party with the following information:

(a) the actual time of the explosion with a precision of one-tenth second and its aggregate yield;

(b) when the planned aggregate yield of a group explosion exceeds 50 kilotons, the actual time of the first individual explosion with a precision of one-tenth second, the time interval between individual explosions with a precision of one milli-second and the yield of each individual explosion; and

(c) confirmation of other information provided in accordance with paragraphs 1, 2, 3 and 4 of this article and explanation of any changes or corrections based on the results of the explosion.

10. At any time, but not later than one year after the explosion, the other Party may request the Party carrying out the explosion to clarify any item of the information provided in accordance with this article. Such clarification shall be provided as soon as practicable, but not later than 30 days after the request is made.

Article III

1. For the purposes of this Protocol:

(a) "designated personnel" means those nationals of the other Party identified to the Party carrying out an explosion as the persons who will exercise the rights and functions provided for in the Treaty and this Protocol; and

(b) "emplacement hole" means the entire interior of any drill-hole, shaft, adit or tunnel in which an explosive and associated cables and other equipment are to be installed.

2. For any explosion with a planned aggregate yield exceeding 100 kilotons but not exceeding 150 kilotons if the Parties, in consultation based on information provided in accordance with Article II and other information that may be introduced by either Party, deem it appropriate for the confirmation of the yield of the explosion, and for any explosion with a planned aggregate yield exceeding 150 kilotons, the Party carrying out the explosion shall allow designated personnel within the areas and at the locations described in Article V to exercise the following rights and functions:

(a) confirmation that the local circumstances, including facilities and installations associated with the project, are consistent with the stated peaceful purposes;

(b) confirmation of the validity of the geological and geophysical information provided in accordance with Article II through the following procedures:

(1) examination by designated personnel of research and measurement data of the Party carrying out the explosion and of rock core or rock fragments removed from each emplacement hole, and of any logs and drill core from existing exploratory holes which shall be provided to designated personnel upon their arrival at the site of the explosion;

(2) examination by designated personnel of rock core or rock fragments as they become available in accordance with the procedures specified in subparagraph 2(b)(3) of this article; and

(3) observation by designated personnel of implementation by the Party carrying out the explosion of one of the following four procedures, unless this right is waived by the other Party:

(i) construction of that portion of each emplacement hole starting from a point nearest the entrance of the emplacement hole which is at a distance, in meters, from the nearest emplacement point equal to 30 times the cube root of the planned yield in kilotons of the explosive to be emplaced at that point and continuing to the completion of the emplacement hole; or

(ii) construction of that portion of each emplacement hole starting from a point nearest the entrance of the emplacement hole which is at a distance, in meters, from the nearest emplacement point equal to six times the cube root of the planned yield in kilotons of the explosive to be emplaced at that point and continuing to the completion of the emplacement hole as well as the removal of rock core or rock fragments from the wall of an existing exploratory hole, which is substantially parallel with and at no point more than 100 meters from the emplacement hole, at locations specified by designated personnel which lie within a distance, in meters, from the same horizon as each emplacement point of 30 times the cube root of the planned yield in kilotons of the explosive to be emplaced at that point; or

(iii) removal of rock core or rock fragments from the wall of each emplacement hole at locations specified by designated personnel which lie within a distance, in meters, from each emplacement point of 30 times the cube root of the planned yield in kilotons of the explosive to be emplaced at each such point; or

(iv) construction of one or more new exploratory holes so that for each emplacement hole there will be a new exploratory hole to the same depth as that of the emplacement of the explosive, substantially parallel with and at no point more than 100 meters from each emplacement hole, from which rock cores would be removed at locations specified by designated personnel which lie within a distance, in meters, from the same horizon as each emplacement point of 30 times the cube root of the planned yield in kilotons of the explosive to be emplaced at each such point:

(c) observation of the emplacement of each explosive, confirmation of the depth of its emplacement and observation of the stemming of each emplacement hole;

(d) unobstructed visual observation of the area of the entrance to each emplacement hole at any time from the time of emplacement of each explosive until all personnel have been withdrawn from the site for the detonation of the explosion; and

(e) observation of each explosion.

3. Designated personnel, using equipment provided in accordance with paragraph 1 of Article IV, shall have the right, for any explosion with a planned aggregate yield exceeding 150 kilotons, to determine the yield of each individual explosion in a group explosion in accordance with the provisions of Article VI.

4. Designated personnel, when using their equipment in accordance with paragraph 1 of Article IV, shall have the right, for any explosion with planned aggregate yield exceeding 500 kilotons, to emplace, install and operate under the observation and with the assistance of personnel of the Party carrying out the explosion, if such assistance is requested by designated personnel, a local seismic network in accordance with the provisions of paragraph 7 of Article IV. Radio links may be used for the transmission of data and control signals between the seismic stations and the control center. Frequencies, maximum power output of radio transmitters, directivity of antennas and times of operation of the local seismic network radio transmitters before the explosion shall be agreed between the Parties in accordance with Article X and time of operation after the explosion shall conform to the time specified in paragraph 7 of Article IV.

5. Designated personnel shall have the right to:

(a) acquire photographs under the following conditions:

(1) the Party carrying out the explosion shall identify to the other Party those personnel of the Party carrying out the explosion who shall take photographs as requested by designated personnel;

(2) photographs shall be taken by personnel of the Party carrying out the explosion in the presence of designated personnel and at the time requested by designated personnel for taking such photographs. Designated personnel shall determine whether these photographs are in conformity with their requests and, if not, additional photographs shall be taken immediately;

(3) photographs shall be taken with cameras provided by the other Party having built-in, rapid developing capability and a copy of each photograph shall be provided at the completion of the development process to both Parties;

(4) cameras provided by designated personnel shall be kept in agreed secure storage when not in use; and

(5) the request for photographs can be made, at any time, of the following:

(i) exterior views of facilities and installations associated with the conduct of the explosion as described in subparagraph 4(a) of Article II;

(ii) geological samples used for confirmation of geological and geo-physical information, as provided for in subparagraph 2(b) of this article and the equipment utilized in the acquisition of such samples;

(iii) emplacement and installation of equipment and associated cables used by designated personnel for yield determination;

(iv) emplacement and installation of the local seismic network used by designated personnel;

(v) emplacement of the explosives and the stemming of the emplacement hole; and

(vi) containers, facilities and installations for storage and operation of equipment used by designated personnel;

(b) photographs of visual displays and records produced by the equipment used by designated personnel and photographs within the control centers taken by cameras which are component parts of such equipment; and

(c) receive at the request of designated personnel and with the agreement of the Party carrying out the explosion supplementary photographs taken by the Party carrying out the explosion.

Article IV

1. Designated personnel in exercising their rights and functions may choose to use the following equipment of either Party, of which choice the Party carrying out the explosion shall be informed not later than 150 days before the beginning of emplace-ment of the explosives:

(a) electrical equipment for yield determination and equipment for a local seismic network as described in paragraphs 3, 4 and 7 of this article; and

(b) geologist's field tools and kits and equipment for recording of field notes.

2. Designated personnel shall have the right in exercising their rights and functions to utilize the following additional equipment which shall be provided by the Party carrying out the explosion, under procedures to be established in accordance with Article X to ensure that the equipment meets the specifications of the other Party: portable short-range communication equipment, field glasses, optical equipment for

surveying and other items which may be specified by the other Party. A description of such equipment and operating instructions shall be provided to the other Party not later than 90 days before the beginning of emplacement of the explosives in connection with which such equipment is to be used.

3. A complete set of electrical equipment for yield determination shall consist of:

(a) sensing elements and associated cables for transmission of electrical power, control signals and data;

(b) equipment of the control center, electrical power supplies and cables for transmission of electrical power, control signals and data; and

(c) measuring and calibration instruments, maintenance equipment and spare parts necessary for ensuring the functioning of sensing elements, cables and equipment of the control center.

4. A complete set of equipment for the local seismic network shall consist of:

(a) seismic stations each of which contains a seismic instrument, electrical power supply and associated cables and radio equipment for receiving and transmission of control signals and data or equipment for recording control signals and data;

(b) equipment of the control center and electrical power supplies; and

(c) measuring and calibration instruments, maintenance equipment and spare parts necessary for ensuring the functioning of the complete network.

5. In case designated personnel, in accordance with paragraph 1 of this article, choose to use equipment of the Party carrying out the explosion for yield determination or for a local seismic network, a description of such equipment and installation and operating instructions shall be provided to the other Party not later than 90 days before the beginning of emplacement of the explosives in connection with which such equipment is to be used. Personnel of the Party carrying out the explosion shall emplace, install and operate the equipment in the presence of designated personnel. After the explosion, designated personnel shall receive duplicate copies of the recorded data. Equipment for yield determination shall be emplaced in accordance with Article VI. Equipment for a local seismic network shall be emplaced in accordance with paragraph 7 of this article.

6. In case designated personnel, in accordance with paragraph 1 of this article, choose to use their own equipment for yield determination and their own equipment for a local seismic network, the following procedures shall apply:

(a) the Party carrying out the explosion shall be provided by the other Party with the equipment and information specified in subparagraphs (a)(1) and (a)(2) of this paragraph not later than 150 days prior to the beginning of emplacement of the explosives in connection with which such equipment is to be used in order to permit the Party carrying out the explosion to familiarize itself with such equipment, if such equipment and information has not been previously provided, which equipment shall be returned to the other Party not later than 90 days before the beginning of emplacement of the explosives. The equipment and information to be provided are:

(1) one complete set of electrical equipment for yield determination as described in paragraph 3 of this aritcle, electrical and mechanical design information, specifications and installation and operating instructions concerning this equipment; and

(2) one complete set of equipment for the local seismic network described in paragraph 4 of this article, including one seismic station, electrical and mechanical design information, specifications and installation and operating instructions concerning this equipment;

(b) not later than 35 days prior to the beginning of emplacement of the explosives in connection with which the following equipment is to be used, two complete sets of electrical equipment for yield determination as described in paragraph 3 of this article and specific installation instructions for the emplacement of the sensing elements based on information provided in accordance with subparagraph 2(a) of Article VI and two complete sets of equipment for the local seismic network as described in paragraph 4 of this article, which sets of equipment shall have the same components and technical characteristics as the corresponding equipment specified in subparagraph 6(a) of this article, shall be delivered in sealed containers to the port of entry;

(c) The Party carrying out the explosion shall choose one of each of the two sets of equipment described above which shall be used by designated personnel in connection with the explosions;

(d) the set or sets of equipment not chosen for use in connection with the explosion shall be at the disposal of the Party carrying out the explosion for a period that may be as long as 30 days after the explosion at which time such equipment shall be returned to the other Party;

(e) the set or sets of equipment chosen for use shall be transported by the Party carrying out the explosion in the sealed containers in which this equipment arrived, after seals of the Party carrying out the explosion have been affixed to them, to the site of the explosion, so that this equipment is delivered to designated personnel for emplacement, installation and operation not later than 20 days before the beginning of emplacement of the explosives. This equipment shall remain in the custody of designated personnel in accordance with paragraph 7 of Article V or in agreed secure storage. Personnel of the Party carrying out the explosion shall have the right to observe the use of this equipment by designated personnel during the time the equipment is at the site of the explosion. Before the beginning of emplacement of the explosives, designated personnel shall demonstrate to personnel of the Party carrying out the explosion that this equipment is in working order;

(f) each set of equipment shall include two sets of components for recording data and associated calibration equipment. Both of these sets of components in the equipment chosen for use shall simultaneously record data. After the explosion, and after duplicate copies of all data have been obtained by designated personnel and the Party carrying out the explosion, one of each of the two sets of components for recording data and associated calibration equipment shall be selected, by an agreed process of chance, to be retained by designated personnel. Designated personnel shall pack and seal such components for recording data and associated calibration equipment which shall accompany them from the site of the explosion to the port of exit; and

(g) all remaining equipment may be retained by the Party carrying out the explosion for a period that may be as long as 30 days, after which time this equipment shall be returned to the other Party.

7. For any explosion with a planned aggregate yield exceeding 500 kilotons, a local seismic network, the number of stations of which shall be determined by designated personnel but shall not exceed the number of explosives in the group plus five, shall be emplaced, installed and operated at agreed sites of emplacement within an area circumscribed by circles of 15 kilometers in radius centered on points on the surface of the earth above the points of emplacement of the explosives during a period beginning not later than 20 days before the beginning of emplacement of the explosives and continuing after the explosion not later than three days unless otherwise agreed between the Parties.

8. The Party carrying out the explosion shall have the right to examine in the presence of designated personnel all equipment, instruments and tools of designated personnel specified in subparagraph 1(b) of this article.

9. The Joint Consultative Commission will consider proposals that either Party may put forward for the joint development of standardized equipment for verification purposes.

Article V

1. Except as limited by the provisions of paragraph 5 of this article, designated personnel in the exercise of their rights and functions shall have access along agreed routes:

(a) for an explosion with a planned aggregate yield exceeding 100 kilotons in accordance with paragraph 2 of Article III:

(1) to the locations of facilities and installations associated with the conduct of the explosion provided in accordance with subparagraph 4(a) of Article II; and

(2) to the locations of activities described in paragraph 2 of Article III; and

(b) for any explosion with a planned aggregate yield exceeding 150 kilotons, in addition to the access described in subparagraph 1(a) of this article:

(1) to other locations within the area circumscribed by circles of 10 kilometers in radius centered on points on the surface of the earth above the points of emplacement of the explosives in order to confirm that the local circumstances are consistent with the stated peaceful purposes;

(2) to the locations of the components of the electrical equipment for yield determination to be used for recording data when, by agreement between the Parties, such equipment is located outside the area described in subparagraph 1(b)(1) of this article; and

(3) to the sites of emplacement of the equipment of the local seismic network provided for in paragraph 7 of Article IV.

2. The Party carrying out the explosion shall notify the other Party of the procedure it has chosen from among those specified in subparagraph 2(b)(3) of Article III not later than 30 days before beginning the implementation of such procedure. Designated personnel shall have the right to be present at the site of the explosion to exercise their rights and functions in the areas and at the locations described in paragraph 1 of this article for a period of time beginning two days before the beginning of the implementation of the procedure and continuing for a period of three days after the completion of this procedure.

3. Except as specified in paragraph 5 of this article, designated personnel shall have the right to be present in the areas and at the locations described in paragraph 1 of this article:

(a) for an explosion with a planned aggregate yield exceeding 100 kilotons but not exceeding 150 kilotons, in accordance with paragraph 2 of Article III, at any time beginning five days before the beginning of emplacement of the explosives and continuing after the explosion and after safe access to evacuated areas has been established according to standards determined by the Party carrying out the explosion for a period of two days; and

(b) for any explosion with a planned aggregate yield exceeding 150 kilotons, at any time beginning 20 days before the beginning of emplacement of the explosives and continuing after the explosion and after safe access to evacuated areas has been established according to standards determined by the Party carrying out the explosion for a period of:

(1) five days in the case of an explosion with a planned aggregate yield exceeding 150 kilotons but not exceeding 500 kilotons; or

(2) eight days in the case of an explosion with a planned aggregate yield exceeding 500 kilotons.

4. Designated personnel shall not have the right to be present in those areas from which all personnel have been evacuated in connection with carrying out an explosion, but shall have the right to re-enter those areas at the same time as personnel of the Party carrying out the explosion.

5. Designated personnel shall not have or seek access by physical, visual or technical means to the interior of the canister containing an explosive, to documentary or other information descriptive of the design of an explosive nor to equipment for control and firing of explosives. The Party carrying out the explosion shall not locate documentary or other information descriptive of the design of an explosive in such ways as to impede the designated personnel in the exercise of their rights and functions.

6. The number of designated personnel present at the site of an explosion shall not exceed:

(a) for the exercise of their rights and functions in connection with the confirmation of the geological and geophysical information in accordance with the provisions of subparagraph 2(b) and applicable provisions of paragraph 5 of Article III—the number of emplacement holes plus three;

(b) for the exercise of their rights and functions in connection with confirming that the local circumstances are consistent with the information provided and with the stated peaceful purposes in accordance with the provisions in subparagraphs 2(a), 2(c), 2(d) and 2(e) and applicable provisions of paragraph 5 of Article III—the number of explosives plus two;

(c) for the exercise of their rights and functions in connection with confirming that the local circumstances are consistent with the information provided and with the stated peaceful purposes in accordance with the provisions in subparagraphs 2(a), 2(c), 2(d) and 2(e) and applicable provisions of paragraph 5 of Article III and in connection with the use of electrical equipment for determination of the yield in accordance with paragraph 3 of Article III—the number of explosives plus seven; and

(d) for the exercise of their rights and functions in connection with confirming that the local circumstances are consistent with the information provided and with the stated peaceful purposes in accordance with the provisions in subparagraph 2(a), 2(c), 2(d) and 2(e) and applicable provisions of paragraph 5 of Article III and in connection with the use of electrical equipment for determination of the yield in accordance with paragraph 3 of Article III and with the use of the local seismic network in accordance with paragraph 4 of Article III—the number of explosives plus 10.

7. The Party carrying out the explosion shall have the right to assign its personnel to accompany designated personnel while the latter exercise their rights and functions.

8. The Party carrying out an explosion shall assure for designated personnel telecommunications with their authorities, transportation and other services appropriate to their presence and to the exercise of their rights and functions at the site of the explosion.

9. The expenses incurred for the transportation of designated personnel and their equipment to and from the site of the explosion, telecommunications provided for in paragraph 8 of this article, their living and working quarters, subsistence and all other personal expenses shall be the responsibility of the Party other than the Party carrying out the explosion.

10. Designated personnel shall consult with the Party carrying out the explosion in order to coordinate the planned program and schedule of activities of designated personnel with the program of the Party carrying out the explosion for the conduct of the project so as to ensure that designated personnel are able to conduct their activities in an orderly and timely way that is compatible with the implementation of the project. Procedures for such consultations shall be established in accordance with Article X.

Article VI

For any explosion with a planned aggregate yield exceeding 150 kilotons, determination of the yield of each explosive used shall be carried out in accordance with the following provisions:

1. Determination of the yield of each individual explosion in the group shall be based on measurements of the velocity of propagation, as a function of time, of the hydrodynamic shock wave generated by the explosion, taken by means of electrical equipment described in paragraph 3 of Article IV.

2. The Party carrying out the explosion shall provide the other Party with the following information:

(a) not later than 60 days before the beginning of emplacement of the explosives, the length of each canister in which the explosive will be contained in the corresponding emplacement hole, the dimensions of the tube or other device used to emplace the canister and the cross-sectional dimensions of the emplacement hole to a distance, in meters, from the emplacement point of 10 times the cube root of its yield in kilotons;

(b) not later than 60 days before the beginning of emplacement of the explosives, a description of materials, including their densities, to be used to stem each emplacement hole; and

(c) not later than 30 days before the beginning of emplacement of the explosives, for each emplacement hole of a group explosion, the local coordinates of the point of emplacement of the explosive, the entrance of the emplacement hole, the point of the emplacement hole most distant from the entrance, the location of the emplacement hole at each 200 meters distance from the entrance and the configuration of any known voids larger than one cubic meter located within the distance, in meters, of 10 times the cube root of the planned yield in kilotons measured from the bottom of the canister containing the explosive. The error in these coordinates shall not exceed one percent of the distance between the emplacement hole and the nearest other emplacement hole or one percent of the distance between the point of measurement and the entrance of the emplacement hole, whichever is smaller, but in no case shall the error be required to be less than one meter.

3. The Party carrying out the explosion shall emplace for each explosive that portion of the electrical equipment for yield determination described in subparagraph 3(a) of Article IV, supplied in accordance with paragraph 1 of Article IV, in the same emplacement hole as the explosive in accordance with the installation instructions supplied under the provisions of paragraph 5 or 6 of Article IV. Such emplacement shall be carried out under the observation of designated personnel. Other equipment specified in subparagraph 3(b) of Article IV shall be emplaced and installed:

(a) by designated personnel under the observation and with the assistance of personnel of the Party carrying out the explosion, if such assistance is requested by designated personnel; or

(b) in accordance with paragraph 5 of Article IV.

4. That portion of the electrical equipment for yield determination described in subparagraph 3(a) of Article IV that is to be emplaced in each emplacement hole shall be located so that the end of the electrical equipment which is farthest from the entrance to the emplacement hole is at a distance, in meters, from the bottom of the canister containing the explosive equal to 3.5 times the cube root of the planned yield in kilotons of the explosive when the planned yield is less than 20 kilotons and three times the cube root of the planned yield in kilotons of the explosive when the planned yield is 20 kilotons or more. Canisters longer than 10 meters containing the explosive shall only be utilized if there is prior agreement between the Parties establishing provisions for their use. The Party carrying out the explosion shall provide the other Party with data on the distribution of density inside any other canister in the emplacement hole with a transverse cross-sectional area exceeding 10 square centimeters located within a distance, in meters, of 10 times the cube root of the planned yield in kilotons of the explosion from the bottom of the canister containing the explosive. The Party carrying out the explosion shall provide the other Party with access to confirm such data on density distribution within any such canister.

5. The Party carrying out an explosion shall fill each emplacement hole, including all pipes and tubes contained therein which have at any transverse section an aggregate cross-sectional area exceeding 10 square centimeters in the region containing the electrical equipment for yield determination and to a distance, in meters, of six times the cube root of the planned yield in kilotons of the explosive from the explosive emplacement point, with material having a density not less than seven-tenths of the average density of the surrounding rock, and from that point to a distance of not less than 00 meters from the explosive emplacement point with material having a density greater than one gram per cubic centimeter.

6. Designated personnel shall have the right to:

(a) confirm information provided in accordance with subparagraph 2(a) of this article;

(b) confirm information provided in accordance with subparagraph 2(b) of this article and be provided, upon request, with a sample of each batch of stemming material as that material is put into the emplacement hole; and

(c) confirm the information provided in accordance with subparagraph 2(c) of this article by having access to the data acquired and by observing, upon their request, the making of measurements.

7. For those explosives which are emplaced in separate holes, the emplacement shall be such that the distance D, in meters, between any explosive and any portion of the electrical equipment for determination of the yield of any other explosive in the group shall be not less than 10 times the cube root of the planned yield in kilotons of the larger explosive of such a pair of explosives. Individual explosions shall be separated by time intervals, in milliseconds, not greater than one-sixth the amount by which the distance D, in meters, exceeds 10 times the cube root of the planned yield in kilotons of the larger explosive of such a pair of explosives.

8. For those explosives in a group which are emplaced in a common emplacement hole, the distance, in meters, between each explosive and any other explosive in that emplacement hole shall be not less than 10 times the cube root of the planned yield in kilotons of the larger explosive of such a pair of explosives, and the explosives shall be detonated in sequential order, beginning with the explosive farthest from the entrance to the emplacement hole, with the individual detonations separated by time intervals, in milliseconds, of not less than one times the cube root of the planned yield in kilotons of the largest explosive in this emplacement hole.

Article VII

1. Designated personnel with their personal baggage and their equipment as provided in Article IV shall be permitted to enter the territory of the Party carrying out the explosion at an entry port to be agreed upon by the Parties, to remain in the territory of the Party carrying out the explosion for the purpose of fulfilling their rights and functions provided for in the Treaty and this Protocol, and to depart from an exit port to be agreed upon by the Parties.

2. At all times while designated personnel are in the territory of the Party carrying out the explosion, their persons, property, personal baggage, archives and documents as well as their temporary official and living quarters shall be accorded the same privileges and immunities as provided in Articles 22, 23, 24, 29, 30, 31, 34 and 36 of the Vienna Convention on Diplomatic Relations of 1961 to the persons, property, personal baggage, archives and documents of diplomatic agents as well as to the premises of diplomatic missions and private residences of diplomatic agents.

3. Without prejudice to their privileges and immunities it shall be the duty of designated personnel to respect the laws and regulations of the State in whose territory the explosion is to be carried out insofar as they do not impede in any way whatsoever the proper exercising of their rights and functions provided for by the Treaty and this Protocol.

Article VIII

The Party carrying out an explosion shall have sole and exclusive control over and full responsibility for the conduct of the explosion.

Article IX

1. Nothing in the Treaty and this Protocol shall affect proprietary rights in information made available under the Treaty and this Protocol and in information which may be disclosed in preparation for and carrying out of explosions; however, claims to such proprietary rights shall not impede implementation of the provisions of the Treaty and this Protocol.

2. Public release of the information provided in accordance with Article II or publication of material using such information, as well as public release of the results of observation and measurements obtained by designated personnel, may take place only by agreement with the Party carrying out an explosion; however, the other Party shall have the right to issue statements after the explosion that do not divulge information in which the Party carrying out the explosion has rights which are referred to in paragraph 1 of this article.

Article X

The Joint Consultative Commission shall establish procedures through which the Parties will, as appropriate, consult with each other for the purpose of ensuring efficient implementation of this Protocol.

DONE at Washington and Moscow, on May 28, 1976.

For the United States of America:

GERALD R. FORD,

The President of the United States of America.

For the Union of Soviet Socialist Republics:

L. BREZHNEV,
General Secretary of the Central Committee of the CPSU.

Agreed Statement

May 13, 1976

The Parties to the Treaty Between the United States of America and the Union of Soviet Socialist Republics on Underground Nuclear Explosions for Peaceful Purposes, hereinafter referred to as the Treaty, agree that under subparagraph 2(c) of Article III of the Treaty:

(a) Development testing of nuclear explosives does not constitute a "peaceful application" and any such development tests shall be carried out only within the boundaries of nuclear weapon test sites specified in accordance with the Treaty between the United States of America and the Union of Soviet Socialist Republics on the Limitation of Underground Nuclear Weapon Tests;

(b) Associating test facilities, instrumentation or procedures related only to testing of nuclear weapons or their effects with any explosion carried out in accordance with the Treaty does not constitute a "peaceful application."

Convention on the Prohibition of Military or Any Other Hostile Use of Environmental Modification Techniques

Use of environmental modification techniques for hostile purposes does not play a major role in military planning at the present time. Such techniques might be developed in the future, however, and would pose a threat of serious damage unless action is taken to prohibit their use. In July 1972, the U.S. Government renounced the use of climate modification techniques for hostile purposes, even if their development were proved to be feasible in the future.

Both the U.S. Senate and the House of Representatives held hearings, beginning in 1972, and the Senate adopted a resolution in 1973 calling for an international agreement "prohibiting the use of any environmental or geophysical modification activity as a weapon of war...." In response to this resolution, the President ordered the Department of Defense to undertake an in-depth review of the military aspects of weather and other environmental modification techniques. The results of this study and a subsequent interagency study led to the U.S. Government's decision to seek agreement with the Soviet Union to explore the possibilities of an international agreement.

During the summit meeting in Moscow in July 1974, President Nixon and General Secretary Brezhnev formally agreed to hold bilateral discussions on how to bring about "the most effective measures possible to overcome the dangers of the use of environmental modification techniques for military purposes." Three sets of discussions were held in 1974 and 1975, resulting in agreement on a common approach and common language.

In August 1975, the chief representatives of the U.S. and the Soviet delegations to the Conference of the Committee on Disarmament (CCD) tabled, in parallel, identical draft texts of a "Convention on the Prohibition of Military or any Other Hostile Use of Environmental Modification Techniques."

The convention defines environmental modification techniques as changing—through the deliberate manipulation of natural processes—the dynamics, composition or structure of the earth, including its biota, lithosphere, hydrosphere, and atmosphere, or of outer space. Changes in weather or climate patterns, in ocean currents, or in the state of the ozone layer or ionosphere, or an upset in the ecological balance of a region are some of the effects which might result from the use of environmental modification techniques.

Intensive negotiations held in the CCD during the spring and summer of 1976 resulted in a modified text and, in addition, to understandings regarding four of the treaty articles. These were transmitted to the U.N. General Assembly for consideration during the fall session.

Article I sets forth the basic commitment: "Each State Party to this convention undertakes not to engage in military or any other hostile use of environmental modification techniques having widespread, long-lasting or severe effects as the means of destruction, damage or injury to any other State Party." An understanding defines the terms "widespread, long-lasting or severe." "Widespread" is defined as "encompassing an area on the scale of several hundred square kilometers"; "long-lasting" is defined as "lasting for a period of months, or approximately a season"; and "severe" is defined as "involving serious or significant disruption or harm to human life, natural and economic resources or other assets."

With regard to peaceful uses of environmental modification techniques, the convention provides that the parties shall have the right to participate in the fullest possible exchange of scientific and technological information.

In addition to the provision for mutual consultation regarding complaints and for recourse to the Security Council, the revised draft establishes the framework for a Consultative Committee of Experts, which would meet on an *ad hoc* basis when so requested by a party, in order to clarify the nature of activities suspected to be in violation of the convention. Responding to the suggestion of many delegations, the revised text incorporates a provision for periodic conferences to review the convention's operation.

During the 1976 fall session, the U.N. General Assembly held extensive debate on the draft convention, including several resolutions relating thereto. On December 10, the General Assembly adopted a resolution by a vote of 96 to 8, with 30 abstentions, which referred the convention to all member nations for their consideration, signature, and ratification, and requested the U.N. Secretary-General to open the convention for signature.

The U.N. Secretary-General officiated at the signing ceremony in Geneva on May 18. The United States joined 33 other nations in signing the convention. The convention entered into force on October 5, 1978, when the 20th state to sign the convention deposited its instrument of ratification. President Carter transmitted the convention to the Senate on September 22, 1978. The Senate gave its advice and consent to ratification on November 28, 1979, by a vote of 98-0. The President ratified the convention December 13, 1979. The convention entered into force for the United States on January 17, 1980, when the United States instrument of ratification was deposited in New York.

Convention on the Prohibition of Military or Any Other Hostile Use of Environmental Modification Techniques

Signed in Geneva May 18, 1977
Entered into force October 5, 1978
Ratification advised by U.S. Senate November 28, 1979
Ratified by U.S. President December 13, 1979
U.S. ratification deposited at New York January 17, 1980

The States Parties to this Convention,

Guided by the interest of consolidating peace, and wishing to contribute to the cause of halting the arms race, and of bringing about general and complete disarmament under strict and effective international control, and of saving mankind from the danger of using new means of warfare,

Determined to continue negotiations with a view to achieving effective progress towards further measures in the field of disarmament,

Recognizing that scientific and technical advances may open new possibilities with respect to modification of the environment,

Recalling the Declaration of the United Nations Conference on the Human Environment adopted at Stockholm on 16 June 1972,

Realizing that the use of environmental modification techniques for peaceful purposes could improve the interrelationship of man and nature and contribute to the preservation and improvement of the environment for the benefit of present and future generations,

Recognizing, however, that military or any other hostile use of such techniques could have effects extremely harmful to human welfare,

Desiring to prohibit effectively military or any other hostile use of environmental modification techniques in order to eliminate the dangers to mankind from such use, and affirming their willingness to work towards the achievement of this objective,

Desiring also to contribute to the strengthening of trust among nations and to the further improvement of the international situation in accordance with the purposes and principles of the Charter of the United Nations,

Have agreed as follows:

Article I

1. Each State Party to this Convention undertakes not to engage in military or any other hostile use of environmental modification techniques having widespread, long-lasting or severe effects as the means of destruction, damage or injury to any other State Party.

2. Each State Party to this Convention undertakes not to assist, encourage or induce any State, group of States or international organization to engage in activities contrary to the provisions of paragraph 1 of this article.

Article II

As used in article I, the term "environmental modification techniques" refers to any technique for changing—through the deliberate manipulation of natural processes—the dynamics, composition or structure of the Earth, including its biota, lithosphere, hydrosphere and atmosphere, or of outer space.

Article III

1. The provisions of this Convention shall not hinder the use of environmental modification techniques for peaceful purposes and shall be without prejudice to the generally recognized principles and applicable rules of international law concerning such use.

2. The States Parties to this Convention undertake to facilitate, and have the right to participate in, the fullest possible exchange of scientific and technological information on the use of environmental modification techniques for peaceful purposes. States Parties in a position to do so shall contribute, alone or together with other States or international organizations, to international economic and scientific co-operation in the preservation, improvement, and peaceful utilization of the environment, with due consideration for the needs of the developing areas of the world.

Article IV

Each State Party to this Convention undertakes to take any measures it considers necessary in accordance with its constitutional processes to prohibit and prevent any activity in violation of the provisions of the Convention anywhere under its jurisdiction or control.

Article V

1. The States Parties to this Convention undertake to consult one another and to co-operate in solving any problems which may arise in relation to the objectives of, or in the application of the provisions of, the Convention. Consultation and co-operation pursuant to this article may also be undertaken through appropriate international procedures within the framework of the United Nations and in accordance with its Charter. These international procedures may include the services of appropriate international organizations, as well as of a Consultative Committee of Experts as provided for in paragraph 2 of this article.

2. For the purposes set forth in paragraph 1 of this article, the Depositary shall, within one month of the receipt of a request from any State Party to this convention, convene a Consultative Committee of Experts. Any State Party may appoint an expert to the Committee whose functions and rules of procedure are set out in the annex, which constitutes an integral part of this Convention. The Committee shall transmit to the Depositary a summary of its findings of fact, incorporating all views and information presented to the Committee during its proceedings. The Depositary shall distribute the summary to all States Parties.

3. Any State Party to this Convention which has reason to believe that any other State Party is acting in breach of obligations deriving from the provisions of the Convention may lodge a complaint with the Security Council of the United Nations. Such a complaint should include all relevant information as well as all possible evidence supporting its validity.

4. Each State Party to this Convention undertakes to co-operate in carrying out any investigation which the Security Council may initiate, in accordance with the provisions of the Charter of the United Nations, on the basis of the complaint received by the

Council. The Security Council shall inform the States Parties of the results of the investigation.

5. Each State Party to this Convention undertakes to provide or support assistance, in accordance with the provisions of the Charter of the United Nations, to any State Party which so requests, if the Security Council decides that such Party has been harmed or is likely to be harmed as a result of violation of the Convention.

Article VI

1. Any State Party to this Convention may propose amendments to the Convention. The text of any proposed amendment shall be submitted to the Depositary who shall promptly circulate it to all States Parties.

2. An amendment shall enter into force for all States Parties to this Convention which have accepted it, upon the deposit with the Depositary of instruments of acceptance by a majority of States Parties. Thereafter it shall enter into force for any remaining State Party on the date of deposit of its instrument of acceptance.

Article VII

This Convention shall be of unlimited duration.

Article VIII

1. Five years after the entry into force of this Convention, a conference of the States Parties to the Convention shall be convened by the Depositary at Geneva, Switzerland. The conference shall review the operation of the Convention with a view to ensuring that its purposes and provisions are being realized, and shall in particular examine the effectiveness of the provisions of paragraph 1 of Article I in eliminating the dangers of military or any other hostile use of environmental modification techniques.

2. At intervals of not less than five years thereafter, a majority of the States Parties to the Convention may obtain, by submitting a proposal to this effect to the Depositary, the convening of a conference with the same objectives.

3. If no conference has been convened pursuant to paragraph 2 of this article within ten years following the conclusion of a previous conference, the Depositary shall solicit the views of all States Parties to the Convention, concerning the convening of such a conference. If one third or ten of the States Parties, whichever number is less, respond affirmatively, the Depositary shall take immediate steps to convene the conference.

Article IX

1. This Convention shall be open to all States for signature. Any State which does not sign the Convention before its entry into force in accordance with paragraph 3 of this article may accede to it at any time.

2. This Convention shall be subject to ratification by signatory States. Instruments of ratification or accession shall be deposited with the Secretary-General of the United Nations.

3. This Convention shall enter into force upon the deposit of instruments of ratification by twenty Governments in accordance with paragraph 2 of this article.

4. For those States whose instruments of ratification or accession are deposited after the entry into force of this Convention, it shall enter into force on the date of the deposit of their instruments of ratification or accession.

5. The Depositary shall promptly inform all signatory and acceding States of the date of each signature, the date of deposit of each instrument of ratification or

accession and the date of the entry into force of this Convention and of any amendments thereto, as well as of the receipt of other notices.

6. This Convention shall be registered by the Depositary in accordance with Article 102 of the Charter of the United Nations.

Article X

This Convention, of which the English, Arabic, Chinese, French, Russian, and Spanish texts are equally authentic, shall be deposited with the Secretary-General of the United Nations, who shall send certified copies thereof to the Governments of the signatory and acceding States.

IN WITNESS WHEREOF, the undersigned, being duly authorized thereto by their respective governments, have signed this Convention, opened for signature at Geneva on the eighteenth day of May, one thousand nine hundred and seventy-seven.

DONE at Gevena on May 18, 1977.

Annex to the Convention
Consultative Committee of Experts

1. The Consultative Committee of Experts shall undertake to make appropriate findings of fact and provide expert views relevant to any problem raised pursuant to paragraph 1 of Article V of this Convention by the State Party requesting the convening of the Committee.

2. The work of the Consultative Committee of Experts shall be organized in such a way as to permit it to perform the functions set forth in paragraph 1 of this annex. The Committee shall decide procedural questions relative to the organization of its work, where possible by consensus, but otherwise by a majority of those present and voting. There shall be no voting on matters of substance.

3. The Depositary or his representative shall serve as the Chairman of the Committee.

4. Each expert may be assisted at meetings by one or more advisers.

5. Each expert shall have the right, through the Chairman, to request from States, and from international organizations, such information and assistance as the expert considers desirable for the accomplishment of the Committee's work.

Understandings Regarding the Convention[1]

Understanding Relating to Article I

It is the understanding of the Committee that, for the purposes of this Convention, the terms, "widespread", "long-lasting" and "severe" shall be interpreted as follows:

(a) "widespread": encompassing an area on the scale of several hundred square kilometres;

(b) "long-lasting": lasting for a period of months, or approximately a season;

(c) "severe": involving serious or significant disruption or harm to human life, natural and economic resources or other assets.

It is further understood that the interpretation set forth above is intended exclusively for this Convention and is not intended to prejudice the interpretation of the same or similar terms if used in connexion with any other international agreement.

Understanding Relating to Article II

It is the understanding of the Committee that the following examples are illustrative of phenomena that could be caused by the use of environmental modification techniques as defined in Article II of the Convention: earthquakes; tsunamis; an upset in the ecological balance of a region; changes in weather patterns (clouds, precipitation, cyclones of various types and tornadic storms); changes in climate patterns; changes in ocean currents; changes in the state of the ozone layer; and changes in the state of the ionosphere.

It is further understood that all the phenomena listed above, when produced by military or any other hostile use of environmental modification techniques, would result, or could reasonably be expected to result, in widespread, long-lasting or severe destruction, damage or injury. Thus, military or any other hostile use of environmental modification techniques as defined in Article II, so as to cause those phenomena as a means of destruction, damage or injury to another State Party, would be prohibited.

It is recognized, moreover, that the list of examples set out above is not exhaustive. Other phenomena which could result from the use of environmental modification techniques as defined in Article II could also be appropriately included. The absence of such phenomena from the list does not in any way imply that the undertaking contained in Article I would not be applicable to those phenomena, provided the criteria set out in that article were met.

Understanding Relating to Article III

It is the understanding of the Committee that this Convention does not deal with the question whether or not a given use of environmental modification techniques for peaceful purposes is in accordance with generally recognized principles and applicable rules of international law.

---

[1]These are not incorporated into the Convention but are part of the negotiating record and were included in the report transmitted by the CCD to the U.N. General Assembly in September 1976.

Understanding Relating to Article VIII

It is the understanding of the Committee that a proposal to amend the Convention may also be considered at any conference of Parties held pursuant to Article VIII. It is further understood that any proposed amendment that is intended for such consideration should, if possible, be submitted to the Depositary no less than 90 days before the commencement of the conference.

Environmental Modification Convention

Country	Date of[1] Signature	Date of Deposit[1] of Ratification	Date of Deposit[1] of Accession
Australia	5/31/78		
Bangladesh			10/ 3/79
Belgium	5/18/77		
Benin	6/10/77		
Bolivia	5/18/77		
Brazil	11/ 9/77		
Bulgaria	5/18/77	5/31/78	
Byelorussian S.S.R.[2]	5/18/77	6/ 7/78	
Canada	5/18/77		
Cape Verde			10/ 3/79
Cuba	9/23/77	4/10/78	
Cyprus	10/ 7/77	4/12/78	
Czechoslovakia	5/18/77	5/12/78	
Denmark	5/18/77	4/19/78	
Ethiopia	5/18/77		
Finland	5/18/77	5/12/78	
German Democratic Republic	5/18/77	5/25/78	
Germany, Federal Republic of	5/18/77		
Ghana	3/21/78	6/22/78	
Holy See	5/27/77		
Hungary	5/18/77	4/19/78	
Iceland	5/18/77		
India	12/10/77	12/15/78	
Iran	5/18/77		
Iraq	8/15/77		
Ireland	5/18/77		
Italy	5/18/77		
Kuwait			1/ 2/80
Laos	4/13/78	10/ 5/78	
Lebanon	5/18/77		
Liberia	5/18/77		
Luxembourg	5/18/77		
Malawi			10/ 5/78
Mongolia	5/18/77	5/19/78	

See footnotes on page 239.

Environmental Modification Convention

Country	Date of[1] Signature	Date of Deposit[1] of Ratification	Date of Deposit[1] of Accession
Morocco	5/18/77		
Netherlands	5/18/77		
Nicaragua	8/11/77		
Norway	5/18/77	2/15/79	
Poland	5/18/77	6/ 8/78	
Portugal	5/18/77		
Romania	5/18/77		
São Tome and Principe			10/ 5/79
Sierra Leone	4/12/78		
Spain	5/18/77	7/19/78	
Sri Lanka	6/ 8/77	4/25/78	
Syrian Arab Republic	8/ 4/77		
Tunisia	5/11/78	5/11/78	
Turkey	5/18/77		
Uganda	5/18/77		
Ukrainian S.S.R.[2]	5/18/77	6/13/78	
Union of Soviet Socialist Republics	5/18/77	5/30/78	
United Kingdom	5/18/77	5/16/78	
United States	5/18/77	1/17/80	
Yemen Arab Republic (Sana)	5/18/77	7/20/77	
Yemen, People's Democratic Republic of (Aden)			6/12/79
Zaire	2/28/78		
Totals[3]	48	21	6

See footnotes on page 239.

Strategic Arms Limitation Talks (SALT II)

In accordance with Article VII of the Interim Agreement in which the sides committed themselves to continue active negotiations on strategic offensive arms, the SALT II negotiations began in November 1972. The primary goal of SALT II was to replace the Interim Agreement with a long-term comprehensive treaty providing broad limits on strategic offensive weapons systems. The principal U.S. objectives as the SALT II negotiations began were to provide for equal numbers of strategic nuclear delivery vehicles for the sides, to begin the process of reduction of these delivery vehicles, and to impose restraints on qualitative developments which could threaten future stability.

Early discussion between the sides focused on the weapon systems to be included, factors involved in providing for equality in numbers of strategic nuclear delivery vehicles, taking into account the important differences between the forces of the two sides, bans on new systems, qualitative limits, and a Soviet proposal to include U.S. forward-based systems. The positions of the sides differed widely on many of these issues.

A major breakthrough occurred at the Vladivostok meeting in November 1974, between President Ford and General Secretary Brezhnev. At this meeting, the sides agreed to a basic framework for the SALT II agreement. Basic elements of the Aide-Memoire, which recorded this agreement, included:

- 2,400 equal aggregate limit on strategic nuclear delivery vehicles (ICBMs, SLBMs, and heavy bombers) of the sides;
- 1,320 equal aggregate limit on MIRV systems;
- ban on construction of new land-based ICBM launchers;
- limits on deployment of new types of strategic offensive arms; and
- important elements of the Interim Agreement (e.g., relating to verification) would be incorporated in the new agreement.

In addition, the Aide-Memoire stated that the duration of the new agreement would be through 1985.

In early 1975, the delegations in Geneva resumed negotiations, working toward an agreement based on this general framework. It was during this time that a Joint Draft Text was first prepared and many limitations were agreed. During the negotiations, however, it became clear that there was fundamental disagreement between the two sides on two major issues: how cruise missiles were to be addressed, and whether the new Soviet bomber known to the United States as Backfire would be considered a heavy bomber and therefore counted in the 2,400 aggregate. While there was disagreement on other issues such as MIRV verification provisions, restrictions on new systems, and missile throw-weight ceilings, progress was made in these areas. However, the issues of cruise missiles and Backfire remained unresolved.

When the new Administration took office in 1977, renewed emphasis was placed on the Strategic Arms Limitation Talks. A comprehensive interagency review of SALT was undertaken. Building on the work of the previous Administration, particularly the Vladivostok accord and the subsequent agreement on many issues in Geneva, the United States made a comprehensive proposal which was presented to the Soviets by Secretary of State Vance in March 1977. This proposal would have added significant reductions and qualitative constraints to the ceilings which were agreed to at Vladivostok. At the same time, the United States also presented an alternative proposal for a SALT II agreement similar to the framework agreed to at Vladivostok, with the Backfire and cruise missile issues deferred until SALT III.

Both proposals were rejected by the Soviets as inconsistent with their understandings of the Vladivostok accord.

In subsequent negotiations, the sides agreed on a general framework for SALT II which accommodated both the Soviet desire to retain the Vladivostok framework for an agreement, and the U.S. desire for more comprehensive limitations in SALT II.

The agreement would consist of three parts:

• A Treaty which would be in force through 1985 based on the Vladivostok accord;

• A Protocol of about 3-years' duration which would cover certain issues such as cruise missile constraints, mobile ICBM limits, and qualitative constraints on ICBMs, while deferring further negotiations on these issues to SALT III;

• A Joint Statement of Principles which would be an agreed set of guidelines for future negotiations.

Within this framework, negotiations to resolve the remaining differences continued on several levels. President Carter, Secretary Vance, and Soviet Foreign Minister Gromyko met in Washington in September 1977. Further high-level meetings were held in Washington, Moscow, and Geneva during 1978 and 1979. In addition, the SALT delegations of the United States and Soviet Union in Geneva were in session nearly continuously since the 1974 Vladivostok meeting to work out agreed Treaty language on those issues where agreement in principle had been reached at the ministerial level.

The completed SALT II agreement was signed by President Carter and General Secretary Brezhnev in Vienna on June 18, 1979. President Carter transmitted it to the Senate on June 22 for its advice and consent to ratification.

Treaty Between the United States of America and the Union of Soviet Socialist Republics on the Limitation of Strategic Offensive Arms

The SALT II Treaty will provide for:

- an equal aggregate limit on the number of strategic nuclear delivery vehicles—ICBM and SLBM launchers, heavy bombers, and air-to-surface ballistic missiles (ASBMs). Initially, this ceiling will be 2,400, as agreed at Vladivostok. The ceiling will be lowered to 2,250 at the end of 1981;
- an equal aggregate limit of 1,320 on the total number of launchers of MIRVed ballistic missiles and heavy bombers with long-range cruise missiles;
- an equal aggregate limit of 1,200 on the total number of launchers of MIRVed ballistic missiles; and
- an equal aggregate limit of 820 on launchers of MIRVed ICBMs.

In addition to these numerical limits, the agreement includes:

- a ban on construction of additional fixed ICBM launchers, and on increases in the number of fixed heavy ICBM launchers;
- a ban on heavy mobile ICBM launchers, and on launchers of heavy SLBMs and ASBMs;
- a ban on flight-testing or deployment of new types of ICBMs, with an exception of one new type of light ICBM for each side;
- a ban on increasing the numbers of warheads on existing types of ICBMs, and a limit of 10 warheads on the one new type of ICBM permitted to each Party, a limit of 14 warheads on SLBMs, and 10 warheads on ASBMs. The number of long-range cruise missiles per heavy bomber is limited to an average of 28; and the number of long-range cruise missiles per heavy bomber of existing types is limited to 20;
- ceilings on the launch weight and throw weight of strategic ballistic missiles and a ban on the conversion of light ICBM launchers to launchers of heavy ICBMs;
- a ban on the Soviet SS-16 ICBM;
- a ban on rapid reload ICBM systems;
- a ban on certain new types of strategic offensive systems which are technologically feasible, but which have not yet been deployed. Such systems include long-range ballistic missiles on surface ships, and ballistic and cruise missile launchers on the seabeds;

- advance notification of certain ICBM test launches; and
- an agreed data base for systems included in various SALT-limited categories.

The Treaty also includes detailed definitions of limited systems, provisions to enhance verification, a ban on circumvention of the provisions of the agreement, and a provision outlining the duties of the SCC in connection with the SALT II Treaty. The duration of the Treaty will be through 1985.

Verification of the SALT II agreement will be by national technical means (NTM), including photo-reconnaissance satellites. The sides have agreed not to interfere with each others' national technical means of verification, and not to use deliberate concealment measures which impede verification by NTM of compliance with the provisions of the agreement. Because specific characteristics of some SALT-limited systems become apparent during the testing phase, monitoring of testing programs is an important aspect of SALT verification. Such monitoring may involve collection of electronic signals known as telemetry which are used during tests to transmit information about systems while they are being tested. Therefore, the sides have agreed not to engage in deliberate denial of telemetric information whenever such denial impedes verification of compliance with the provisions of the agreement.

In addition to these provisions of the agreement which directly address the question of verification, counting and distinguishability rules, as well as some constraints on specific systems, are incorporated into the agreement specifically for verification purposes.

To facilitate verification of the MIRV limits, the sides have agreed that once a missile has been tested with MIRVs, then all missiles of that type shall be considered to be equipped with MIRVs, even if that missile type has also been tested with a non-MIRV payload. Additionally, the sides have agreed that once a launcher contains or launches a MIRVed missile, than all launchers of that type shall be considered to be launchers of MIRVed missiles and would be included in the 1,320 limit. Similar counting rules have been adopted for cruise missiles and for heavy bombers.

A constraint included for verification purposes is a ban on production, testing, and deployment of the Soviet SS-16 ICBM. This missile appeared to share a number of components with the Soviet SS-20, an intermediate range ballistic missile (IRBM). As the Parties had agreed that land-based launchers of ballistic missiles which are not ICBMs should not be converted into launchers of ICBMs, the U.S. sought this ban on the SS-16 in order to prevent verification problems which might have arisen if the SS-16 program had gone forward, since in that case distinguishing between SS-16 and SS-20 deployments would have been very difficult.

Pursuant to a Memorandum of Understanding, the sides have exchanged data on the numbers of weapons in SALT-limited categories, and will maintain this agreed data base through regular updates at each session of the Standing Consultative Commission. Although the United States does not require (and does not rely upon) this data for verification purposes, maintenance of the agreed data base will ensure that both parties are applying the provisions of the Treaty in a consistent manner.

The Protocol to the Treaty will remain in force until December 31, 1981. In the Protocol the sides have agreed to ban deployment of mobile ICBM launchers and flight-testing of ICBMs from such launchers. Development of such systems short of flight-testing would be permitted. (After the Protocol period, the Treaty specifically permits the deployment of mobile ICBM launchers.)

Additionally, the Protocol bans deployment, but not testing, of cruise missiles capable of ranges in excess of 600 kilometers on ground- and sea-based launchers. (The Protocol does not limit deployment of such systems after its expiration in 1981.)

Finally, the Protocol includes a ban on flight testing and deployment of air-to-surface ballistic missiles (ASBMs).

The Joint Statement of Principles, the third element of the SALT II agreement, establishes a basic framework for the next stage of SALT negotiations, SALT III. The sides have agreed on the following general goals to be achieved in the next round of talks:

- significant and substantial reductions in the number of strategic offensive arms;
- further qualitative limitations on strategic offensive arms; and
- resolution of the issues included in the Protocol.

The sides will also consider other steps to enhance strategic stability, and either side may bring up any other topic relevant to the limitation of strategic arms.

The Joint Statement of Principles also establishes the principle that cooperative measures may be used to ensure adequate verification of a SALT III agreement, raising the possibility of thus going beyond reliance on national technical means alone.

Treaty Between the United States of America and the Union of Soviet Socialist Republics on the Limitation of Strategic Offensive Arms*

Signed at Vienna June 18, 1979

The United States of America and the Union of Soviet Socialist Republics, hereinafter referred to as the Parties,

Conscious that nuclear war would have devastating consequences for all mankind,

Proceeding from the Basic Principles of Relations Between the United States of America and the Union of Soviet Socialist Republics of May 29, 1972,

Attaching particular significance to the limitation of strategic arms and determined to continue their efforts begun with the Treaty on the Limitation of Anti-Ballistic Missile Systems and the Interim Agreement on Certain Measures with Respect to the Limitation of Strategic Offensive Arms, of May 26, 1972,

Convinced that the additional measures limiting strategic offensive arms provided for in this Treaty will contribute to the improvement of relations between the Parties, help to reduce the risk of outbreak of nuclear war and strengthen international peace and security,

Mindful of their obligations under Article VI of the Treaty on the Non-Proliferation of Nuclear Weapons,

Guided by the principle of equality and equal security,

Recognizing that the strengthening of strategic stability meets the interests of the Parties and the interests of international security,

Reaffirming their desire to take measures for the further limitation and for the further reduction of strategic arms, having in mind the goal of achieving general and complete disarmament,

Declaring their intention to undertake in the near future negotiations further to limit and further to reduce strategic offensive arms,

Have agreed as follows:

---

*The text of the SALT II Treaty and Protocol, as signed in Vienna, is accompanied by a set of Agreed Statements and Common Understandings, also signed by Presidents Carter and Brezhnev, which is prefaced as follows:

In connection with the Treaty Between the United States of America and the Union of Soviet Socialist Republics on the Limitation of Strategic Offensive Arms, the Parties have agreed on the following Agreed Statements and Common Understandings undertaken on behalf of the Government of the United States and the Government of the Union of Soviet Socialist Republics.

As an aid to the reader, the texts of the Agreed Statements and Common Understandings are beneath the articles of the Treaty or Protocol to which they pertain.

Article I

Each Party undertakes, in accordance with the provisions of this Treaty, to limit strategic offensive arms quantitatively and qualitatively, to exercise restraint in the development of new types of strategic offensive arms, and to adopt other measures provided for in this Treaty.

Article II

For the purposes of this Treaty:

1. Intercontinental ballistic missile (ICBM) launchers are land-based launchers of ballistic missiles capable of a range in excess of the shortest distance between the northeastern border of the continental part of the territory of the United States of America and the northwestern border of the continental part of the territory of the Union of Soviet Socialist Republics, that is, a range in excess of 5,500 kilometers.

First Agreed Statement. The term "intercontinental ballistic missile launchers," as defined in paragraph 1 of Article II of the Treaty, includes all launchers which have been developed and tested for launching ICBMs. If a launcher has been developed and tested for launching an ICBM, all launchers of that type shall be considered to have been developed and tested for launching ICBMs.

First Common Understanding. If a launcher contains or launches an ICBM, that launcher shall be considered to have been developed and tested for launching ICBMs.

Second Common Understanding. If a launcher has been developed and tested for launching an ICBM, all launchers of that type, except for ICBM test and training launchers, shall be included in the aggregate numbers of strategic offensive arms provided for in Article III of the Treaty, pursuant to the provisions of Article VI of the Treaty.

Third Common Understanding. The one hundred and seventy-seven former Atlas and Titan I ICBM launchers of the United States of America, which are no longer operational and are partially dismantled, shall not be considered as subject to the limitations provided for in the Treaty.

Second Agreed Statement. After the date on which the Protocol ceases to be in force, mobile ICBM launchers shall be subject to the relevant limitations provided for in the Treaty which are applicable to ICBM launchers, unless the Parties agree that mobile ICBM launchers shall not be deployed after that date.

---

2. Submarine-launched ballistic missile (SLBM) launchers are launchers of ballistic missiles installed on any nuclear-powered submarine or launchers of modern ballistic missiles installed on any submarine, regardless of its type.

Agreed Statement. Modern submarine-launched ballistic missiles are: for the United States of America, missiles installed in all nuclear-powered submarines; for the Union of Soviet Socialist Republics, missiles of the type installed in nuclear-powered submarines made operational since 1965; and for both Parties, submarine-launched ballistic missiles first flight-tested since 1965 and installed in any submarine, regardless of its type.

---

3. Heavy bombers are considered to be:

(a) currently, for the United States of America, bombers of the B-52 and B-1 types, and for the Union of Soviet Socialist Republics, bombers of the Tupolev-95 and Myasishchev types;

(b) in the future, types of bombers which can carry out the mission of a heavy bomber in a manner similar or superior to that of bombers listed in subparagraph (a) above;

(c) types of bombers equipped for cruise missiles capable of a range in excess of 600 kilometers; and

(d) types of bombers equipped for ASBMs.

First Agreed Statement. The term "bombers," as used in paragraph 3 of Article II and other provisions of the Treaty, means airplanes of types initially constructed to be equipped for bombs or missiles.

Second Agreed Statement. The Parties shall notify each other on a case-by-case basis in the Standing Consultative Commission of inclusion of types of bombers as heavy bombers pursuant to the provisions of paragraph 3 of Article II of the Treaty; in this connection the Parties shall hold consultations, as appropriate, consistent with the provisions of paragraph 2 of Article XVII of the Treaty.

Third Agreed Statement. The criteria the Parties shall use to make case-by-case determinations of which types of bombers in the future can carry out the mission of a heavy bomber in a manner similar or superior to that of current heavy bombers, as referred to in subparagraph 3(b) of Article II of the Treaty, shall be agreed upon in the Standing Consultative Commission.

Fourth Agreed Statement. Having agreed that every bomber of a type included in paragraph 3 of Article II of the Treaty is to be considered a heavy bomber, the Parties further agree that:

(a) airplanes which otherwise would be bombers of a heavy bomber type shall not be considered to be bombers of a heavy bomber type if they have functionally related observable differences which indicate that they cannot perform the mission of a heavy bomber;

(b) airplanes which otherwise would be bombers of a type equipped for cruise missiles capable of a range in excess of 600 kilometers shall not be considered to be bombers of a type equipped for cruise missiles capable of a range in excess of 600 kilometers if they have functionally related observable differences which indicate that they cannot perform the mission of a bomber equipped for cruise missiles capable of a range in excess of 600 kilometers, except that heavy bombers of current types, as designated in subparagraph 3(a) of Article II of the Treaty, which otherwise would be of a type equipped for cruise missiles capable of a range in excess of 600 kilometers shall not be considered to be heavy bombers of a type equipped for cruise missiles capable of a range in excess of 600 kilometers if they are distinguishable on the basis of externally observable differences from heavy bombers of a type equipped for cruise missiles capable of a range in excess of 600 kilometers; and

(c) airplanes which otherwise would be bombers of a type equipped for ASBMs shall not be considered to be bombers of a type equipped for ASBMs if they have functionally related observable differences which indicate that they cannot perform the mission of a bomber equipped for ASBMs, except that heavy bombers of current types, as designated in subparagraph 3(a) of Article II of the Treaty, which otherwise would be of a type equipped for ASBMs shall not be considered to be heavy bombers of a type equipped for ASBMs if they are distinguishable on the basis of externally observable differences from heavy bombers of a type equipped for ASBMs.

First Common Understanding. Functionally related observable differences are differences in the observable features of airplanes which indicate whether or not these airplanes can perform the mission of a heavy bomber, or whether or not they can perform the mission of a bomber equipped for cruise missiles capable of a range in excess of 600 kilometers or whether or not they can perform the mission of a bomber equipped for ASBMs. Functionally related observable differences shall be verifiable by national technical means. To this end, the Parties may take, as appropriate, cooperative measures contributing to the effectiveness of verification by national technical means.

Fifth Agreed Statement. Tupolev-142 airplanes in their current configuration, that is, in the configuration for anti-submarine warfare, are considered to be airplanes of a type different from types of heavy bombers referred to in subparagraph 3(a) of Article II of the Treaty and not subject to the Fourth Agreed Statement to paragraph 3 of Article II of the Treaty. This Agreed Statement does not preclude improvement of Tupolev-142 airplanes as an anti-submarine system, and does not prejudice or set a precedent for designation in the future of types of airplanes as heavy bombers pursuant to subparagraph 3(b) of Article II of the Treaty or for application of the Fourth Agreed Statement to paragraph 3 of Article II of the Treaty to such airplanes.

Second Common Understanding. Not later than six months after entry into force of the Treaty the Union of Soviet Socialist Republics will give its thirty-one Myasishchev airplanes used as tankers in existence as of the date of signature of the Treaty functionally related observable differences which indicate that they cannot perform the mission of a heavy bomber.

Third Common Understanding. The designations by the United States of America and by the Union of Soviet Socialist Republics for heavy bombers referred to in subparagraph 3(a) of Article II of the Treaty correspond in the following manner:

Heavy bombers of the types designated by the United States of America as the B-52 and the B-1 are known to the Union of Soviet Socialist Republics by the same designations;

Heavy bombers of the type designated by the Union of Socialist Republics as the Tupolev-95 are known to the United States of America as heavy bombers of the Bear type; and

Heavy bombers of the type designated by the Union of Soviet Socialist Republics as the Myasishchev are known to the United States of America as heavy bombers of the Bison type.

---

4. Air-to-surface ballistic missiles (ASBMs) are any such missiles capable of a range in excess of 600 kilometers and installed in an aircraft or on its external mountings.

5. Launchers of ICBMs and SLBMs equipped with multiple independently targetable reentry vehicles (MIRVs) are launchers of the types developed and tested for launching ICBMs or SLBMs equipped with MIRVs.

First Agreed Statement. If a launcher has been developed and tested for launching an ICBM or an SLBM equipped with MIRVs, all launchers of that type shall be considered to have been developed and tested for launching ICBMs or SLBMs equipped with MIRVs.

First Common Understanding. If a launcher contains or launches an ICBM or an SLBM equipped with MIRVs, that launcher shall be considered to have been developed and tested for launching ICBMs or SLBMs equipped with MIRVs.

Second Common Understanding. If a launcher has been developed and tested for launching an ICBM or an SLBM equipped with MIRVs, all launchers of that type, except for ICBM and SLBM test and training launchers, shall be included in the corresponding aggregate numbers provided for in Article V of the Treaty, pursuant to the provisions of Article VI of the Treaty.

Second Agreed Statement. ICBMs and SLBMs equipped with MIRVs are ICBMs and SLBMs of the types which have been flight-tested with two or more independently targetable reentry vehicles, regardless of whether or not they have also been flight-tested with a single reentry vehicle or with multiple reentry vehicles which are not independently targetable. As of the date of signature of the Treaty, such ICBMs and SLBMS are: for the United States of America, Minuteman III ICBMs, Poseidon C-3 SLBMs, and Trident C-4 SLBMs; and for the Union of Soviet Socialist Republics, RS-16, RS-18, RS-20 ICBMs and RSM-50 SLBMs.

Each Party will notify the other Party in the Standing Consultative Commission on a case-by-case basis of the designation of the one new type of light ICBM, if equipped with MIRVs, permitted pursuant to paragraph 9 of Article IV of the Treaty when first flight-tested; of designations of additional types of SLBMs equipped with MIRVs when first installed on a submarine; and of designations of types of ASBMs equipped with MIRVs when first flight-tested.

Third Common Understanding. The designations by the United States of America and by the Union of Soviet Socialist Republics for ICBMs and SLBMs equipped with MIRVs correspond in the following manner:

Missiles of the type designated by the United States of America as the Minuteman III and known to the Union of Soviet Socialist Republics by the same designation, a light ICBM that has been flight-tested with multiple independently targetable reentry vehicles;

Missiles of the type designated by the United States of America as the Poseiden C-3 and known to the Union of Soviet Socialist Republics by the same designation, an SLBM that was first flight-tested in 1968 and that has been flight-tested with multiple independently targetable reentry vehicles;

Missiles of the type designated by the United States of America as the Trident C-4 and known to the Union of Soviet Socialist Republics by the same designation, an SLBM that was first flight-tested in 1977 and that has been flight-tested with multiple independently targetable reentry vehicles;

Missiles of the type designated by the Union of Soviet Socialist Republics as the RS-16 and known to the United States of America as the SS-17, a light ICBM that has been flight-tested with a single reentry vehicle and with multiple independently targetable reentry vehicles;

Missiles of the type designated by the Union of Soviet Socialist Republics as the RS-18 and known to the United States of America as the SS-19, the heaviest in terms of launch-weight and throw-weight of light ICBMs, which has been flight-tested with a single reentry vehicle and with multiple independently targetable reentry vehicles;

Missiles of the type designated by the Union of Soviet Socialist Republics as the RS-20 and known to the United States of America as the SS-18, the heaviest in terms of launch-weight and throw-weight of heavy ICBMs, which has been flight-tested with a single reentry vehicle and with multiple independently targetable reentry vehicles;

Missiles of the type designated by the Union of Soviet Socialist Republics as the RSM-50 and known to the United States of America as the SS-N-18, an SLBM that has been flight-tested with a single reentry vehicle and with multiple independently targetable reentry vehicles.

Third Agreed Statement. Reentry vehicles are independently targetable:

(a) if, after separation from the booster, maneuvering and targeting of the reentry vehicles to separate aim points along trajectories which are unrelated to each other are accomplished by means of devices which are installed in a self-contained dispensing mechanism or on the reentry vehicles, and which are based on the use of electronic or other computers in combination with devices using jet engines, including rocket engines, or aerodynamic systems;

(b) if maneuvering and targeting of the reentry vehicles to separate aim points along trajectories which are unrelated to each other are accomplished by means of other devices which may be developed in the future.

Fourth Common Understanding. For the purposes of this Treaty, all ICBM launchers in the Derazhnya and Pervomaysk areas in the Union of Soviet Socialist Republics are included in the aggregate numbers provided for in Article V of the Treaty.

Fifth Common Understanding. If ICBM or SLBM launchers are converted, constructed or undergo significant changes to their principal observable structural design features after entry into force of the Treaty, any such launchers which are launchers of missiles equipped with MIRVs shall be distinguishable from launchers of missiles not equipped with MIRVs, and any such launchers which are launchers of missiles not equipped with MIRVs shall be distinguishable from launchers of missiles equipped with MIRVs, on the basis of externally observable design features of the launchers. Submarines with launchers of SLBMs equipped with MIRVs shall be distinguishable from submarines with launchers of SLBMs not equipped with MIRVs on the basis of externally observable design features of the submarines.

This Common Understanding does not require changes to launcher conversion or construction programs, or to programs including significant changes to the principal observable structural design features of launchers, underway as of the date of signature of the Treaty.

---

6. ASBMs equipped with MIRVs are ASBMs of the types which have been flight-tested with MIRVs.

First Agreed Statement. ASBMs of the types which have been flight-tested with MIRVs are all ASBMs of the types which have been flight-tested with two or more independently targetable reentry vehicles, regardless of whether or not they have also been flight-tested with a single reentry vehicle or with multiple reentry vehicles which are not independently targetable.

Second Agreed Statement. Reentry vehicles are independently targetable:

(a) if, after separation from the booster, maneuvering and targeting of the reentry vehicles to separate aim points along trajectories which are unrelated to each other are accomplished by means of devices which are installed in a self-contained dispensing mechanism or on the reentry vehicles, and which are based on the use of electronic or other computers in combination with devices using jet engines, including rocket engines, or aerodynamic systems;

(b) if maneuvering and targeting of the reentry vehicles to separate aim points along trajectories which are unrelated to each other are accomplished by means of other devices which may be developed in the future.

---

7. Heavy ICBMs are ICBMs which have a launch-weight greater or a throw-weight greater than that of the heaviest, in terms of either launch-weight or throw-weight, respectively, of the light ICBMs deployed by either Party as of the date of signature of this Treaty.

First Agreed Statement. The launch-weight of an ICBM is the weight of the fully loaded missile itself at the time of launch.

Second Agreed Statement. The throw-weight of an ICBM is the sum of the weight of:

(a) its reentry vehicle or reentry vehicles;
(b) any self-contained dispensing mechanisms or other appropriate devices for targeting one reentry vehicle, or for releasing or for dispensing and targeting two or more reentry vehicles; and
(c) its penetration aids, including devices for their release.

Common Understanding. The term "other appropriate devices," as used in the definition of the throw-weight of an ICBM in the Second Agreed Statement to paragraph 7 of Article II of the Treaty, means any devices for dispensing and targeting two or more reentry vehicles; and any devices for releasing two or more reentry vehicles or for targeting one reentry vehicle, which cannot provide their reentry vehicles or reentry vehicle with additional velocity of more than 1,000 meters per second.

---

8. Cruise missiles are unmanned, self-propelled, guided, weapon-delivery vehicles which sustain flight through the use of aerodynamic lift over most of their flight path and which are flight-tested from or deployed on aircraft, that is, air-launched cruise missiles, or such vehicles which are referred to as cruise missiles in subparagraph 1(b) of Article IX.

First Agreed Statement. If a cruise missile is capable of a range in excess of 600 kilometers, all cruise missiles of that type shall be considered to be cruise missiles capable of a range in excess of 600 kilometers.

First Common Understanding. If a cruise missile has been flight-tested to a range in excess of 600 kilometers, it shall be considered to be a cruise missle capable of a range in excess of 600 kilometers.

Second Common Understanding. Cruise missiles not capable of a range in excess of 600 kilometers shall not be considered to be of a type capable of a range in excess of 600 kilometers if they are distinguishable on the basis of externally observable design features from cruise missiles of types capable of a range in excess of 600 kilometers.

Second Agreed Statement. The range of which a cruise missile is capable is the maximum distance which can be covered by the missile in its standard design mode flying until fuel exhaustion, determined by projecting its flight path onto the Earth's sphere from the point of launch to the point of impact.

Third Agreed Statement. If an unmanned, self-propelled, guided vehicle which sustains flight through the use of aerodynamic lift over most of its flight path has been flight-tested or deployed for weapon delivery, all vehicles of that type shall be considered to be weapon-delivery vehicles.

Third Common Understanding. Unmanned, self-propelled, guided vehicles which sustain flight through the use of aerodynamic lift over most of their flight path and are not weapon-delivery vehicles, that is, unarmed, pilotless, guided vehicles, shall not be considered to be cruise missiles if such vehicles are distinguishable from cruise missiles on the basis of externally observable design features.

Fourth Common Understanding. Neither Party shall convert unarmed, pilotless, guided vehicles into cruise missiles capable of a range in excess of 600 kilometers, nor shall either Party convert cruise missiles capable of a range in excess of 600 kilometers into unarmed, pilotless, guided vehicles.

Fifth Common Understanding. Neither Party has plans during the term of the Treaty to flight-test from or deploy on aircraft unarmed, pilotless, guided vehicles which are capable of a range in excess of 600 kilometers. In the future, should a Party have such plans, that Party will provide notification thereof to the other Party well in advance of such flight-testing or deployment. This Common Understanding does not apply to target drones.

Article III

1. Upon entry into force of this Treaty, each Party undertakes to limit ICBM launchers, SLBM launchers, heavy bombers, and ASBMs to an aggregate number not to exceed 2,400.

2. Each Party undertakes to limit, from January 1, 1981, strategic offensive arms referred to in paragraph 1 of this Article to an aggregate number not to exceed 2,250, and to initiate reductions of those arms which as of that date would be in excess of this aggregate number.

3. Within the aggregate numbers provided for in paragraphs 1 and 2 of this Article and subject to the provisions of this Treaty, each Party has the right to determine the composition of these aggregates.

4. For each bomber of a type equipped for ASBMs, the aggregate numbers provided for in paragraphs 1 and 2 of this Article shall include the maximum number of such missiles for which a bomber of that type is equipped for one operational mission.

5. A heavy bomber equipped only for ASBMs shall not itself be included in the aggregate numbers provided for in paragraphs 1 and 2 of this Article.

6. Reductions of the numbers of strategic offensive arms required to comply with the provisions of paragraphs 1 and 2 of this Article shall be carried out as provided for in Article XI.

Article IV

1. Each Party undertakes not to start construction of additional fixed ICBM launchers.

2. Each Party undertakes not to relocate fixed ICBM launchers.

3. Each Party undertakes not to convert launchers of light ICBMs, or of ICBMs of older types deployed prior to 1964, into launchers of heavy ICBMs of types deployed after that time.

4. Each Party undertakes in the process of modernization and replacement of ICBM silo launchers not to increase the original internal volume of an ICBM silo launcher by

more than thirty-two percent. Within this limit each Party has the right to determine whether such an increase will be made through an increase in the original diameter or in the original depth of an ICBM silo launcher, or in both of these dimensions.

Agreed Statement. The word "original" in paragraph 4 of Article IV of the Treaty refers to the internal dimensions of an ICBM silo launcher, including its internal volume, as of May 26, 1972, or as of the date on which such launcher becomes operational, whichever is later.

Common Understanding. The obligations provided for in paragraph 4 of Article IV of the Treaty and in the Agreed Statement thereto mean that the original diameter or the original depth of an ICBM silo launcher may not be increased by an amount greater than that which would result in an increase in the original internal volume of the ICBM silo launcher by thirty-two percent solely through an increase in one of these dimensions.

---

5. Each Party undertakes:

(a) not to supply ICBM launcher deployment areas with intercontinental ballistic missiles in excess of a number consistent with normal deployment, maintenance, training, and replacement requirements;

(b) not to provide storage facilities for or to store ICBMs in excess of normal deployment requirements at launch sites of ICBM launchers;

(c) not to develop, test, or deploy systems for rapid reload of ICBM launchers.

Agreed Statement. The term "normal deployment requirements," as used in paragraph 5 of Article IV of the Treaty, means the deployment of one missile at each ICBM launcher.

---

6. Subject to the provisions of this Treaty, each Party undertakes not to have under construction at any time strategic offensive arms referred to in paragraph 1 of Article III in excess of numbers consistent with a normal construction schedule.

Common Understanding. A normal construction schedule, in paragraph 6 of Article IV of the Treaty, is understood to be one consistent with the past or present construction practices of each Party.

---

7. Each Party undertakes not to develop, test, or deploy ICBMs which have a launch-weight greater or a throw-weight greater than that of the heaviest, in terms of either launch-weight or throw-weight, respectively, of the heavy ICBMs, deployed by either Party as of the date of signature of this Treaty.

First Agreed Statement. The launch-weight of an ICBM is the weight of the fully loaded missile itself at the time of launch.

Second Agreed Statement. The throw-weight of an ICBM is the sum of the weight of:

(a) its reentry vehicle or reentry vehicles;

(b) any self-contained dispensing mechanisms or other appropriate devices for targeting one reentry vehicle, or for releasing or for dispensing and targeting two or more reentry vehicles; and

(c) its penetration aids, including devices for their release.

Common Understanding. The term "other appropriate devices," as used in the definition of the throw-weight of an ICBM in the Second Agreed Statement to paragraph 7 of Article IV of the Treaty, means any devices for dispensing and targeting two or more reentry vehicles; and any devices for releasing two or more reentry vehicles or for targeting one reentry vehicle, which cannot provide their reentry vehicles or reentry vehicle with additional velocity of more than 1,000 meters per second.

---

8. Each Party undertakes not to convert land-based launchers of ballistic missiles which are not ICBMs into launchers for launching ICBMs, and not to test them for this purpose.

Common Understanding. During the term of the Treaty, the Union of Soviet Socialist Republics will not produce, test, or deploy ICBMs of the type designated by the Union of Soviet Socialist Republics as the RS-14 and known to the United States of America as the SS-16, a light ICBM first flight-tested after 1970 and flight-tested only with a single reentry vehicle; this Common Understanding also means that the Union of Soviet Socialist Republics will not produce the third stage of that missile, the reentry vehicle of that missile, or the appropriate device for targeting the reentry vehicle of that missile.

9. Each Party undertakes not to flight-test or deploy new types of ICBMs, that is, types of ICBMs not flight-tested as of May 1, 1979, except that each Party may flight-test and deploy one new type of light ICBM.

First Agreed Statement. The term "new types of ICBMs," as used in paragraph 9 of Article IV of the Treaty, refers to any ICBM which is different from those ICBMs flight-tested as of May 1, 1979 in any one or more of the following respects:

(a) the number of stages, the length, the largest diameter, the launch-weight, or the throw-weight, of the missile;

(b) the type of propellant (that is, liquid or solid) of any of its stages.

First Common Understanding. As used in the First Agreed Statement to paragraph 9 of Article IV of the Treaty, the term "different," referring to the length, the diameter, the launch-weight, and the throw-weight, of the missile, means a difference in excess of five percent.

Second Agreed Statement. Every ICBM of the one new type of light ICBM permitted to each Party pursuant to paragraph 9 of Article IV of the Treaty shall have the same number of stages and the same type of propellant (that is, liquid or solid) of each stage as the first ICBM of the one new type of light ICBM launched by that Party. In addition, after the twenty-fifth launch of an ICBM of that type, or after the last launch before deployment begins of ICBMs of that type, whichever occurs earlier, ICBMs of the one new type of light ICBM permitted to that Party shall not be different in any one or more of the following respects: the length, the largest diameter, the launch-weight, or the throw-weight, of the missile.

A Party which launches ICBMs of the one new type of light ICBM permitted pursuant to paragraph 9 of Article IV of the Treaty shall promptly notify the other Party of the date of the first launch and of the date of either the twenty-fifth or the last launch before deployment begins of ICBMs of that type, whichever occurs earlier.

Second Common Understanding. As used in the Second Agreed Statement to paragraph 9 of Article IV of the Treaty, the term "different," referring to the length, the diameter, the launch-weight, and the throw-weight, of the missile, means a difference in excess of five percent from the value established for each of the above parameters as of the twenty-fifth launch or as of the last launch before deployment begins, whichever occurs earlier. The values demonstrated in each of the above parameters during the last twelve of the twenty-five launches or during the last twelve launches before deployment begins, whichever twelve launches occur earlier, shall not vary by more than ten percent from any other of the corresponding values demonstrated during those twelve launches.

Third Common Understanding. The limitations with respect to launch-weight and throw-weight, provided for in the First Agreed Statement and the First Common Understanding to paragraph 9 of Article IV of the Treaty, do not preclude the flight-testing or the deployment of ICBMs with fewer reentry vehicles, or fewer penetration aids, or both, than the maximum number of reentry vehicles and the maximum number of penetration aids with which ICBMs of that type have been flight-tested as of May 1, 1979, even if this results in a decrease in launch-weight or in throw-weight in excess of five percent.

In addition to the aforementioned cases, those limitations do not preclude a decrease in launch-weight or in throw-weight in excess of five percent, in the case of the flight-testing or the deployment of ICBMs with a lesser quantity of propellant, including the propellant of a self-contained dispensing mechanism or other appropriate device, than the maximum quantity of propellant, including the propellant of a self-contained dispensing mechanism or other appropriate device, with which ICBMs of that type have been flight-tested as of May 1, 1979, provided that such an ICBM is at the same time flight-tested or deployed with fewer reentry vehicles, or fewer penetration aids, or both, than the maximum number of reentry vehicles and the maximum number of penetration aids with which ICBMs of that type have been flight-tested as of May 1, 1979, and the decrease in launch-weight and throw-weight in such cases results only from the reduction in the number of reentry vehicles, or penetration aids, or both, and the reduction in the quantity of propellant.

Fourth Common Understanding. The limitations with respect to launch-weight and throw-weight, provided for in the Second Agreed Statement and the Second Common Understanding to paragraph 9 of Article IV of the Treaty, do not preclude the flight-testing or the deployment of ICBMs of the one new type of light ICBM permitted to each Party pursuant to paragraph 9 of Article IV of the Treaty with fewer reentry vehicles, or fewer penetration aids, or both, than the maximum number of reentry vehicles and the maximum number of penetration aids with which ICBMs of that type have been flight-tested, even if this results in a decrease in launch-weight or in throw-weight in excess of five percent.

In addition to the aforementioned cases, those limitations do not preclude a decrease in launch-weight or in throw-weight in excess of five percent, in the case of the flight-testing or the deployment of ICBMs of that type with a lesser quantity of propellant, including the propellant of a self-contained dispensing mechanism or other appropriate device, than the maximum quantity of propellant, including the propellant of a self-contained dispensing mechanism or other appropriate device, with which ICBMs of that type have been flight-tested, provided that such an ICBM is at the same time flight-tested or deployed with fewer reentry vehicles, or fewer penetration aids, or both, than the maximum number of reentry vehicles and the maximum number of penetration aids with which ICBMs of that type have been flight-tested, and the decrease In launch-weight and throw-weight In such cases results only from the reduction in the number of reentry vehicles, or penetration aids, or both, and the reduction in the quantity of propellant.

10. Each Party undertakes not to flight-test or deploy ICBMs of a type flight-tested as of May 1, 1979 with a number of reentry vehicles greater than the maximum number of reentry vehicles with which an ICBM of that type has been flight-tested as of that date.

First Agreed Statement. The following types of ICBMs and SLBMs equipped with MIRVs have been flight-tested with the maximum number of reentry vehicles set forth below:

For the United States of America

ICBMs of the Minuteman III type—seven reentry vehicles;
SLBMs of the Poseidon C-3 type—fourteen reentry vehicles;
SLBMs of the Trident C-4 type—seven reentry vehicles.

For the Union of Soviet Socialist Republics

ICBMs of the RS-16 type—four reentry vehicles;
ICBMs of the RS-18 type—six reentry vehicles;
ICBMs of the RS-20 type—ten reentry vehicles;
SLBMs of the RSM-50 type—seven reentry vehicles.

Common Understanding. Minuteman III ICBMs of the United States of America have been deployed with no more than three reentry vehicles. During the term of the Treaty, the United States of America has no plans to and will not flight-test or deploy missiles of this type with more than three reentry vehicles.

Second Agreed Statement. During the flight-testing of any ICBM, SLBM, or ASBM after May 1, 1979, the number of procedures for releasing or for dispensing may not exceed the maximum number of reentry vehicles established for missiles of corresponding types as provided for in paragraphs 10, 11, 12, and 13 of Article IV of the Treaty. In this Agreed Statement "procedures for releasing or for dispensing" are understood to mean maneuvers of a missile associated with targeting and releasing or dispensing its reentry vehicles to aim points, whether or not a reentry vehicle is actually released or dispensed. Procedures for releasing anti-missile defense penetration aids will not be considered to be procedures for releasing or for dispensing a reentry vehicle so long as the procedures for releasing anti-missile defense penetration aids differ from those for releasing or for dispensing reentry vehicles.

Third Agreed Statement. Each Party undertakes:

(a) not to flight-test or deploy ICBMs equipped with multiple reentry vehicles, of a type flight-tested as of May 1, 1979, with reentry vehicles the weight of any of which is less than the weight of the lightest of those reentry vehicles with which an ICBM of that type has been flight-tested as of that date;

(b) not to flight-test or deploy ICBMs equipped with a single reentry vehicle and without an appropriate device for targeting a reentry vehicle, of a type flight-tested as of May 1, 1979, with a reentry vehicle the weight of which is less than the weight of the lightest reentry vehicle on an ICBM of a type equipped with MIRVs and flight-tested by that Party as of May 1, 1979; and

(c) not to flight-test or deploy ICBMs equipped with a single reentry vehicle and with an appropriate device for targeting a reentry vehicle, of a type flight-tested as of May 1, 1979, with a reentry vehicle the weight of which is less than fifty percent of the throw-weight of that ICBM.

---

11. Each Party undertakes not to flight-test or deploy ICBMs of the one new type permitted pursuant to paragraph 9 of this Article with a number of reentry vehicles greater than the maximum number of reentry vehicles with which an ICBM of either Party has been flight-tested as of May 1, 1979, that is, ten.

First Agreed Statement. Each Party undertakes not to flight-test or deploy the one new type of light ICBM permitted to each Party pursuant to paragraph 9 of Article IV of the Treaty with a number of reentry vehicles greater than the maximum number of reentry vehicles with which an ICBM of that type has been flight-tested as of the twenty-fifth launch or the last launch before deployment begins of ICBMs of that type, whichever occurs earlier.

Second Agreed Statement. During the flight-testing of any ICBM, SLBM, or ASBM after May 1, 1979 the number of procedures for releasing or for dispensing may not exceed the maximum number of reentry vehicles established for missiles of corresponding types as provided for in paragraphs 10, 11, 12, and 13 of Article IV of the Treaty. In this Agreed Statement "procedures for releasing or for dispensing" are understood to mean maneuvers of a missile associated with targeting and releasing or dispensing its reentry vehicles to aim points, whether or not a reentry vehicle is actually released or dispensed. Procedures for releasing anti-missile defense penetration aids will not be considered to be procedures for releasing or for dispensing a reentry vehicle so long as the procedures for releasing anti-missile defense penetration aids differ from those for releasing or for dispensing reentry vehicles.

---

12. Each Party undertakes not to flight-test or deploy SLBMs with a number of reentry vehicles greater than the maximum number of reentry vehicles with which an SLBM of either Party has been flight-tested as of May 1, 1979, that is, fourteen.

First Agreed Statement. The following types of ICBMs and SLBMs equipped with MIRVs have been flight-tested with the maximum number of reentry vehicles set forth below:

For the United States of America

ICBMs of the Minuteman III type—seven reentry vehicles;
SLBMs of the Poseidon C-3 type—fourteen reentry vehicles;
SLBMs of the Trident C-4 type—seven reentry vehicles.

For the Union of Soviet Socialist Republics

ICBMs of the RS-16 type—four reentry vehicles;
ICBMs of the RS-18 type—six reentry vehicles;
ICBMs of the RS-20 type—ten reentry vehicles;
SLBMs of the RSM-50 type—seven reentry vehicles.

Second Agreed Statement. During the flight-testing of any ICBM, SLBM, or ASBM after May 1, 1979 the number of procedures for releasing or for dispensing may not exceed the maximum number of reentry vehicles established for missiles of corresponding types as provided for in paragraphs 10, 11, 12, and 13 of Article IV of the Treaty. In this Agreed Statement "procedures for releasing or dispensing" are understood to mean maneuvers of a missile associated with targeting and releasing or dispensing its reentry vehicles to aim points, whether or not a reentry vehicle is actually released or dispensed. Procedures for releasing anti-missile defense penetration aids will not be considered to be procedures for releasing or for dispensing a reentry vehicle so long as the procedures for releasing anti-missile defense penetration aids differ from those for releasing or for dispensing reentry vehicles.

---

13. Each Party undertakes not to flight-test or deploy ASBMs with a number of reentry vehicles greater than the maximum number of reentry vehicles with which an ICBM of either Party has been flight-tested as of May 1, 1979, that is, ten.

Agreed Statement. During the flight-testing of any ICBM, SLBM, or ASBM after May 1, 1979 the number of procedures for releasing or for dispensing may not exceed the maximum number of reentry vehicles established for missiles of corresponding types as provided for in paragraphs 10, 11, 12, and 13 of Article IV of the Treaty. In this Agreed Statement "procedures for releasing or for dispensing" are understood to mean maneuvers of a missile associated with targeting and releasing or dispensing its reentry vehicles to aim points, whether or not a reentry vehicle is actually released or dispensed. Procedures for releasing anti-missile defense penetration aids will not be considered to be procedures for releasing or for dispensing a reentry vehicle so long as the procedures for releasing anti-missile defense penetration aids differ from those for releasing or for dispensing reentry vehicles.

---

14. Each Party undertakes not to deploy at any one time on heavy bombers equipped for cruise missiles capable of a range in excess of 600 kilometers a number of such cruise missiles which exceeds the product of 28 and the number of such heavy bombers.

First Agreed Statement. For the purposes of the limitation provided for in paragraph 14 of Article IV of the Treaty, there shall be considered to be deployed on each heavy bomber of a type equipped for cruise missiles capable of a range in excess of 600 kilometers the maximum number of such missiles for which any bomber of that type is equipped for one operational mission.

Second Agreed Statement. During the term of the Treaty no bomber of the B-52 or B-1 types of the United States of America and no bomber of the Tupolev-95 or Myasishchev types of the Union of Soviet Socialist Republics will be equipped for more than twenty cruise missiles capable of a range in excess of 600 kilometers.

Article V

1. Within the aggregate numbers provided for in paragraphs 1 and 2 of Article III, each Party undertakes to limit launchers of ICBMs and SLBMs equipped with MIRVs, ASBMs equipped with MIRVs, and heavy bombers equipped for cruise missiles

capable of a range in excess of 600 kilometers to an aggregate number not to exceed 1,320.

2. Within the aggregate number provided for in paragraph 1 of this Article, each Party undertakes to limit launchers of ICBMs and SLBMs equipped with MIRVs, and ASBMs equipped with MIRVs to an aggregate number not to exceed 1,200.

3. Within the aggregate number provided for in paragraph 2 of this Article, each Party undertakes to limit launchers of ICBMs equipped with MIRVs to an aggregate number not to exceed 820.

4. For each bomber of a type equipped for ASBMs equipped with MIRVs, the aggregate numbers provided for in paragraphs 1 and 2 of this Article shall include the maximum number of ASBMs for which a bomber of that type is equipped for one operational mission.

Agreed Statement. If a bomber is equipped for ASBMs equipped with MIRVs, all bombers of that type shall be considered to be equipped for ASBMs equipped with MIRVs.

---

5. Within the aggregate numbers provided for in paragraphs 1, 2, and 3 of this Article and subject to the provisions of this Treaty, each Party has the right to determine the composition of these aggregates.

Article VI

1. The limitations provided for in this Treaty shall apply to those arms which are:

   (a) operational;
   (b) in the final stage of construction;
   (c) in reserve, in storage, or mothballed;
   (d) undergoing overhaul, repair, modernization, or conversion.

2. Those arms in the final stage of construction are:

   (a) SLBM launchers on submarines which have begun sea trials;
   (b) ASBMs after a bomber of a type equipped for such missiles has been brought out of the shop, plant, or other facility where its final assembly or conversion for the purpose of equipping it for such missiles has been performed;
   (c) other strategic offensive arms which are finally assembled in a shop, plant, or other facility after they have been brought out of the shop, plant, or other facility where their final assembly has been performed.

3. ICBM and SLBM launchers of a type not subject to the limitation provided for in Article V, which undergo conversion into launchers of a type subject to that limitation, shall become subject to that limitation as follows:

   (a) fixed ICBM launchers when work on their conversion reaches the stage which first definitely indicates that they are being so converted;
   (b) SLBM launchers on a submarine when that submarine first goes to sea after their conversion has been performed.

Agreed Statement. The procedures referred to in paragraph 7 of Article VI of the Treaty shall include procedures determining the manner in which mobile ICBM launchers of a type not subject to the limitation provided for in Article V of the Treaty, which undergo conversion into launchers of a type subject to that limitation, shall become subject to that limitation, unless the Parties agree that mobile ICBM launchers shall not be deployed after the date on which the Protocol ceases to be in force.

---

4. ASBMs on a bomber which undergoes conversion from a bomber of a type equipped for ASBMs which are not subject to the limitation provided for in Article V into a bomber of a type equipped for ASBMs which are subject to that limitation shall become subject to that limitation when the bomber is brought out of the shop, plant, or other facility where such conversion has been performed.

5. A heavy bomber of a type not subject to the limitation provided for in paragraph 1 of Article V shall become subject to that limitation when it is brought out of the shop, plant, or other facility where it has been converted into a heavy bomber of a type equipped for cruise missiles capable of a range in excess of 600 kilometers. A bomber of a type not subject to the limitation provided for in paragraph 1 or 2 of Article III shall become subject to that limitation and to the limitation provided for in paragraph 1 of Article V when it is brought out of the shop, plant, or other facility where it has been converted into a bomber of a type equipped for cruise missiles capable of a range in excess of 600 kilometers.

6. The arms subject to the limitations provided for in this Treaty shall continue to be subject to these limitations until they are dismantled, are destroyed, or otherwise cease to be subject to these limitations under procedures to be agreed upon.

Agreed Statement. The procedures for removal of strategic offensive arms from the aggregate numbers provided for in the Treaty, which are referred to in paragraph 6 of Article VI of the Treaty, and which are to be agreed upon in the Standing Consultative Commission, shall include:

(a) procedures for removal from the aggregate numbers, provided for in Article V of the Treaty, of ICBM and SLBM launchers which are being converted from launchers of a type subject to the limitation provided for in Article V of the Treaty, into launchers of a type not subject to that limitation;

(b) procedures for removal from the aggregate numbers, provided for in Articles III and V of the Treaty, of bombers which are being converted from bombers of a type subject to the limitations provided for in Article III of the Treaty or in Articles III and V of the Treaty into airplanes or bombers of a type not so subject.

Common Understanding. The procedures referred to in subparagraph (b) of the Agreed Statement to paragraph 6 of Article VI of the Treaty for removal of bombers from the aggregate numbers provided for in Articles III and V of the Treaty shall be based upon the existence of functionally related observable differences which indicate whether or not they can perform the mission of a heavy bomber, or whether or not they can perform the mission of a bomber equipped for cruise missiles capable of a range in excess of 600 kilometers.

---

7. In accordance with the provisions of Article XVII, the Parties will agree in the Standing Consultative Commission upon procedures to implement the provisions of this Article.

Article VII

1. The limitations provided for in Article III shall not apply to ICBM and SLBM test and training launchers or to space vehicle launchers for exploration and use of outer

space. ICBM and SLBM test and training launchers are ICBM and SLBM launchers used only for testing or training.

Common Understanding. The term "testing," as used in Article VII of the Treaty, includes research and development.

---

2. The Parties agree that:

(a) there shall be no significant increase in the number of ICBM or SLBM test and training launchers or in the number of such launchers of heavy ICBMs;

(b) construction or conversion of ICBM launchers at test ranges shall be undertaken only for purposes of testing and training;

(c) there shall be no conversion of ICBM test and training launchers or of space vehicle launchers into ICBM launchers subject to the limitations provided for in Article III.

First Agreed Statement. The term "significant increase," as used in subparagraph 2(a) of Article VII of the Treaty, means an increase of fifteen percent or more. Any new ICBM test and training launchers which replace ICBM test and training launchers at test ranges will be located only at test ranges.

Second Agreed Statement. Current test ranges where ICBMs are tested are located: for the United States of America, near Santa Maria, California, and at Cape Canaveral, Florida; and for the Union of Soviet Socialist Republics, in the areas of Tyura-Tam and Plesetskaya. In the future, each Party shall provide notification in the Standing Consultative Commission of the location of any other test range used by that Party to test ICBMs.

First Common Understanding. At test ranges where ICBMs are tested, other arms, including those not limited by the Treaty, may also be tested.

Second Common Understanding. Of the eighteen launchers of fractional orbital missiles at the test range where ICBMs are tested in the area of Tyura-Tam, twelve launchers shall be dismantled or destroyed and six launchers may be converted to launchers for testing missiles undergoing modernization.

Dismantling or destruction of the twelve launchers shall begin upon entry into force of the Treaty and shall be completed within eight months, under procedures for dismantling or destruction of these launchers to be agreed upon in the Standing Consultative Commission. These twelve launchers shall not be replaced.

Conversion of the six launchers may be carried out after entry into force of the Treaty. After entry into force of the Treaty, fractional orbital missiles shall be removed and shall be destroyed pursuant to the provisions of subparagraph 1(c) of Article IX and of Article XI of the Treaty and shall not be replaced by other missiles, except in the case of conversion of these six launchers for testing missiles undergoing modernization. After removal of the fractional orbital missiles, and prior to such conversion, any activities associated with these launchers shall be limited to normal maintenance requirements for launchers in which missiles are not deployed. These six launchers shall be subject to the provisions of Article VII of the Treaty and, if converted, to the provisions of the Fifth Common Understanding to paragraph 5 of Article II of the Treaty.

Article VIII

1. Each Party undertakes not to flight-test cruise missiles capable of a range in excess of 600 kilometers or ASBMs from aircraft other than bombers or to convert such aircraft into aircraft equipped for such missiles.

Agreed Statement. For purposes of testing only, each Party has the right, through initial construction or, as an exception to the provisions of paragraph 1 of Article VIII of the Treaty, by conversion, to equip for cruise missiles capable of a range in excess of 600 kilometers or for ASBMs no more than sixteen airplanes, including airplanes which are prototypes of bombers equipped for such missiles. Each Party also has the right, as an exception to the provisions of paragraph 1 of Article VIII of the Treaty, to flight-test from such airplanes cruise missiles capable of a range in excess of 600 kilometers and, after the date on which the Protocol ceases to be in force, to flight-test ASBMs from such airplanes as well, unless the Parties agree that they will not flight-test ASBMs after that date. The limitations provided for in Article III of the Treaty shall not apply to such airplanes.

The aforementioned airplanes may include only:

(a) airplanes other than bombers which, as an exception to the provisions of paragraph 1 of Article VIII of the Treaty, have been converted into airplanes equipped for cruise missiles capable of a range in excess of 600 kilometers or for ASBMs;

(b) airplanes considered to be heavy bombers pursuant to subparagraph 3(c) or 3(d) of Article II of the Treaty; and

(c) airplanes other than heavy bombers which, prior to March 7, 1979, were used for testing cruise missiles capable of a range in excess of 600 kilometers.

The airplanes referred to in subparagraphs (a) and (b) of this Agreed Statement shall be distinguishable on the basis of functionally related observable differences from airplanes which otherwise would be of the same type but cannot perform the mission of a bomber equipped for cruise missiles capable of a range in excess of 600 kilometers or for ASBMs.

The airplanes referred to in subparagraph (c) of this Agreed Statement shall not be used for testing cruise missiles capable of a range in excess of 600 kilometers after the expiration of a six-month period from the date of entry into force of the Treaty, unless by the expiration of that period they are distinguishable on the basis of functionally related observable differences from airplanes which otherwise would be of the same type but cannot perform the mission of a bomber equipped for cruise missiles capable of a range in excess of 600 kilometers.

First Common Understanding. The term "testing," as used in the Agreed Statement to paragraph 1 of Article VIII of the Treaty, includes research and development.

Second Common Understanding. The Parties shall notify each other in the Standing Consultative Commission of the number of airplanes, according to type, used for testing pursuant to the Agreed Statement to paragraph 1 of Article VIII of the Treaty. Such notification shall be provided at the first regular session of the Standing Consultative Commission held after an airplane has been used for such testing.

Third Common Understanding. None of the sixteen airplanes referred to in the Agreed Statement to paragraph 1 of Article VIII of the Treaty may be replaced, except in the event of the involuntary destruction of any such airplane or in the case of the dismantling or destruction of any such airplane. The procedures for such replacement and for removal of any such airplane from that number, in case of its conversion, shall be agreed upon in the Standing Consultative Commission.

---

2. Each Party undertakes not to convert aircraft other than bombers into aircraft which can carry out the mission of a heavy bomber as referred to in subparagraph 3(b) of Article II.

Article IX

1. Each Party undertakes not to develop, test, or deploy:

(a) ballistic missiles capable of a range in excess of 600 kilometers for installation on waterborne vehicles other than submarines, or launchers of such missiles;

Common Understanding to subparagraph (a). The obligations provided for in subparagraph 1(a) of Article IX of the Treaty do not affect current practices for transporting ballistic missiles.

(b) fixed ballistic or cruise missile launchers for emplacement on the ocean floor, on the seabed, or on the beds of internal waters and inland waters, or in the subsoil thereof, or mobile launchers of such missiles, which move only in contact with the ocean floor, the seabed, or the beds of internal waters and inland waters, or missiles for such launchers;

Agreed Statement to subparagraph (b). The obligations provided for in subparagraph 1(b) of Article IX of the Treaty shall apply to all areas of the ocean floor and the seabed, including the seabed zone referred to in Articles I and II of the 1971 Treaty on the Prohibition of the Emplacement of Nuclear Weapons and Other Weapons of Mass Destruction on the Seabed and the Ocean Floor and in the Subsoil Thereof.

(c) systems for placing into Earth orbit nuclear weapons or any other kind of weapons of mass destruction, including fractional orbital missiles;

Common Understanding to subparagraph (c). The provisions of subparagraph 1(c) of Article IX of the Treaty do not require the dismantling or destruction of any existing launchers of either Party.

(d) mobile launchers of heavy ICBMs;
(e) SLBMs which have a launch-weight greater or a throw-weight greater than that of the heaviest, in terms of either launch-weight or throw-weight, respectively, of the light ICBMs deployed by either Party as of the date of signature of this Treaty, or launchers of such SLBMs; or
(f) ASBMs which have a launch-weight greater or a throw-weight greater than that of the heaviest, in terms of either launch-weight or throw-weight, respectively, of the light ICBMs deployed by either Party as of the date of signature of this Treaty.

First Agreed Statement to subparagraphs (e) and (f). The launch-weight of an SLBM or of an ASBM is the weight of the fully loaded missile itself at the time of launch.

Second Agreed Statement to subparagraphs (e) and (f). The throw-weight of an SLBM or of an ASBM is the sum of the weight of:

(a) its reentry vehicle or reentry vehicles;
(b) any self-contained dispensing mechanisms or other appropriate devices for targeting one reentry vehicle, or for releasing or for dispensing and targeting two or more reentry vehicles; and
(c) its penetration aids, including devices for their release.

Common Understanding to subparagraphs (e) and (f). The term "other appropriate devices," as used in the definition of the throw-weight of an SLBM or of an ASBM in the Second Agreed Statement to subparagraphs 1(e) and 1(f) of Article IX of the Treaty, means any devices for dispensing and targeting two or more reentry vehicles; and any devices for releasing two or more reentry vehicles or for targeting one reentry vehicle, which cannot provide their reentry vehicles or reentry vehicle with additional velocity of more than 1,000 meters per second.

---

2. Each Party undertakes not to flight-test from aircraft cruise missiles capable of a range in excess of 600 kilometers which are equipped with multiple independently targetable warheads and not to deploy such cruise missiles on aircraft.

Agreed Statement. Warheads of a cruise missile are independently targetable if maneuvering or targeting of the warheads to separate aim points along ballistic trajectories or any other flight paths, which are unrelated to each other, is accomplished during a flight of a cruise missile.

Article X

Subject to the provisions of this Treaty, modernization and replacement of strategic offensive arms may be carried out.

Article XI

1. Strategic offensive arms which would be in excess of the aggregate numbers provided for in this Treaty as well as strategic offensive arms prohibited by this Treaty shall be dismantled or destroyed under procedures to be agreed upon in the Standing Consultative Commission.

2. Dismantling or destruction of strategic offensive arms which would be in excess of the aggregate number provided for in paragraph 1 of Article III shall begin on the date of the entry into force of this Treaty and shall be completed within the following periods from that date: four months for ICBM launchers; six months for SLBM launchers; and three months for heavy bombers.

3. Dismantling or destruction of strategic offensive arms which would be in excess of the aggregate number provided for in paragraph 2 of Article III shall be initiated no later than January 1, 1981, shall be carried out throughout the ensuing twelve-month period, and shall be completed no later than December 31, 1981.

4. Dismantling or destruction of strategic offensive arms prohibited by this Treaty shall be completed within the shortest possible agreed period of time, but not later than six months after the entry into force of this Treaty.

Article XII

1. In order to ensure the viability and effectiveness of this Treaty, each Party undertakes not to circumvent the provisions of this Treaty, through any other state or states, or in any other manner.

Article XIII

1. Each Party undertakes not to assume any international obligations which would conflict with this Treaty.

Article XIV

The Parties undertake to begin, promptly after the entry into force of this Treaty, active negotiations with the objective of achieving, as soon as possible, agreement on further measures for the limitation and reduction of strategic arms. It is also the objective of the Parties to conclude well in advance of 1985 an agreement limiting strategic offensive arms to replace this Treaty upon its expiration.

Article XV

1. For the purpose of providing assurance of compliance with the provisions of this Treaty, each Party shall use national technical means of verification at its disposal in a manner consistent with generally recognized principles of international law.

2. Each party undertakes not to interfere with the national technical means of verification of the other Party operating in accordance with paragraph 1 of this Article.

3. Each Party undertakes not to use deliberate concealment measures which impede verification by national technical means of compliance with the provisions of this Treaty. This obligation shall not require changes in current construction, assembly, conversion, or overhaul practices.

First Agreed Statement. Deliberate concealment measures, as referred to in paragraph 3 of Article XV of the Treaty, are measures carried out deliberately to hinder or deliberately to impede verification by national technical means of compliance with the provisions of the Treaty.

Second Agreed Statement. The obligation not to use deliberate concealment measures, provided for in paragraph 3 of Article XV of the Treaty, does not preclude the testing of anti-missile defense penetration aids.

First Common Understanding. The provisions of paragraph 3 of Article XV of the Treaty and the First Agreed Statement thereto apply to all provisions of the Treaty, including provisions associated with testing. In this connection, the obligation not to use deliberate concealment measures includes the obligation not to use deliberate concealment measures associated with testing, including those measures aimed at concealing the association between ICBMs and launchers during testing.

Second Common Understanding. Each Party is free to use various methods of transmitting telemetric information during testing, including its encryption, except that, in accordance with the provisions of paragraph 3 of Article XV of the Treaty, neither Party shall engage in deliberate denial of telemetric information, such as through the use of telemetry encryption, whenever such denial impedes verfication of compliance with the provisions of the Treaty.

Third Common Understanding. In addition to the obligations provided for in paragraph 3 of Article XV of the Treaty, no shelters which impede verification by national technical means of compliance with the provisions of the Treaty shall be used over ICBM silo launchers.

Article XVI

1. Each Party undertakes, before conducting each planned ICBM launch, to notify the other Party well in advance on a case-by-case basis that such a launch will occur, except for single ICBM launches from test ranges or from ICBM launcher deployment areas, which are not planned to extend beyond its national territory.

First Common Understanding. ICBM launches to which the obligations provided for in Article XVI of the Treaty apply, include, among others, those ICBM launches for which advance notification is required pursuant to the provisions of the Agreement on Measures to Reduce the Risk of Outbreak of Nuclear War Between the United States of America and the Union of Soviet Socialist Republics, signed September 30, 1971, and the Agreement Between the Government of the United States of America and the Government of the Union of Soviet Socialist Republics on the Prevention of Incidents On and Over the High Seas, signed May 25, 1972. Nothing in Article XVI of the Treaty is intended to inhibit advance notification, on a voluntary basis, of any ICBM launches not subject to its provisions, the advance notification of which would enhance confidence between the Parties.

Second Common Understanding. A multiple ICBM launch conducted by a Party, as distinct from single ICBM launches referred to in Article XVI of the Treaty, is a launch which would result in two or more of its ICBMs being in flight at the same time.

Third Common Understanding. The test ranges referred to in Article XVI of the Treaty are those covered by the Second Agreed Statement to paragraph 2 of Article VII of the Treaty.

2. The Parties shall agree in the Standing Consultative Commission upon procedures to implement the provisions of this Article.

Article XVII

1. To promote the objectives and implementation of the provisions of this Treaty, the Parties shall use the Standing Consultative Commission established by the Memorandum of Understanding Between the Government of the United States of America and the Government of the Union of Soviet Socialist Republics Regarding the Establishment of a Standing Consultative Commission of December 21, 1972.

2. Within the framework of the Standing Consultative Commission, with respect to this Treaty, the Parties will:

(a) consider questions concerning compliance with the obligations assumed and related situations which may be considered ambiguous;
(b) provide on a voluntary basis such information as either Party considers necessary to assure confidence in compliance with the obligations assumed;

(c) consider questions involving unintended interference with national technical means of verification, and questions involving unintended impeding of verification by national technical means of compliance with the provisions of this Treaty;

(d) consider possible changes in the strategic situation which have a bearing on the provisions of this Treaty;

(e) agree upon procedures for replacement, conversion, and dismantling or destruction, of strategic offensive arms in cases provided for in the provisions of this Treaty and upon procedures for removal of such arms from the aggregate numbers when they otherwise cease to be subject to the limitations provided for in this Treaty, and at regular sessions of the Standing Consultative Commission, notify each other in accordance with the aforementioned procedures, at least twice annually, of actions completed and those in process;

(f) consider, as appropriate, possible proposals for further increasing the viability of this Treaty, including proposals for amendments in accordance with the provisions of this Treaty;

(g) consider, as appropriate, proposals for further measures limiting strategic offensive arms.

3. In the Standing Consultative Commission the Parties shall maintain by category the agreed data base on the numbers of strategic offensive arms established by the Memorandum of Understanding Between the United States of America and the Union of Soviet Socialist Republics Regarding the Establishment of a Data Base on the Numbers of Strategic Offensive Arms of June 18, 1979.

Agreed Statement. In order to maintain the agreed data base on the numbers of strategic offensive arms subject to the limitations provided for in the Treaty in accordance with paragraph 3 of Article XVII of the Treaty, at each regular session of the Standing Consultative Commission the Parties will notify each other of and consider changes in those numbers in the following categories: launchers of ICBMs; fixed launchers of ICBMs; launchers of ICBMs equipped with MIRVs; launchers of SLBMs; launchers of SLBMs equipped with MIRVs; heavy bombers; heavy bombers equipped for cruise missiles capable of a range in excess of 600 kilometers; heavy bombers equipped only for ASBMs; ASBMs; and ASBMs equipped with MIRVs.

Article XVIII

Each Party may propose amendments to this Treaty. Agreed amendments shall enter into force in accordance with the procedures governing the entry into force of this Treaty.

Article XIX

1. This Treaty shall be subject to ratification in accordance with the constitutional procedures of each Party. This Treaty shall enter into force on the day of the exchange of instruments of ratification and shall remain in force through December 31, 1985, unless replaced earlier by an agreement further limiting strategic offensive arms.

2. This Treaty shall be registered pursuant to Article 102 of the Charter of the United Nations.

3. Each Party shall, in exercising its national sovereignty, have the right to withdraw from this Treaty if it decides that extraordinary events related to the subject matter of this Treaty have jeopardized its supreme interests. It shall give notice of its decision to the other Party six months prior to withdrawal from the Treaty. Such notice shall

include a statement of the extraordinary events the notifying Party regards as having jeopardized its supreme interests.

DONE at Vienna on June 18, 1979, in two copies, each in the English and Russian languages, both texts being equally authentic.

For the United States of America:

JIMMY CARTER

President of the United States of America

For the Union of Soviet Socialist Republics:

L. BREZHNEV,

General Secretary of the CPSU, Chairman of the Presidium of the Supreme Soviet of the U.S.S.R.

Protocol to the Treaty Between the United States of America and the Union of Soviet Socialist Republics on the Limitation of Strategic Offensive Arms

The United States of America and the Union of Soviet Socialist Republics, hereinafter referred to as the Parties,

Having agreed on limitations on strategic offensive arms in the Treaty,

Have agreed on additional limitations for the period during which this Protocol remains in force, as follows:

Article I

Each Party undertakes not to deploy mobile ICBM launchers or to flight-test ICBMs from such launchers.

Article II

1. Each Party undertakes not to deploy cruise missiles capable of a range in excess of 600 kilometers on sea-based launchers or on land-based launchers.

2. Each Party undertakes not to flight-test cruise missiles capable of a range in excess of 600 kilometers which are equipped with multiple independently targetable warheads from sea-based launchers or from land-based launchers.

Agreed Statement. Warheads of a cruise missile are independently targetable if maneuvering or targeting of the warheads to separate aim points along ballistic trajectories or any other flight paths, which are unrelated to each other, is accomplished during a flight of a cruise missile.

---

3. For the purposes of this Protocol, cruise missiles are unmanned, self-propelled, guided, weapon-delivery vehicles which sustain flight through the use of aerodynamic lift over most of their flight path and which are flight-tested from or deployed on sea-based or land-based launchers, that is, sea-launched cruise missiles and ground-launched cruise missiles, respectively.

First Agreed Statement. If a cruise missile is capable of a range in excess of 600 kilometers, all cruise missiles of that type shall be considered to be cruise missiles capable of a range in excess of 600 kilometers.

First Common Understanding. If a cruise missile has been flight-tested to a range in excess of 600 kilometers, it shall be considered to be a cruise missile capable of a range in excess of 600 kilometers.

Second Common Understanding. Cruise missiles not capable of a range in excess of 600 kilometers shall not be considered to be of a type capable of a range in excess of 600 kilometers if they are distinguishable on the basis of externally observable design features from cruise missiles of types capable of a range in excess of 600 kilometers.

231

Second Agreed Statement. The range of which a cruise missile is capable is the maximum distance which can be covered by the missile in its standard design mode flying until fuel exhaustion, determined by projecting its flight path onto the Earth's sphere from the point of launch to the point of impact.

Third Agreed Statement. If an unmanned, self-propelled, guided vehicle which sustains flight through the use of aerodynamic lift over most of its flight path has been flight-tested or deployed for weapon delivery, all vehicles of that type shall be considered to be weapon-delivery vehicles.

Third Common Understanding. Unmanned, self-propelled, guided vehicles which sustain flight through the use of aerodynamic lift over most of their flight path and are not weapon-delivery vehicles, that is, unarmed, pilotless, guided vehicles, shall not be considered to be cruise missiles if such vehicles are distinguishable from cruise missiles on the basis of externally observable design features.

Fourth Common Understanding. Neither Party shall convert unarmed, pilotless, guided vehicles into cruise missiles capable of a range in excess of 600 kilometers, nor shall either Party convert cruise missiles capable of a range in excess of 600 kilometers into unarmed, pilotless, guided vehicles.

Fifth Common Understanding. Neither Party has plans during the term of the Protocol to flight-test from or deploy on sea-based or land-based launchers unarmed, pilotless, guided vehicles which are capable of a range in excess of 600 kilometers. In the future, should a Party have such plans, that Party will provide notification thereof to the other Party well in advance of such flight-testing or deployment. This Common Understanding does not apply to target drones.

Article III

Each Party undertakes not to flight-test or deploy ASBMs.

Article IV

This Protocol shall be considered an integral part of the Treaty. It shall enter into force on the day of the entry into force of the Treaty and shall remain in force through December 31, 1981, unless replaced earlier by an agreement on further measures limiting strategic offensive arms.

DONE at Vienna on June 18, 1979, in two copies, each in the English and Russian languages, both texts being equally authentic.

For the United States of America:

JIMMY CARTER

President of the United States of America

For the Union of Soviet Socialist Republics:

L. BREZHNEV

General Secretary of the CPSU, Chairman of the Presidium of the Supreme Soviet of the U.S.S.R.

Memorandum of Understanding Between the United States of America and the Union of Soviet Socialist Republics Regarding the Establishment of a Data Base on the Numbers of Strategic Offensive Arms

For the purposes of the Treaty Between the United States of America and the Union of Soviet Socialist Republics on the Limitation of Strategic Offensive Arms, the Parties have considered data on numbers of strategic offensive arms and agree that as of November 1, 1978 there existed the following numbers of strategic offensive arms subject to the limitations provided for in the Treaty which is being signed today.

	U.S.A.	U.S.S.R.
Launchers of ICBMs	1,054	1,398
Fixed launchers of ICBMs	1,054	1,398
Launchers of ICBMs equipped with MIRVs	550	576
Launchers of SLBMs	656	950
Launchers of SLBMs equipped with MIRVs	496	128
Heavy bombers	574	156
Heavy bombers equipped for cruise missiles capable of a range in excess of 600 kilometers	0	0
Heavy bombers equipped only for ASBMs	0	0
ASBMs	0	0
ASBMs equipped with MIRVs	0	0

At the time of entry into force of the Treaty the Parties will update the above agreed data in the categories listed in this Memorandum.

DONE at Vienna on June 18, 1979, in two copies, each in the English and Russian languages, both texts being equally authentic.

For the United States of America

RALPH EARLE II

Chief of the United States Delegation to the Strategic Arms Limitation Talks

For the Union of Soviet Socialist Republics

V. KARPOV

Chief of the U.S.S.R. Delegation to the Strategic Arms Limitation Talks

Statement of Data on the Numbers of Strategic Offensive Arms as of the Date of Signature of the Treaty

The United States of America declares that as of June 18, 1979 it possesses the following numbers of strategic offensive arms subject to the limitations provided for in the Treaty which is being signed today:

Launchers of ICBMs	1,054
Fixed launchers of ICBMs	1,054
Launchers of ICBMs equipped with MIRVs	550
Launchers of SLBMs	656
Launchers of SLBMs equipped with MIRVs	496
Heavy bombers	573
Heavy bombers equipped for cruise missiles capable of a range in excess of 600 kilometers	3
Heavy bombers equipped only for ASBMs	0
ASBMs	0
ASBMs equipped with MIRVs	0

June 18, 1979

RALPH EARLE II

Chief of the United States Delegation to the Strategic Arms Limitation Talks

I certify that this is a true copy of the document signed by Ambassador Ralph Earle II entiled "Statement of Data on the Numbers of Strategic Offensive Arms as of the Date of Signature of the Treaty" and given to Ambassador V. Karpov on June 18, 1979 in Vienna, Austria.

THOMAS GRAHAM, JR.

General Counsel
United States Arms Control and Disarmament Agency

Statement of Data on the Numbers of Strategic Offensive Arms as of the Date of Signature of the Treaty

The Union of Soviet Socialist Republics declares that as of June 18, 1979, it possesses the following numbers of strategic offensive arms subject to the limitations provided for in the Treaty which is being signed today:

Launchers of ICBMs	1,398
Fixed launchers of ICBMs	1,398

Launchers of ICBMs equipped with MIRVs	608
Launchers of SLBMs	950
Launchers of SLBMs equipped with MIRVs	144
Heavy bombers	156
Heavy bombers equipped for cruise missiles capable of a range in excess of 600 kilometers	0
Heavy bombers equipped only for ASBMs	0
ASBMs	0
ASBMs equipped with MIRVs	0

June 18, 1979

V. KARPOV

Chief of the U.S.S.R. Delegation to the Strategic Arms Limitation Talks

Translation certified by:
W.D. Krimer,
Senior Language Officer,
Division of Language Services, U.S. Department of State

WILLIAM D. KRIMER

Joint Statement of Principles and Basic Guidelines for Subsequent Negotiations on the Limitation of Strategic Arms

The United States of America and the Union of Soviet Socialist Republics, hereinafter referred to as the Parties,

Having concluded the Treaty on the Limitation of Strategic Offensive Arms,

Reaffirming that the strengthening of strategic stability meets the interests of the Parties and the interests of international security,

Convinced that early agreement on the further limitation and further reduction of strategic arms would serve to strengthen international peace and security and to reduce the risk of outbreak of nuclear war,

Have agreed as follows:

First, The Parties will continue to pursue negotiations, in accordance with the principle of equality and equal security, on measures for the further limitation and reduction in the numbers of strategic arms, as well as for their further qualitative limitation.

In furtherance of existing agreements between the Parties on the limitation and reduction of strategic arms, the Parties will continue, for the purposes of reducing and averting the risk of outbreak of nuclear war, to seek measures to strengthen strategic stability by, among other things, limitations on strategic offensive arms most destabilizing to the strategic balance and by measures to reduce and to avert the risk of surprise attack.

Second. Further limitations and reductions of strategic arms must be subject to adequate verification by national technical means, using additionally, as appropriate, cooperative measures contributing to the effectiveness of verification by national technical means. The Parties will seek to strengthen verification and to perfect the operation of the Standing Consultative Commission in order to promote assurance of compliance with the obligations assumed by the Parties.

Third. The Parties shall pursue in the course of these negotiations, taking into consideration factors that determine the strategic situation, the following objectives:

1) significant and substantial reductions in the numbers of strategic offensive arms;

2) qualitative limitations on strategic offensive arms, including restrictions on the development, testing, and deployment of new types of strategic offensive arms and on the modernization of existing strategic offensive arms;

3) resolution of the issues included in the Protocol to the Treaty Between the United States of America and the Union of Soviet Socialist Republics on the Limitation of Strategic Offensive Arms in the context of the negotiations relating to the implementation of the principles and objectives set out herein.

Fourth. The Parties will consider other steps to ensure and enhance strategic stability, to ensure the equality and equal security of the Parties, and to implement the above principles and objectives. Each Party will be free to raise any issue relative to the further limitation of strategic arms. The Parties will also consider further joint measures, as appropriate, to strengthen international peace and security and to reduce the risk of outbreak of nuclear war.

Vienna, June 18, 1979

For the United States of America

JIMMY CARTER

President of the United States of America

For the Union of Soviet Socialist Republics

L. BREZHNEV

General Secretary of the CPSU, Chairman of the Presidium of the Supreme Soviet of the U.S.S.R.

Soviet Backfire Statement

On June 16, 1979, President Brezhnev handed President Carter the following written statement [original Russian text was attached]:

"The Soviet side informs the US side that the Soviet 'Tu-22M' airplane, called 'Backfire' in the USA, is a medium-range bomber, and that it does not intend to give this airplane the capability of operating at intercontinental distances. In this connection, the Soviet side states that it will not increase the radius of action of this airplane in such a way as to enable it to strike targets on the territory of the USA. Nor does it intend to give it such a capability in any other manner, including by in-flight refueling. At the same time, the Soviet side states that it will not increase the production rate of this airplane as compared to the present rate."

President Brezhnev confirmed that the Soviet Backfire production rate would not exceed 30 per year.

President Carter stated that the United States enters into the SALT II Agreement on the basis of the commitments contained in the Soviet statement and that it considers the carrying out of these commitments to be essential to the obligations assumed under the Treaty.

CYRUS VANCE

Footnotes

1. Dates given are the earliest dates on which countries signed the agreements or deposited their ratifications or accessions—whether in Washington, London, Moscow, or New York. In the case of a country that was a dependent territory which became a party through succession, the date given is the date on which the country gave notice that it would continue to be bound by the terms of the agreement.
2. The United States regards the signature and ratification by the Byelorussian S.S.R. and the Ukrainian S.S.R. as already included under the signature and ratification of the Union of Soviet Socialist Republics.
3. This total does not include actions by the Byelorussian S.S.R. and the Ukrainian S.S.R. (See footnote 2.)

U.S. ARMS CONTROL AND DISARMAMENT AGENCY

Publication 105

August 1980

For sale by the Superintendent of Documents, U.S. Government Printing Office
Washington, D.C. 20402

☆ U.S. GOVERNMENT PRINTING OFFICE: 1980 O—318-287